The Doll

by Contemporary Artists

The Doll
by Contemporary Artists

Krystyna Poray Goddu & Wendy Lavitt

Photographs by Lynton Gardiner

Abbeville Press ❧ Publishers
New York ❧ London ❧ Paris

For Joseph, Anna, and Jack

For Mel, Kathy and Kerry, John, and Meredith

JACKET, FRONT: detail of *La Petite Fille Debout* by Héloise (see plate 66). JACKET, BACK: upper left—*The Fairy Queen* by Linda Kertzman (see plate 98); upper right—*Lobster Man* by Scott Gray (see plate 104); lower right—*Carnivale* by Nancy Wiley (see plate 74); lower left—*Snowshoe Santa* by Mary Alice Byerly (see plate 38). Pages 2–3: *The Queen of the Night and General Star and the Starlets* by Peter Wolf (see plate 106). Page 5: *East Wind on Cherry Tree Lane* by Nancy Wilson (see plate 29).

EDITOR: Susan Costello
DESIGNER: Celia Fuller
PRODUCTION EDITOR: Owen Dugan
PRODUCTION MANAGER: Lou Bilka

Frank Sinatra image, plate 17, courtesy of Sheffield Enterprises, Inc.

First edition
10 9 8 7 6 5 4 3 2 1

Library of Congress Cataloging-in-Publication Data
Goddu, Krystyna Poray.
    The doll by contemporary artists / by Krystyna Poray Goddu and
Wendy Lavitt ; photographs by Lynton Gardiner.
        p.   cm.
    Includes bibliographical references.
    ISBN 1-55859-840-5
    1. Dolls—History—20th century.   I. Lavitt, Wendy.   II. Title.
NK4894.A2G63   1995
688.7'221'09045—dc20   95-9795

Contents

Preface ❦ 6

Early Artists ❦ 8

Portraits of Real People ❦ 28

Figures from Literature ❦ 50

Holiday Inspirations ❦ 68

Reflections of Cultural Diversity ❦ 90

Contemporary Children ❦ 110

Women of the Imagination ❦ 132

Characters ❦ 152

Fantasies ❦ 170

Beyond Dolls ❦ 192

Appendices ❦ 212
Glossary · The Artists · Bibliography · Sources

Index ❦ 223

Preface

In a small corner of the art world, a quiet but extraordinary revolution has been taking place over the past fifteen years. It may be traced to the autumn of 1982 when the first issue of *Dolls—The Collector's Magazine* appeared. In that issue less than twenty percent of its contents was devoted to contemporary artist dolls; the bulk of the magazine featured antique, or commercially made, examples. In today's issues, the balance has shifted dramatically, with contemporary artist dolls representing more than three-quarters of the publication's contents. It is clear to all who have been watching that they have indeed witnessed a revolution. It is this exciting turn of artistic focus and collecting interest that has inspired this book.

The roots of this movement lie in the early years of this century, when a few key European artists turned their attention to dolls. We begin our exploration of contemporary dolls with these women, acknowledging them as the precursors of doll artistry as it exists today. It is even more important, though, to look at the dollmakers who came directly after them, most of them Americans, because with their work, the concept of the dressed, posable three-dimensional human figure as simultaneously doll and art object began to come alive.

After considering the work of several of these important early doll-makers, we begin to look at contemporary dolls. Most of the dolls shown and discussed in this book were created in the past ten years, by artists in many different countries, following the growing recognition of doll artistry as an acceptable creative medium. Among them, many were created in 1993 and 1994, as this book was being prepared for publication. The pieces we have selected represent, as a whole, the international state of the art as it appeared in the mid-1990s.

We prepared this book to reflect, in its organization and movement, the development of the artistic intent and imagination. We begin with portraits of actual people, where the artist's aim is to portray an existing character, dead or living, and move on to literary characters, holiday figures, and representations of other cultures, through which the artist is creatively interpreting an existing idea. Then we delve further into the individual imagination, as the artist begins to represent human characters entirely of his or her own inspiration, and continue with fantasy creatures, where the artist goes beyond purely human figures. We end with nearly abstract creations, through which the artist is pushing the limits of the term "doll." We hope that the reader will find that the book has a movement and progression from the very realistic to the abstract, and that in its movement it is about much more than just dolls—that it is about the development of the artistic imagination as expressed through the medium of the doll.

This book represents, on each of our parts, the culmination of more than a decade of the study of antique and contemporary dolls. During this time, Krystyna Poray Goddu served as founding editor of *Dolls* magazine, reporting on the work of developing doll artists and the discoveries being made by researchers on antique dolls. Wendy Lavitt was researching the previously untapped field of American folk art, seeking out examples of American folk dolls and exploring the work of contemporary doll artists. We both believe that antique as well as contemporary dolls have not received their proper due as objects worthy of study, and deserve much further scholarship and serious consideration.

That said, we are at a very exciting moment in the study of contemporary art dolls. It is extraordinarily rare to have the opportunity to witness the development of a new art form. We feel privileged to be part of this moment and to be among the first to record it. We hope we have passed on to our readers a sense of this privilege and this excitement. Most of all, we hope that the words and images in this book will inspire our readers toward a new way of seeing art.

Krystyna Poray Goddu
Wendy Lavitt

Early Artists

 To trace doll artistry back to its true beginnings, we would have to go back centuries. People have been creating objects of a human form, be they decorative items or playthings, since ancient times. The earliest dolls had a twofold purpose; today we have come full circle to this double identity. The ancient Egyptians buried tiny painted wooden dolls representing servants and tradespeople with their dead. For the artists of the late twentieth century, the doll has become a multi-faceted medium of artistic expression. Between the ancients and the moderns lie centuries when dolls have been, first and foremost, playthings.

Plate 1
Käthe Kruse,
Doll I,
15 in. (38.1 cm),
1911–14

Dolls as toys have their own rich tradition. Some of the toymakers of centuries past were artists; at the very least, many of them were masters of their art. And there have been pockets of time when artists turned to dollmaking and

9

dollmakers became known as artists. But not until the second half of this century did there arise the identified phenomenon of the doll as art.

Early in this century, several important dollmakers conceived of their dolls as art, albeit art for children to play with. The influences of these dollmakers—women like Marion Kaulitz, Berthe Noufflard, Käthe Kruse, and later Sasha Morgenthaler—can still be seen in the work of today's doll artists. These early twentieth-century makers were followed by artists who never considered children when creating their pieces and, often, didn't themselves designate their creations "dolls." They worked in a broad variety of media, from needle sculpture to wax, wood, and the traditional porcelain, and they are the pioneers of contemporary doll artistry.

In the first decades of this century, Germany and France both saw the rise of artistic movements that promoted the idea that fine artists should turn their talents to toys in general, and to dolls in particular. In Germany, this movement was centered in Munich. A 1908 exhibition, *Art Dolls,* at the Hermann Tietz department store in Munich was organized by the head of the store's toy department, Max Schreiber, and featured dolls that were meant to look like everyday children, as opposed to the romanticized, wide-eyed, silk-and-satin-clothed dolls that wealthy children had been playing with for decades.

One of the participants in this exhibit was an artist named Marion Kaulitz, who went on to start a movement she called Puppen Reform (Doll Reform) and to establish a workshop in Gmünd, south of Munich, for the creation of her realistic dolls. Her creations, relatively few of which can be found today, became known as the Munich Art Dolls or the Marion Kaulitz Art Dolls; they were exhibited throughout Germany and elsewhere in Europe for several years, often winning awards and citations for their originality. (Three are noted to have been shown in a 1912 German art exhibit at the Newark Museum in Newark, New Jersey.) Kaulitz apparently came up with ideas for the dolls and then worked on them with other artists. The dolls' heads were of a plaster-like material, which Kaulitz painted, and the dolls—often dressed in regional costumes, in simple school clothes, or even as street urchins—represented various races. Contemporary accounts applaud Kaulitz for bringing realism to dolls.

In Paris, meanwhile, the French were tired of what they perceived as a German invasion of their toy market. In the beginning years of the century, open discussion in the media deriding the quantity and poor quality of German toys led to the establishment, in 1901, of an annual competition called the Concours Lepine. Begun by the prefect of Paris, Monsieur Lepine, its purpose was to encourage artisans to create toys via museum and gallery exhibitions on the themes of toys and dolls, art and children, as well as through competitions for the creation of dolls. Among the artists who eventually participated in this movement was the painter Berthe Noufflard.

Born Berthe Langweil in 1886, Noufflard was the daughter of an eminent Parisian antiques dealer. She started painting early, and was exhibiting and selling her work by the age of twenty. In 1911 she married a fellow painter, Alfred Noufflard. In 1915, during a period of enforced wartime exile in Italy, the couple's first daughter, Henriette, was born. That same year Berthe created and modeled her first dolls. By 1916 some of these, mostly figures of young girls, including one resembling Red Riding Hood, had made their way back to Paris, where they were part of an exhibit at the Musée des Arts Décoratifs entitled *Jouets Artistiques* (Toys by Artists). Half of the ninety-one exhibitors chose to create dolls for the display.

Noufflard's dolls were never produced in large numbers, although there is correspondence between her and several manufacturers indicating that larger-scale production may have been her goal. Contemporary articles praise Noufflard's child dolls—which had elongated bodies of stuffed cloth with heads, lower arms, and legs of a thick plaster—for looking natural and alive, and being pleasing both to children and to artists.

The last-known appearance of Berthe Noufflard's dolls seems to have been in 1924, when she and her husband held a joint exhibition of their paintings and Berthe's dolls at the Galeries Simonson in Paris. This double display of paintings and dolls was highly unusual for that time, and reflects the artistic light in which Berthe Noufflard regarded her dolls.

The dolls produced by the German maker Käthe Kruse, whose dollmaking career spanned nearly five decades, from 1911 to 1956, were unquestionably created as children's toys. The high quality of their craftsmanship, their aesthetic appeal, and their very distinctive style places them among the finest artistic creations of any age. Probably more contemporary creators of children's dolls claim to have been influenced by Kruse than by any other maker. Her influence is most evident in the work of cloth artists like R. John Wright (see "Figures from Literature") and Maggie Iacono (see "Contemporary Children"), whose soft and rounded children bear a look that can be traced back to Kruse.

Like many dollmakers, Käthe Kruse made her first doll for her own child. Kruse was born Katharina Simon, in Breslau, Germany, in 1883. Her first career was as an actress, performing to critical acclaim throughout Europe. Her meeting with the successful sculptor, Max Kruse, drew her into a world of creativity and intellectual curiosity and, quickly, into motherhood.

After the birth of her first child, Maria, in December 1902, Käthe Kruse gave up acting. When three-year-old Maria asked for a doll, her father refused to buy the unappealing, hard and cold porcelain examples he found in the shops of Berlin. "Make your own dolls," he wrote to Käthe in a letter. Käthe did, creating the head from a potato and filling a knotted kitchen towel with sand to make the body. The doll had a short life, due to the fragility of its materials, but the enthusiastic response of her two daughters to this doll that moved and felt like a real baby pushed Käthe to continue her progressively more successful experiments in dollmaking.

It wasn't until 1910 that the outside world got a glimpse of Kruse's dolls. She was invited to participate in an exhibition of homemade toys sponsored by the Hermann Tietz department store in Berlin. Kruse modeled a head after a classic baroque sculpture by François Duquesne, covered the model with cloth, and then filled it with wax. She handpainted the head and attached it to a nettle-cloth body filled with wood shavings. The doll was an immediate success at the exhibit, and a manufacturing contract, then orders, quickly followed. Käthe Kruse's commercial dollmaking career, in which she participated actively until 1956, was underway. (After she stopped working, her children ran the company until 1990, when it was bought by Stephen and Andrea Kathrin Christenson and the family of Prince Albrecht zu Castell-Castell, who continue today as owners of this very active toymaking concern.)

Kruse's earliest commercially produced dolls were the boy and girl known as *Doll I* (plate 1). They were created between 1911 and 1933; the fifteen-inch-high boy was made before 1914. His pudgy, wide-hipped body is firmly stuffed with nettle cloth. His arms are sewn on, while his legs have disk joints sewn into the upper thigh and pelvis and attached by a cotter pin. The roundness of his body is achieved by the trunk's eight-piece cloth construction. The boy's hands and head help identify him as a very early *Doll I:* The thumbs are separate, the fingers are individually seamed, and his head is of hand-molded nettle cloth. Later dolls have sewn-on thumbs and machine-molded nettle-cloth heads. The soft back of the head is sewn on to the molded face mask, then stuffed with deer hair and wood shavings. After being primed and sanded, the head was painted by hand. The boy shown has especially beautiful painting, including the characteristic *Doll I* brown curl that falls on his forehead. Because different

artists hand-painted Kruse's dolls, even those coming from the same mold can vary greatly from one another.

    Contemporary artists are quick to note that, in strictest terms, Kruse would not be accepted as an "artist" today. She did not create her original head, traditionally judged as the most important part of a doll. She became a manufacturer of dolls, in charge of a workshop where she trained and supervised seamstresses and painters, rather than an artist solely creating one-of-a-kind pieces and small editions. Yet these same modern-day artists immediately acknowledge the profound influence of her aesthetic. The firm stuffed body, the molded cloth head, the hand-painted eyes and the unsmiling expression are the distinctive characteristics that give Kruse's dolls a timeless emotional and visual appeal. Conceived and produced as toys, these are now sought-after collector's items and the inspiration for many of today's artists.

    Years after Kruse had begun successful production of her dolls, another creative woman faced a similar dilemma. Like Kruse, the Swiss-born Sasha

Morgenthaler had also married an artist; and like Kruse, Morgenthaler wanted to create a doll with which a child could identify, one with a changeable expression and a realistic figure, one that could survive ordinary play: in short, a beautiful, realistic, affordable, and durable toy.

Born Sasha von Sinner in Bern, in 1893, into an unconventional, cosmopolitan, and artistic household, she was a quiet and creative child who, according to her older sister, lived in her own fantasy world, sketching and painting. The painter Paul Klee, a frequent visitor to the von Sinner house, encouraged her creative talents and advised sending her, at the age of sixteen, to the School of Fine Arts in Geneva. Sasha (as she is always known) then went on to study painting, sculpture, and anatomy in Switzerland and Germany where, in 1914, she met the painter Ernst Morgenthaler, whom she married in 1916.

Morgenthaler, Paul Klee, Wassily Kandinsky, and other artists of the time with whom Sasha was friendly were active in a movement called the Blaue Reiter (Blue Rider), which encouraged any means of artistic expression as worthwhile. Sasha, who eventually gave up painting, was very much a part of this artistic milieu. The Morgenthalers lived in Zurich from 1919 on, and by 1924 they had three children, for whom Sasha began creating animals and dolls.

In 1926 she created a rag doll for her two-year-old daughter, Barbara. The dearth of affordable and pleasing dolls for her own children slowly fostered her determination to create a sensitive, durable, and inexpensive play doll. "I tried to recreate my dreams," she wrote in an autobiographical note late in her life, "and since that time I am completely occupied with making realistic dolls which children love because they have real living expressions. It is the relationship of asymmetrical proportions that gives this realistic effect. An asymmetrical design of the dolls which must at the same time have an internal wholeness, that is the reason for the fact that one can achieve a wide range of expressions and moods with my dolls."

For some years Sasha pursued other endeavors, but in 1941 she turned again to dollmaking. She tried wax for the heads, hoping to achieve the tautness and transparency of youthful skin. The bodies were a stuffed cotton knit. Both media were eventually used, along with a variety of others.

Years of experimentation and struggle to achieve her technical goals followed, as Sasha worked both alone and with helpers. In 1944 she and her team introduced six-piece, all-wax dolls. Sasha developed a basic face, with four variations, for her older children dolls, as well as another variation for the babies and toddlers. Her goal for the faces was that they be peaceful, with only the illusion of expression, that they be non-nationalistic, neutral, simple, and harmonious. She wanted to achieve a face capable of many moods, so that every child could read into her own doll the expression she needed to find there.

The most successful asymmetrical body was eventually achieved in the late 1940s, in the medium of a synthetic resin, a forerunner of hard plastic. Nevertheless, Sasha continued to use several different media, including all-plaster and cloth, for the bodies through the late 1960s. Working with her small team, she eventually achieved all her goals but one; the dolls were still so expensive that only the wealthiest children could play with them. In 1963 she had her dolls produced briefly by the German company of Götz, and these dolls are beautiful and quite rare today. But they did not meet Sasha's standards and so, in 1965, an English couple, John and Sara Doggart, took over production. Until 1986, the Doggarts' north-England company, Trendon, manufactured inexpensive, sixteen-inch-high vinyl "Sashas" with rooted hair, which became, as Sasha had dreamed, the beloved playmates of a generation of children. In 1986 production of the Sashas ended, when the Doggarts retired without finding anyone capable of carrying on production to their specifications. Today, even these mass-produced Sashas are eagerly collected.

The many dolls produced by Sasha herself are even more highly sought after. The *Girl* (plate 2) in a blue-and-white dress dates from the late 1940s. Nineteen inches high, she has a gypsum head with a stockinette body and labeled clothing. She is an all-original, except for her felt shoes, which were replaced by Sasha Morgenthaler's workshop, and bears the undefined, muted, and magical aura that is evoked by the very name Sasha.

An American woman with goals similar to Sasha's was the artist Dewees Cochran (1892–1991), who worked during more or less the same time period. It is interesting that neither the extensive writings about Cochran nor her own autobiography, *As If They Might Speak,* mentions Sasha's work, for the two women, while very different in their artistic sensibility and style, worked toward similar aims. Cochran, who garnered much publicity and counted the prominent society of the United States as her steady clientele, never saw the successful, long-range production of her dolls that Sasha eventually was able to establish. Cochran did, however, make her living from her dollmaking, creating one-of-a-kind commissioned portraits as well as designing pieces for production. She also managed to draw continual attention to her natural figures as much more than children's toys. Finally, as one of the charter members of the National Institute of American Doll Artists (NIADA) in 1963, she set the standard for artists who aspired to create realistic figures. The contemporary children of the American Robert Tonner (who makes fashionable women as well; see "Women of the Imagination"), for example, are clear descendants of Cochran's modern youngsters.

Like Sasha Morgenthaler, Pennsylvania-born Dewees Cochran had an artistic background; she attended the School of Industrial Art and the Pennsylvania Academy of Fine Arts, studying painting and modeling there. Her marriage to fellow artist Paul Helbeck took the couple to Europe in the 1920s, where, for ten years, Cochran pursued art history and painting, including a study of nineteenth-century physiognomy types, which was later a strong influence on the development of her dollmaking.

When the couple returned to the United States in 1933, Cochran thought of dollmaking as a means of earning a living, and soon decided that conquering New York was necessary to her financial success. At Saks Fifth Avenue, the offhand suggestion of a buyer that she "do something realistic, more lifelike than these dolls in the case," led Cochran to the idea of making a doll to order, to look just like a specific child. This idea was to shape her entire career.

From 1934 on, Cochran created many variations on the concept of dolls that were the likenesses of actual children, starting with the *Portrait Dolls,* made of carved balsa wood with silk bodies stuffed with kapok, real hair wigs, and handsewn clothing, which were commissioned by well-known people like Mrs. Irving Berlin, wife of the popular composer.

As demand for these figures grew, Cochran sought ways to make her work easier and to bring her prices down, while maintaining quality. She tried technical innovations like the substitution of plastic wood for balsa, then hit upon the idea of developing six basic face styles of American children. In this way, upon receiving an order for a portrait, she could pick the suitable shape from one of six molds, instead of starting from scratch with a Plasticine mold for each child. She would then capture the essence of each individual subject in the painting of the features, the wig, and the clothing. The development of the six face shapes themselves came from months of research of physiognomy types, at the New York Public Library, as well as from photographs from the city's modeling agencies. (One is reminded of Sasha's creation of four basic, if more abstract, facial types for her older children dolls.)

From 1936 to 1939 the Effanbee Doll Company produced four of Cochran's types as a series of all-composition dolls; they were called *America's Children* and later, *Look-Alikes,* and were hailed as being striking likenesses of actual children. Both Cochran's *Portrait Dolls* and the Effanbee dolls received great publicity,

the most exciting being the April 9, 1939, cover of
Life magazine, which featured a child with her *Look-
Alike* doll.

After World War II, Cochran developed more
concepts, including the mass-produced *Cindy* doll,
which disappointed the artist for its lack of quality,
and the latex *Grow-Up* dolls. The latter idea, which
came into being in 1952, involved three girls and two
boys who would "grow up" in doll form, from age
five through twenty. This series was pronounced one
of the outstanding doll innovations of the twentieth
century by the Bethnal Green Museum of Childhood in London. Cochran was commended for having succeeded in her creation of dolls that grew up
in face and body, while maintaining their distinct
looks and "personalities" throughout. The lifelike
proportions of the body of Cochran's one-of-a-kind
Vultex portrait, *Diana McManus* (plate 3), commissioned in 1970, illustrate beautifully the artist's
achievement of a realistically constructed American
character doll.

Another Pennsylvania native ranks at the very
top of the list when it comes to legendary American
dollmakers: Dorothy Heizer (1881–1973), whose
pioneering artistry in creating cloth figures has never

been surpassed. Like Cochran, Heizer had her early artistic training at the Pennsylvania Academy of Fine Arts, where she studied portraiture, anatomy, and
sculpture. The resulting creations of each artist could not, however, be more
different. Heizer is known for her elegant, accurate historical portraits, for what
she called "sculpturing in fabric," and for intricate costume work, which often
included beading done by hand. Heizer's sensibility influenced artists in an
entirely different way than Cochran did, but the two women share the position
of preeminence among American doll artists. Like Cochran, Heizer was one of
the charter members of NIADA.

Heizer's interest in dollmaking is often traced to an experience she had
at the age of eight, when she saw a French lady doll in a shop window and
dreamed of having her own lady doll for which she could make clothes. A year

later the young girl exchanged the bodies and heads of two dolls and created a fashion figure for which she made costumes. At the age of eleven, she designed and made paper dolls with wardrobes, which she sold to F.A.O. Schwarz in Philadelphia. In spite of these early signs of interest in dollmaking, Heizer did not actually return to it until 1920, as an adult of nearly forty. Instead, she went to art school, then suffered a nervous breakdown that caused her to give up both school and the idea of art as a career. She married and raised a family.

In 1920, for a church bazaar in Essex Fells, New Jersey, where she then lived with her family, the artist dressed three purchased bisque dolls. She quickly moved from the dressing of these figures to the creation of rag dolls with painted features. She then began making fashion figures, always refining further, and showed them commercially. In 1923 the Corticelli Silk Company commissioned a portrait doll of Irene Castle, which was to be the first of Heizer's many portraits. Years of commissions, exhibitions, sales, and publicity followed. Heizer did not devote herself to full-time dollmaking, however, until her husband's death in 1936. After this time she perfected many of her techniques, painting, rather than dyeing, the crepe-de-chine "skin" of her figures, and padding the skeletons with eiderdown. After 1940, she fixed on a standard size of eight-and-one-half inches for her figures, which had previously varied in size.

Henry VIII (plate 4), from the 1540 portrait by Hans Holbein the Younger, was first created in 1935, though the example shown was commissioned in 1956 by the artist Margaret Finch (see "Figures from Literature" and "Fantasies"). He is a prime example of Heizer's gift for both portraiture and costuming. (She is known to have counted the beads on costumes in paintings in order to accurately reproduce the clothing.) "He is so magnificent of stance and attitude; the life seems to stream out of him," wrote Finch to Heizer, upon ordering the doll. The older artist responded: "I am glad you have chosen Henry, for I think he's one of the most interesting people to do, and I believe you are right when you say that he gets over to one the feeling of life more than any of the others." The king wears a typically lavish and elegant Heizer costume: a black velvet jerkin embroidered with gold beads and a black-and-gold-printed velvet cloak trimmed with brown fur.

Today, Heizer's creations are probably more sought-after than those of any other twentieth-century American doll artist. For most contemporary artists, whether or not they have been directly influenced by her work, she represents the pinnacle of achievement in this field.

Also renowned as a portrait sculptor, but of a very different style, and

working in a very different medium, was Lewis Sorensen (1910–1985), who chose the uncommon material of wax for his work. While wax holds an important place in the tradition of British dollmaking, it is very seldom used today. Among the few who work in wax is the English team of Paul Crees and Peter Coe (see "Portraits of Real People").

Sorensen's interest in dolls began in childhood; at the age of eleven he made dolls out of flour sacks, stuffed with cotton pilfered from a worn-out couch. He began making dolls in earnest in 1930. Before achieving the wax formula that he became known for, Sorensen, who had also loved to sew as a boy, worked as a dress designer and made dolls in his spare time. He worked first in cloth and later, in 1940, tried a homemade composition of flour, salt, and water, which he attempted to sculpt into a portrait of an Indian. The end result was not quite what he planned; he ended up with a thirty-two-inch-high hobo instead.

In 1943 Sorensen made his *Mormon Pioneers*—portraits of early settlers—in composition. This group of dolls was the first of his to be widely acclaimed, and had the honor of being featured in historical doll books, such as Eleanor St. George's *Dolls of Yesterday* (1948), which focused almost exclusively on antique dolls. In making the *Mormon Pioneers,* Sorensen looked back to his Mormon heritage and ahead to a career of dollmaking. "These dolls were the first to lead me into serious dollmaking," he wrote later. "I began to realize a person could make a comfortable living making portrait and fashion dolls." He went on to create Marie Antoinette, the Gibson Girl, and other signature dolls.

Sorensen didn't develop his wax process until after World War II, however, when he moved to Bremerton, Washington. Experimenting with materials, he eventually devised a special wax composition, and in 1950, introduced a complete set of presidents and their wives in this medium. (Among those who ordered the sets was Eleanor Roosevelt.) These earliest wax dolls were dipped wax over composition; eventually he began to make the dolls in poured wax.

It is easier to see Sorensen's work than that of many other early doll artists, for he is well represented in museums. There is an especially good collection of his figures at The McCurdy Historical Doll Museum in Provo, Utah—including *Queen Anne* (plate 5), which dates from the early 1950s— and at The Hobby City Doll and Toy Museum in Anaheim, California. In fact, Sorensen built museums of his own in California, in Santa Cruz and Monterey, after moving to that state in 1950. He also created a host of life-sized figures, for which he became well known; the best known of these is probably Abraham Lincoln, from 1951, which was seen several times on television. Sorensen's unmistakable, often craggy-looking figures are collected today as distinctive portraits fashioned from a difficult medium.

Martha Thompson (1903–1964) worked in the more popular medium of porcelain and, like many of her peers, found the greatest satisfaction in creating portraits both of historical characters and of people who were making history in her own lifetime—such as Mamie Eisenhower, Jacqueline Kennedy, and Princess Grace and Prince Rainier of Monaco. Her bisque molded-hair creations are distinguished by their delicacy and elegance. Thompson also fashioned dolls from her own imagination, although she referred to them as simply her "doodling." In a letter to another American doll artist, Helen Bullard (quoted by Bullard in the January 1958 issue of the *Toy Trader*), she wrote: "I just mess around with the clay until something happens that I like. I can do a dozen doodles with little effort in the time it takes me to make one satisfactory portrait doll." Among her "doodles" was a little girl, representing the era of 1905–10, whom she named *Betsey Sheffield* (plate 6); created in 1953, along with a *Little Brother* figure, the dolls were presented as a gift to her sister's and brother's church in Sheffield, Alabama. The dolls were sold at a raffle, with the proceeds going for a long-needed carpet for the church.

"Up to this time," Thompson wrote in the *Toy Trader* in July 1954, "I had designed nine original types of dolls, so the next would be the tenth. Now, I do believe in tithing. So it seemed fitting that I should design this one for some purpose to help others, and what could be more appropriate than a new church carpet? So my tenth doll was dedicated to the little Episcopal church at Sheffield, and the doll, Betsey Sheffield, would have a whole set of godmothers to sponsor her. The wardrobes could be designed and executed by these church ladies." And so they were, with styles taken from the pages of the 1907 *Delineators,* a popular fashion magazine of the early twentieth century.

It is fitting that Thompson created *Betsey Sheffield* and *Little Brother* for a cause of her sister's, for her very first attempt at dollmaking, in 1928, was at the request of her sister, who needed dolls for a kindergarten project. Thompson modeled Ivory soap for the heads and hands, and attached them to cloth bodies. After the soap dolls, the artist tried unsuccessfully to work in unfired clay, and eventually, by 1947, discovered porcelain. She first made replicas of bisques and parians, soon turning to portraits of living and historical people, as well as a few literary figures, such as a set of Louisa May Alcott's *Little Women,* made between 1951 and 1960.

Thompson, who grew up in Huntsville, Alabama, was an artistic child and went on to study art in Boston at the Museum of Fine Arts School, the New School of Design, and the Massachusetts School of Art. She had a professional career as a textbook illustrator and commercial artist before her marriage, in 1929, and the birth of her two children. One of her great frustrations was in trying to find time for her dollmaking in her busy family life. The dolls she did create are still highly admired today, especially by contemporary artists and doll specialists, for the refined sculpting, the delicate attention to detail, and the sensitive rendering of character.

The porcelain work of Gertrude Florian (1903–1973) is also characterized by a formality and elegance that bespeaks an earlier time. Florian overcame numerous limitations—isolation, lack of materials for creation, and few opportunities for exhibition—and persisted in making dolls during the 1930s. Living in Detroit, she showed her work and won ribbons at state fairs and hobby shows, but few sales resulted. Department stores like J. L. Hudson and Marshall Fields were not interested in representing an unknown dollmaker, and after four years, Florian gave up the endeavor. In 1941, however, she received a commission to make seventy-five ten-inch dolls and several life-sized ones in period costumes for a Christmas display at J. L. Judson, and this commission revived her hopes and spirits enough that she returned to dollmaking.

Florian went on to create a wide variety of pieces, from miniature nuns to portraits of Al Jolson and Francis Scott Key to her famous *Mother and Baby in the Rocking Chair* (1951), which has served as inspiration for many artists since it was first exhibited at a national convention of the United Federation of Doll Clubs (UFDC) in Detroit in that year. According to artist Helen Bullard, who wrote about Florian in the first volume of her book *The American Doll Artist,* Florian found that doll collectors

Plate 6
Martha Thompson,
Betsey Sheffield,
15 in. (39.1 cm), 1953

wanted Italian-style madonnas, rather than the healthy young American mothers the artist wanted to use as models. One day, Bullard wrote (quoting a passage from Janet Johl's book, *Your Dolls and Mine*), Florian opened her door to see "a girl with an earthy chunk of a baby just out of the tub, in one arm. The baby had that soft rosy look with little rolls of fat, and almost transparent skin tones." Inspired by this couple, she began creating mothers with babies, all leading up to her *Mother and Baby in the Rocking Chair*, about which Bullard later wrote in her 1984 autobiographical monograph, *My People in Wood:* "I had never seen a doll with inner meaning, and the experience affected me just as Mary Cassatt's paintings of mothers and little girls did."

In the 1960s, as Florian took her place in the top ranks of artists, she began making special sets of heads and limbs for the annual UFDC conventions, selling them to eager collectors who then put them on bodies and costumed them. Among these was the fourteen-inch *Mercer Girl* (plate 7), made in 1968 for a convention held in Seattle, Washington, representing the women recruited by Asa Mercer in the 1860s to go to Seattle and work as teachers and at other worthy professions.

Florian's medium was porcelain, but she is said to have developed a "secret" durable bisque formula, which nobody has ever uncovered. To create her dolls, she would make a mold of her sculpture, then a wax cast for the fine detail, and then make a second mold, from which she actually made the pieces. A great deal of her time was spent mixing paints in pursuit of lifelike flesh tones. The hair is usually sculpted, although some of her dolls do have human-hair wigs (such as Priscilla and John Alden, made in 1953 as a special commission from the Mayflower Hotel in Plymouth, Michigan). Today Florian's works are well represented in museums such as The Detroit Children's Museum in Michigan, the Flag Museum in Baltimore, and the Alfred P. Sloan Museum in Flint, Michigan (which is home to the work of several early doll artists).

Seeing Florian's *Mother and Baby in the Rocking Chair* in 1951 was the beginning of Helen Bullard's crusade on behalf of American doll artists. Born in 1902, Bullard, a wood sculptor, had

Plate 7

Gertrude Florian, *Mercer Girl*, 14 in. (35.6 cm), 1968

established, in 1949, a successful dollmaking cottage industry in Tennessee called Holly Dolls, which carved and dressed simple ten-inch wooden girls of Bullard's design. Upon seeing Florian's piece, Bullard suddenly recognized, as she wrote in *My People in Wood*, that dollmaking was "a field with endless possibilities—an Art, no less." She now began to create her own more complex wooden dolls, such as *Caroline of 1880*, an early feminist rebel, and a spectacular scene of three Alice in Wonderlands, which she called *Alice Fantasy*, consisting of a six-and-one-half-inch Alice, a two-inch "Drink Me" Alice, and an eighteen-inch "Eat Me" Alice.

At the same time, as Bullard began to meet, and see the work of, talented artists such as Heizer, Cochran, and Thompson, she embarked upon a lifelong fight for national recognition of the art of dollmaking, writing monographs in the *Toy Trader* and eventually publishing a number of books on doll artists. Her two-volume work, *The American Doll Artist*, has for years been the only source of information on these early artists.

Bullard went beyond writing in her crusade. A feisty, outspoken, and high-spirited woman, she understood that there was strength in numbers, and that artists who worked in isolation, in a field that was not recognized as legitimate art, needed to band together. "I think my real contribution," she said in a 1985 interview, "was seeing that we could help each other, if we were organized." In 1963 Bullard gathered together three of the foremost doll artists of the day—Magge Head, Gertrude Florian, and Fawn Zeller—to found the National Institute of American Doll Artists (NIADA), an organization that, more than thirty years later, has more than fifty artist members and nearly two hundred patrons, who support and promote the work of the artists. (The other charter members included Dewees Cochran, Dorothy Heizer, Ellery Thorpe, Martha Thompson, Halle Blakely, Lewis Sorensen, and Muriel Bruyere.) The group's aim was to work together toward a common goal: the recognition of original handmade dolls as fine art. In August 1963 NIADA held its first exhibition of members' work, and since that time, yearly exhibitions have been held at annual conferences.

Bullard continued to make wooden dolls until 1981; her work is sculptural and usually historical. Among her achievements were several groups representing Americans over the centuries. The *American Couple Circa 1708* (plate 8) is one of nine couples from her 1962 series, the American Family, portraying nine generations from 1630 through 1900. Her figures are generally strong and primitive in appeal: "I am not a portraitist, and I am not a realist," she reflected in 1985, "I am an impressionist. But there is a lot of realism; for example, in [the doll I made of] Gertrude Stein's face. You recognize her at once." Although

Bullard's own work has not had a major influence on contemporary doll artists, her unquestionable importance in the history of dollmaking lies in the unique triple role she played as writer, organizer, and artist.

A still-active charter member of NIADA, Fawn Zeller bridges the early years of doll artistry in isolation to today's bustling, multilayered world of dollmaking. Working from the start in porcelain, Zeller is known for the creation of more than one hundred one-of-a-kind portrait dolls of exceptional accuracy, as well as a few limited editions and souvenir dolls created for national conventions of the UFDC. Among the limited editions was fifteen-inch *Polly Piedmont* (plate 9), originally created for North Carolina's Piedmont Doll Club and first seen publicly at the 1965 UFDC convention in Washington, D.C. The all-porcelain girl with molded hair and painted features still serves as the Piedmont Doll Club's mascot today.

In spite of her widely acknowledged stature as a "grand lady of dollmaking," Zeller is a perfectionist who is often less than satisfied with her dolls. She came to dollmaking from a career as a portrait painter and researches her portraits exhaustively, both as individuals and as representations of their period in terms of costume and historical positioning. She works with her own mixture of porcelain slip that renders the porcelain—which she uses for the heads, hands and legs—pliable for shaping. (The bodies are wrapped wire frames.) Although Zeller's entire body of work is recognized as outstanding, she is especially celebrated for her lifelike male figures, such as Franklin Roosevelt, Winston Churchill, and Dwight D. Eisenhower. Franklin Roosevelt is a poignant example of her passionate attention to detail; under his costume the doll wears an exact replica of the metal brace the man wore.

In her first decades of dollmaking—the 1940s and 1950s—Zeller often

Plate 9
Fawn Zeller,
Polly Piedmont,
15 in. (38.1 cm), 1965

compared notes with fellow artist Martha Thompson, but even so, she was basically working alone, in a trial-and-error process familiar to all the early twentieth-century artists. "We didn't have the books, kits and other stores of information available today," Zeller says. "We were truly pioneers then." Today this pioneer is hailed by others as much for her generosity in sharing her knowledge and experience as for her refined mastery of the porcelain process. Maggie Finch says, "She set an incredible standard and was an inspiration to all of us. I'll never forget her tips on how she inserted eyelashes one at a time. She is a very giving person." Her giving has included a 1984 book, *Fawn Zeller's Porcelain Dollmaking Techniques*, written by Sibyl McFadden, which reveals, step-by-step, her methods for everything from working with molds to painting china and carving. She has also been active in numerous doll clubs and arts organizations and, in the early 1960s, opened a museum in Inverness, Florida, that existed for four years.

After more than fifty years of dollmaking, Zeller is still filling orders. In 1989 she looked for a new challenge and decided to create eleven fashion heads, representing styles from 1779 to 1887. "Fashion changed so drastically in that time frame," she explains. "It presented a challenge to show the evolution in hairstyles and bonnets."

In considering Fawn Zeller's work, we stride forward into the world of contemporary dolls. The artists who have come after these pioneers have, in many instances, overtaken them in technical skill, range of subject matter, and creative freedom. Certainly many of the boundaries that existed for doll artists fifty years ago have been removed by those who followed them. Materials have changed; methods have been refined. Yet the need to bring into being an evocative three-dimensional human figure that provokes a strong emotional response is always at the heart of these creations.

The chapters that follow will trace the development of contemporary dolls thematically, looking at them always as their creators conceived them. The chapters move from realistic portraits to interpretations of characters, cultures, and images to children and adults conceived entirely in the artist's imagination, and conclude with fantasy creations and pieces that bear little of what defines a doll, sometimes retaining just one intangible aspect or attribute through which the piece keeps a toehold on this fascinating, always changing medium.

Portraits of
Real People

For generations dolls have been made to represent real people, chronicling a moment in the lives of historical personages, celebrities, and ordinary folk. Today's portrait doll artists continue the tradition of realistic depiction as well as artistic interpretation. To capture the essence of their subjects, these artists must be adept at portraying such nebulous qualities as attitude and stance in the faces and bodies of their dolls. The best portrait dolls evoke emotional responses as they mirror life's vicissitudes on a miniature scale.

A number of doll artists specialize in historical figures. These makers share a special gift for expressing the mood of a particular period in history combined with a love of research that can involve months of study in libraries

Plate 10
Alexander and
Marina Royzman,
Vaslav Nijinsky,
20 in. (50.8 cm), 1993

and costume wings of museums around the world. No detail is too small for their attention, as they faithfully record a moment in the lives of their subjects.

Kathy Redmond has been called a doll artist for connoisseurs. Admirers of her sculptured porcelain figures are as likely to be found in the world of decorative arts as in the world of dolls. Redmond began sculpting bronze figures in college, mastering a difficult medium before she turned to porcelain. Unlike most doll artists working with porcelain, Redmond eschews molds, preferring to carve and paint each piece by hand. "If a client wants a repeat of a subject, I make a completely new version from start to finish," Redmond notes. Viewers of some of Redmond's "duplicates" are amazed how each doll exactly portrays the subject but retains an individuality. The most popular repeats include versions of King Henry VIII and his wives, Queen Elizabeth I, Queen Victoria, and the first ladies of the White House.

Viewers marvel at the detail Redmond is able to carve into the porcelain. Jewels dazzle, ribbons curl, and lace fragments into myriad filigree patterns. Redmond has been compared to the masters of trompe l'oeil and is pleased when people can't resist the urge to touch her dolls to check for themselves if the lace is real. She immerses herself in the lives of her subjects and strives to interpret in porcelain rather than merely replicate. Often, she elongates her figures, creating a stylized elegance that makes it easy to recognize a Redmond doll.

In Redmond's studies of European royalty over a twenty-year period, portraits of Queen Victoria are a recurring theme. "The first Queen Victoria doll I made," Redmond recalls, "was about eighteen years ago after I finished reading *Queen Victoria* by Cecil Woodham Smith. I suppose I was already under the influence of Victoriana, as my mother had always collected with great relish Victorian dolls, furniture, and figurines. I was equally enthralled by the Victoria-Albert love story."

Redmond constantly seeks new ways to challenge herself in her chosen medium. Until recently she sculpted her dolls to the shoulder before attaching muslin bodies. Her newest pleasure is to sculpt down to the waist, a technique that adds interest to the figures but requires careful attention in handling. *Young Queen Victoria* (plate 11) was the first "bisque-to-hip" Victoria figure that Redmond attempted. She remembers it as one of her most ambitious projects, noting, "Even grasping the unfired clay figure was difficult. It was tricky not to break the delicate bisque lace while holding the clay doll to work on the hair or face. The deep carving of the lace and other detail work took forever. I fashioned the crown and the hair braid around the ear separately and anchored them

Plate 11
Kathy Redmond,
Young Queen Victoria,
13 in. (33 cm), 1992
(Photo: Courtesy of Kathy
Redmond)

to the wetted-down doll head. As I carved, I would refer to the wonderful paintings of the young Victoria by Franz Winterhalter and listen to my tapes of the Brandenburg Concertos."

Carole Piper is an English dollmaker, who, like Redmond, is fascinated with the monarchy. Her interest in royalty was kindled during the five years she worked as a court dressmaker in the late 1950s, fashioning clothes for members of the royal family. For years she has chronicled the comings and goings of the royals through her portrait dolls, and she plans to continue depicting them, even though their recent troubles have adversely affected the public's interest. She has made many versions of Queen Elizabeth II, subtly altering each portrait as the queen aged. "In depicting the queen, I tried to reveal her as people know her best," Piper allows. "She can look quite severe—I hope that the slight smile on her face has softened that look. I have kept making her hair a bit grayer—some customers seem surprised, but I like to portray her as she is."

Before making a doll, Piper consults her extensive library about the royal family. She faithfully copies royal insignias, jewelry, and costumes, delighting in reproducing the smallest detail. For example, *Queen Elizabeth II* (plate 12) wears her "personal orders" attached to her sash—the insignias are decorated with bejeweled miniature portraits of her father and grandfather. Piper spends at least a week modeling the head, while constantly referring to her photo file. She works in her kitchen, and often sculpts with battered kitchen utensils, which she prefers to conventional sculpting tools. "I like to look at the head I am working on at odd times. I might be cooking, and all of a sudden I'll notice a defect I hadn't seen before," Piper says.

After the porcelain head and limbs are finished, Piper attaches them to a wire-armature cloth body. When it's time for costuming, her years working for Norman Hartnell, dresser of the royal family, prove invaluable. "I learned how to cut and make patterns, to embroider and do beading," Piper notes. She allows herself artistic license with her costumes, choosing to design what she feels the royal family would be likely to wear rather than to copy specific outfits.

After Piper married and left her job to raise a family, she discovered dollmaking during the 1970s. When she came upon the work of Dorothy Heizer and Martha Thompson, she knew she wanted to follow in their footsteps. As Piper mastered the medium of porcelain and became known for her historical portraits, she experimented with dolls representing children. Recently she has found a sense of freedom in these dolls, which are a welcome change from the more precise royals. When asked to name her favorite member of the royal family, Piper quickly volunteered, "The Queen Mum. She has always been loving and outgoing throughout her life. She has shown a very caring nature, especially during both world wars. She's everyone's favorite grandmother!" In the

Plate 12
Carole Piper,
Queen Elizabeth II,
20 in. (50.8 cm), 1993

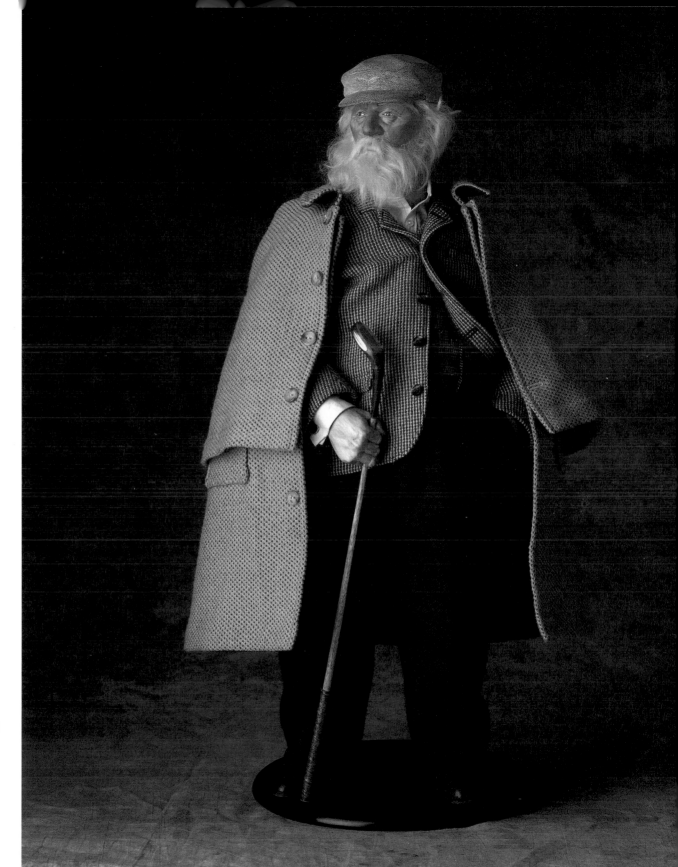

Plate 13
Michael Langton,
Old Tom Morris,
22 in. (55.9 cm), 1993
(Photo: Courtesy of
Michael Langton)

future Piper would like to make the Queen Mum as a young woman, Queen Mary, and some of the older historical figures. "If nothing else," Piper says, "in two hundred years they will at least have a curiosity value." Her many fans would be quick to argue that they will leave a more important legacy.

Another established artist who found inspiration in the British Isles is New Hampshire woodworker and NIADA artist Michael Langton. Langton's evocative portrait, *Old Tom Morris* (plate 13), the world's first professional golfer, from Saint Andrews, Scotland, caused a sensation when Langton made it available for purchase at a golf collectors' show. So many people wanted to buy the piece that in the interests of fairness Langton put all the names of the would-be buyers into a container, shuffled them, and proceeded to give the lucky winner the option of purchasing Old Tom for the predetermined price. Langton, as usual, had spent inordinate amounts of time researching and then making the piece, including taking a trip to Saint Andrews, where he consulted David Joy, a native of Saint Andrews and the local expert on Tom Morris. Details that the trip provided prompted Langton to hire a weaver, Jan Croteau, to make the fabrics for Old Tom's cape, jacket, and vest in the one-third-inch-scale pattern. The hat is carved wood and the golf club Old Tom holds is a one-third-inch-scale model of a real Tom Morris club. In his pocket is a working watch, set for Saint Andrews time. Such minute attention to detail and exceptional carving skills were among the reasons why *Esquire* magazine elected Langton into the 1984 register of outstanding Americans under forty. Out of a field of 5,000 candidates, 271 were chosen. Langton was the only dollmaker in the group.

Langton's natural talents as an artist were largely undirected until a serious motorcycle accident when he was twenty-one gave him "a new impetus to getting my artwork done." Langton's interests were split between his love of working with wood (exercised in furniture design and construction) and his sculpture. When he was asked to create a wooden doll that Katharine Hepburn would use in the movie *On Golden Pond,* Langton found he could employ both of his passions in one project. The discovery that his sculptural interests could be joined with woodworking established the foundation of Langton's dollmaking career. He decided to dedicate all of his time and available resources to the development of an art form whose horizons seemed endless. "It is wonderful," he says, "to be in the realm of *what* to do in art rather than *how* to do it. The craft is not the subordinate partner in this business of art, but a willing equal participant—this union, to me, means artistic freedom."

Canadian artists Martha Boers and her sister Marianne Reitsma, known

for their fantasy dolls, became interested in creating a series of figures of famous artists and their works. To challenge themselves artistically, they chose a renowned artist of the Renaissance, Leonardo da Vinci. At the outset they were dismayed to find a good deal of information about his works but little about him personally. In all their research they found one self-portrait of Leonardo and one small profile sketch. Reitsma began by sculpting the head, which she found daunting. "Leonardo was my first old man head," she remembers, "and since he was bald, the head had to be perfect. There could be no bumps or lumps, which can normally be hidden by hair." While Reitsma worked on the head, Boers began researching the clothing. "In Leonardo's day clothes were rather simple and shapeless but involved lots of drapery," she notes. "After sewing and staining the fabric (they didn't wash their clothes much then), the tunic was soaked, propped up inside, and laid on a heat source to dry. Finally it was put on the doll and the final draping checked. I then added the beard and hair of wispy white mohair to the now finished head." As the artists work, they continually critique and evaluate the efforts of each other. When Reitsma viewed the hair, she said it was too straight. Boers admits, "I had created the hair from memory, so I looked at Leonardo's self-portrait, and sure enough, his hair was wavy, necessitating a new wig." For the painting on the easel, a representation of the *Mona Lisa,* the artists decided to enlarge it and to make it "a work in progress," so that it did not have to look exactly like the painting. Reitsma adds, "It was important to us that the painting be 'real' and not just a cut-out picture glued to a canvas like so many other artists do."

Boers and Reitsma agree that the most enjoyable part of the process involved creating a "messy" studio environment. Taking wooden bowls and jars that had been painted to look like old china bowls and glass jars, the artists dipped the bottoms in thin paint and made rings on the furniture. They gleefully splattered paint on the floor and crate, piled rolls of Leonardo's works onto a computer, shrinking them, and printing them in sepia on old, yellowed newsprint. Reitsma even confesses to using actual postage-size paint rags in the piece, noting, "Nothing looks as authentic, as when you use it. We'd spill a tiny bit of paint, and then madly wipe it up with the tiny rags. It was a lot of fun!"

A desire to celebrate the life of a legendary missionary led Ann McNichols of Naples, Florida, to make *The Deaconess* (plate 15). When Deaconess Harriet Bedell died in 1969, local newspapers recounted her work with the Seminoles. "And the Seminoles came to know her and call her with affection our White Bird," one account began. As McNichols learned more about the inspirational life of Harriet Bedell, she felt compelled to "translate the lines of caring and giving" into a portrait doll. She studied photographs of the deaconess from newspaper files, assuming that her habit was black and white. McNichols planned to order black fabric for the deaconess's costume, but then discovered a description of the deaconess's habit from the curator of the Collier County Museum, indicating it was navy blue. McNichols quickly changed her order to navy blue serge. She copied in miniature the silver cross the deaconess always wore around her neck, and wired the tiny copper glasses through her head for strength, painting them silver before fitting the plastic lenses, which were hand-cut and filed. McNichols created the young Seminole boy holding the deaconess's hand to represent the many Seminole children who loved her.

Growing up in the small community of Naples in the 1950s, McNichols was the daughter of the owners of the town's only art gallery. Fortunately, she was encouraged in her endeavors by artists who exhibited at the gallery. After graduating from high school, McNichols attended a performing arts school before transferring to the Ringling Art School in Sarasota, Florida. Dollmaking, which had once been a hobby, became an art as McNichols studied porcelain, painting, and drawing from Florida teachers.

As McNichols defined her art, she often chose as subjects the Seminoles, whom she admired for their strength and independence. "The Seminoles have many unique characteristics," she notes. "Their colorful clothing and distinctive hairstyles and jewelry make them wonderful subjects. I've made about ten Seminole prototypes for editions of ten to fifteen dolls." As McNichols delved into Seminole customs, she became curious about other tribes and started making dolls from other Indian nations. "I developed a love for ethnic dolls," she explains, "and as one doll leads to another, I am usually planning my next project before I'm at the end of the last one. I consider it an honor to express the proud heritage of such noble people."

Alexander and Marina Royzman make beautiful portrait dolls that reflect their makers' Russian heritage and experiences in their recently adopted country, the United States. Before coming to America in 1990, the Royzmans had creative careers in Russia, Alexander Royzman in cinematography and Marina Royzman in book illustration. Although they were not dollmakers, dolls were part of their lives, for Alexander Royzman occasionally included dolls in his movies and photographs, including a series, *Children and Dolls*, that was exhibited throughout Russia. The Royzmans began to experiment with making dolls, using some of them in sets they designed. Once they were in America, the Royzmans hit upon the idea of making portrait dolls of the great performers in Russian ballets as a way of preserving their heritage. "We wanted to show the beauty and elasticity of the human body and capture the spirit of the ballet," the Royzmans explain. They worked from old engravings and photographs along with ballet programs from many

Plate 15
Ann McNichols,
The Deaconess,
20 in. (50.8 cm), 1991

countries. At first they had little money for materials. Marina Royzman remembers the early days with a smile. "In the beginning of our dollmaking career—which was also the beginning of our life here—we had to find inexpensive materials. We decided to sew the doll bodies out of cloth and to use Sculpey for the heads, arms and legs. To fashion a body with a needle and thread was challenging, but soon, we fell in love with fabrics and textures."

The outstanding performances and the exciting life of Vaslav Nijinsky inspired the Royzmans to depict him in the famous ballet, *Le Spectre de la Rose.* They were determined to portray him as a dancer who revolutionized the sense of rhythm in the ballet. An aura of voluptuousness and the almost discernible scent of roses attests to the Royzmans' skill in costuming as well as their ability to capture a pose. "We worked from many pictures," Marina Royzman explains, pausing to find just the right words in English. "We chose a pose that we considered the most graceful, one that showed Nijinsky at the top of his form. While we wanted to be exact, we also wanted to add our feelings to the piece." For the costume the Royzmans selected the most luxurious silks, embellished with gold thread embroidery. The sensuous silk-chiffon roses are surrounded by hand-painted leaves that at first presented a challenge to the Royzmans. "We wanted them to stay in position, not to fall limply," Marina Royzman says, "and we came up with the idea of using spray starch to keep them in place. This was particularly important in the garland. After we had the garland in place, we thought the leaves needed more highlighting, so we painted on various colors until we achieved a more luminous quality." When *Vaslav Nijinsky* (plate 10) was finished to their satisfaction, it was evident that as a cloth sculpture he would attract the plaudits and sighs of admiration that the actual Nijinsky received on stage.

In England Paul Crees and Peter Coe also see the world as a stage and devote their lives to creating portraits celebrating its players. Their many admirers believe the British dollmaking team have coaxed the art of wax portraiture into a new realm. Comparing their creations with such legendary Victorian artists as Pierotti, Marsh, and Montanari, collectors eagerly await each new edition of the celebrity-inspired dolls. Since editions are small (never more than fifty and usually only ten to twenty pieces), competition is fierce for Crees and Coe's lifelike interpretations of such captivating women as Vivien Leigh, Barbra Streisand, and Elizabeth Taylor. "I've always loved glamour," Crees points out, in explaining his preoccupation with the stars. "It probably stemmed from growing up in the drab confines of postwar England and burying myself in the world of old films and TV where these incredibly beautiful women wore lovely clothes while leading exciting lives."

As a young man, Crees loved art and fashion, a trait that led to his first job as a costume assistant on the musical version of *Gone with the Wind* in London's West End. After a stint at Exeter making costumes and sets for the Northcott Theatre, Crees began working for Britain's oldest repertory theater, the Old Vic, where his knowledge of costuming greatly benefited from the theater's multi-faceted productions. While working in the theater Crees began experimenting with dollmaking by sculpting a head of Marlene Dietrich. "I've always been a fan of Dietrich and have one of the largest collections of Dietrich memorabilia in the world," Crees notes. "Making replicas of Dietrich and dressing them in costumes from her most celebrated films was a natural progression for me. From Dietrich I went on to Garbo, and I was off and running." These first dolls were one-of-a-kinds made of plaster of paris and scrim-covered carved styrofoam. In 1980 Crees was discovered at a local gallery in Bath by Ann Parker, founder of the British Doll Artists Association, who invited him to become the first male member of that august body of artists. While at the Bristol Old Vic, Crees met Peter Coe, whose background in costume design matched his own. Discovering they were kindred spirits, by 1980 they had become a team. On the advice of a sculptor friend they changed over to the medium of poured wax after finding their first attempts at hand-carving plaster of paris too time-consuming.

Today both artists jointly undertake the sculpting. Crees models and paints most of the heads, while Coe concentrates on the difficult task of wax pouring and doll construction. They both sculpt the hands and legs. They recently decided to make detachable arms that snap on to the upper shoulder. Another innovation has been a seamless chest plate that extends down to the stomach, allowing a décolletage gown to reveal a completely natural body. Crees fashions all his own molds from plaster of paris. The flesh-tinted wax is then heated in a custom-made industrial melter until molten and ready to pour. Coe constantly seeks to employ the latest technological advances: he developed and refined the unique matte-finish wax formula, yielding a flexible product that lets the component parts bend under pressure, thereby reducing the chance of breakage.

The artists agree that one of the most enjoyable parts of the process is deciding on who will be their next subject. After much give-and-take before settling on a person, they study countless photos, books, and videos. For the few one-of-a-kind dolls they produce each year, Crees and Coe will go all out on costuming; they admit they can devote enormous chunks of time if they

know they will never have to repeat the same task again. For *Gloria* (plate 16), a limited edition of ten, the artists treated the piece as if it were a one-of-a-kind piece, confessing, "We were swept away by Swanson's commanding persona and felt compelled to recreate one of her most glamorous but intricate costumes. She is swathed in a wine-colored peignoir with gold sequins and bugle-beaded appliqué worn over a pajama suit of gold-tissue lamé." One of their most successful portrait dolls, *Gloria* captures the star's overbearing hauteur as well as her beauty. Viewers are mesmerized by the artistry of the hands, delicately but theatrically posed with each nail individually sculpted and varnished.

When Crees and Coe entered the field of poured-wax dolls, they found little research available and very few artists working in the medium. Of necessity self-taught, Crees and Coe hope they have succeeded in keeping alive an age-old tradition of dollmaking that was in danger of disappearing.

Along with Crees and Coe, Connecticut artist Clark Hanford shares an affinity for the glamorous stars of the stage and screen, sculpting such luminaries as Marlene Dietrich, Bette Davis, Katharine Hepburn, Lucille Ball, Marilyn Monroe, and Elizabeth Taylor. During the last few years Hanford has been designing cabinets to house his sculptures: not traditional glass display cabinets, but solid pieces of furniture containing "surprises." For *Frank Sinatra* (plate 17), Hanford designed a forty-two-inch floor model of a 1940s radio. It is finished in black walnut veneer and plays early Sinatra tunes. When the front is opened, a perfectly lit Frank Sinatra is found inside. Hanford worked in hydrostone, a plasterlike material used in dental work and interior architectural moldings. As he studied the many available photographs of Sinatra, Hanford was surprised to observe that one of Sinatra's ears appeared different from the other. He noticed that most still shots of Sinatra showed the side of his face with the "good" ear. Apparently, Sinatra's

Plate 16
Paul Crees and
Peter Coe,
Gloria,
27 in. (68.6 cm), 1993

birth had been difficult, necessitating a forceps delivery that resulted in a mangled ear. The most challenging part of the process for Hanford involved the hair, as it was the first man for which Hanford had made a wig. (A previous Fred Astaire had molded-on hair.) "In order to make a realistic head of hair, I had to show Sinatra's thinning hairline by inserting less hair at the top and front sides," Hanford reveals. Frank Sinatra already owns a Marlene Dietrich doll by Hanford, and the artist hopes Sinatra will want to add this piece to his collection.

Plate 17
Clark Hanford,
Frank Sinatra,
34 in. (86.4 cm), 1993

Hanford grew up in Connecticut but moved to England in 1970 after studying at Ealing and Goldsmith colleges in London. After establishing a trendy clothing shop, he began sculpting two- to three-foot figures for the shop. At first, he thought of them more as models than as dolls, but always made them "dressed and looking as real as possible." Hanford was surprised when clients started buying the sculptures as well as the clothing, prompting him to consider sculpting as a profession. In May 1987 Hanford met with Joan Collins when his portrait sculpture of her launched her new line of loungewear. "Through my sculptures," Hanford says, "I have entered an exciting world. Right now I am working on Elizabeth Taylor as Cleopatra, and then I plan to redo her as she appeared in real life during the 1960s." Hanford's goal is to keep making dolls that will keep alive the world of entertainment and preserve an important part of America's cultural history.

Nerissa Shaub loves children—both "naughty" and "nice"—and delights in capturing their real-life poses. She does not shy away from portraying children in their least endearing moments, saying, "I want my dolls to reflect the human personality rather than portray an idealized version."

Frances's Children—1953 (plate 18) is an affectionate reminiscence of growing up in Lancaster, Pennsylvania, and partaking in the annual trip to Hagar's

Department Store for a visit with Santa Claus. ("Frances" is Shaub's mother.) Shaub (in the red coat) sits on Santa's knee, clutching a bag of penny candy. She is wearing her "good" coat with its matching hat, along with the black patent-leather Mary-Janes that were de rigueur for all special occasions. Shaub, who remembers ordinarily wearing her sister's hand-me-downs, is dressed in her own white "party dress" that matches her sister's frock. Her brother wears a cast-off coat from one of his sisters—do we imagine that he looks uncomfortable because he is wearing pink? (When Shaub sent her mother a picture of the piece, her mother wrote back, "You have captured [Bill's] expression quite well, but doesn't he look forlorn in his sister's outgrown coat? I do believe that coat happened to be light blue, so it wouldn't have looked like a 'castoff.'" Shaub insists the coat was pink; and in any event the pink coat immediately captures the viewer's attention, anchoring an uneasiness in what superficially appears to be a happy family portrait. "We were all very shy as children," Shaub remembers, "and we were probably terrified sitting in this stranger's lap. I am sure we were looking at my mother for reassurance." Shaub's ability to portray this subtle air of uncertainty is a tribute to her skill as an artist.

Dollmaking is just one of the many forms of artistic expression that have interested Shaub throughout the years. She is also an interior designer, painter, furniture designer, and architectural renderer. This multifaceted career has not prevented her from making over 2,800 dolls for private collectors who often commission her work. In 1979 she started making cloth dolls while teaching art and interior design as a full-time college instructor. In 1984 she participated in her first toy fair under the auspices of doll impresario Tom Boland. She sold out her first collection of limited-edition dolls and discovered she could not keep up with the demand for her dolls. She has since turned to making one-of-a-kind pieces, finding them more compatible with what she calls "my short attention span." Since Shaub is happiest skipping from one project to another, working with one-of-a-kind dolls offers her the freedom she desires. In her studio she challenges herself by experimenting with whatever captures her fancy. She has made anthropomorphic animal dolls, clown dolls, fantasy dolls, and portrait dolls, as well as three-dimensional vignettes. When Shaub finds an old painting or photograph containing children that appeal to her, she will make her own version, creating dolls representing the children. She places them on a baseboard in front of a painted background based on the original painting or photograph. The resulting vignette distills the emotions inherent in the scene with a directness that is always present in Shaub's work.

Plate 18
Nerissa Shaub,
Frances's Children—
1953,
22 in. (55.9 cm), 1994

Shaub makes most of her portrait dolls with Cernit over a clay base. She usually begins a project with a sketch. She then molds the parts, which are cleaned and fired. She will either paint or coat them with Cernit or dip them in wax. For *Frances's Children—1953* Shaub painted the dolls with oil paints after the firing process. "I painted more opaquely than I usually do," she notes, "and then I brushed wax over the paint to remove the shine."

Despite Shaub's interest in various media, she always returns to doll portraiture. She has found it deeply satisfying to recapture her childhood by creating dolls of herself and her siblings at various ages. The tragic death of her sister, Barbara, in 1990 was eased by dollmaking. "I made a thirty-inch Cernit

Plate 19
Photograph of
Isabella, a six-year-
old Belgian girl

doll, a likeness of myself in kindergarten. She helped me in my grieving/healing
process. I held her, talked to her, and cried with her," Shaub remembers. "My
dolls are a vehicle for expressing my emotions." Her many admirers key into the
feelings Shaub portrays and regard Nerissa (as she is known in the doll world)
as a kindred spirit of the children she creates—undaunted by adulthood, with
the honesty of children who are allowed to be themselves.

   Karin Schmidt, a doll artist from Russelheim, Germany, shares Nerissa
Shaub's joy in recreating the natural innocence and liveliness of childhood.
Her one-of-a-kind porcelain dolls are studies of children of varied races and
cultures. While her favorite models are children from South America, Africa,
and the Orient, she also accepts commissions for portrait dolls of European
and American subjects.

   Schmidt traces her dollmaking career to a beloved lost childhood doll
that represented the security she craved as a child of war-torn Germany. Born
in 1940 in eastern Germany, Schmidt suffered in the war: Her father was killed
and her mother was deported by the Russians, leaving her to be cared for by
neighbors. After a reunion with her mother seven years later, life regained a
semblance of normality. Schmidt received her own toys including a celluloid
doll, to which she transferred many of her anxieties, making it an inseparable

Plate 20
Karin Schmidt,
Isabella,
31 in. (78.7 cm), 1994
(Photo: Courtesy of
Karin Schmidt)

companion. When Schmidt was fourteen, her mother finally thought it best to throw away the doll—a decision that still pains Schmidt today, and which she considers the impetus for her desire to make dolls as an adult.

At first Schmidt reproduced antique dolls, moving on to original work as she grew more skilled. Her talent was apparent; between 1983 and 1988 she won several awards, a success that encouraged her to undertake dollmaking as a career. In 1988 she made her first portrait doll, which was so well received that she added a new category to her repertoire: child portraiture.

Schmidt works from photographs as she tries to capture the "soul" of the child. "I want to express a mood; therefore I pay great attention to the sculpting of the mouth and the area around the eyes," she explains. "Since a doll cannot communicate by speaking, I make it communicate by its expression." *Isabella* (plates 19 and 20), a portrait doll of a six-year-old Belgian girl, is typical of Schmidt's one-of-a-kind portrait dolls. Her head, shoulders, arms, and legs are porcelain, while the body is kid leather stuffed with lamb's wool. With *Isabella* Schmidt wished to emphasize her sunny disposition and faunlike innocence. To that end *Isabella*'s tiny face is framed by a wide-brimmed hat over her schoolgirl bangs. A shy smile lights up her face along with the twinkle in her eyes. She lives up to Schmidt's claim, "My dolls have something to say!"

Collectors of Schmidt's dolls are now able to obtain a small number of limited-edition dolls. A recent collaboration with Germany's Goetz Dolls (known for quality vinyl dolls) has resulted in a one-hundred-piece porcelain limited edition of three Schmidt designs and an annual limited edition in vinyl.

For NIADA artist Pat Brooks of Summerton, South Carolina, portrait dolls of children represent the majority of the approximately 350 dolls she has made since 1977. For years she received accolades for her one-of-a-kind basswood dolls, which she called her "babes in wood." Recently, Brooks has added porcelain and Sculpey to her repertoire, and is planning to expand her horizons even further by turning to limited editions. "I feel the small dolls I've been doing for some time would lend themselves to resin," she confides. "I am looking forward to being involved from start to finish, producing fifteen to twenty-five dolls that would be more affordable than my one-of-a-kinds." Brooks's success with her porcelain dolls for the Ashton-Drake Galleries and the basswood doll she designed for the Hamilton Collection (her 1993 *Waiting for Santa* is expected to sell out its edition of 15,000) has convinced her to move into limited editions while still making the one-of-a-kind portrait dolls that catapulted her to fame.

Brooks's success as a dollmaker is not surprising: She was born into an artistic family who owned a doll factory in Massachusetts. As a child she made dolls and doll clothes and studied art in her parents' home studio from the time she could hold a pencil. She studied oil portraiture, life drawing, and ceramics in night school in her late teens. While taking a crafts course at night school, Brooks discovered a "how-to" book with directions for making a wooden doll. She thought the doll might be an interesting project for her course, and followed the directions, substituting the more attractive basswood instead of the recommended sugar pine. As Brooks made contacts in the doll world, she began to visualize a career as a doll artist: "I discovered there was a market for my handcarved dolls when I participated in my first doll show in 1978, where I received my first seven orders. At the time I had two preschool-aged daughters and another child on the way, and the idea of doing something I totally loved, while staying at home to raise my children, was immensely appealing." In Brooks's hands basswood glowed until it resembled porcelain, and handmade accessories personalized each doll. From the beginning, her dolls—many of which were modeled after her children—were captivating viewers with their technical virtuosity and emotional appeal.

Plate 21

Patricia Ryan Brooks,
Cora Mae Sanborn,
8½ in. (21.6 cm), 1992

The portrait doll, *Cora Mae Sanborn* (plate 21), was commissioned by Edythe Sanborn as a remembrance of her sister as a child. Brooks worked from a sepia photograph taken shortly before World War I. "I copied it as closely as possible in Super Sculpey, even to the ring the doll wears on her middle finger," Brooks notes, "but I couldn't resist adding the 'china' doll she holds on her lap." Edythe Sanborn was so thrilled with the doll that she immediately asked Brooks to do her brother, her other sister, and even herself as children. A dedicated collector, Sanborn now owns sixteen of Brooks's dolls.

Gina Bellous, a California artist, has been making miniature portrait dolls in porcelain since 1986, working from an array of photographs her clients send to her. While her dolls are cherished as family heirlooms, they are also highly regarded as examples of fine miniature figures. Bellous, like so many doll artists with backgrounds in art during college, was

still mainly self-taught in her chosen field. Since she could not find a class in miniature dollmaking in her area, she took a course in porcelain doll-making and applied the techniques she learned to one-inch-scale dolls. At first Bellous experimented with wedding-cake dolls, using commercial molds but resculpting and dressing them as brides and grooms. She ran a small ad in a bridal magazine and was amazed at the large response. As Bellous grew more confident, she began altering the dolls more, until they scarcely resembled dolls from commercial molds. Today she still uses commercial molds as a base for some of her dolls. "I want to keep the price of my dolls reasonable, and by not spending time building a base, I can keep up with a sizable volume of orders," Bellous notes. "For special dolls such as *Jaymie* (plates 22, 23), a portrait of my son that I kept for myself, I create an original sculpture." When Bellous uses a commercial mold, she always credits the designer of the mold in a certificate describing the doll that is sent along with the doll to each client.

Jaymie represents a true labor of love for Bellous. He is portrayed at two years old, the second version in a series that Bellous plans to continue along with a series of her daughter at one-year intervals. "With *Jaymie* I had the advantage of working from a live model, although he is so active, I could only study him when he was asleep," Bellous reveals. "I would stand in front of his crib, sketching his nose, his mouth, his eyes—it was exciting." For his clothing Bellous made a tiny, hand-sewn sailor cap and a sweater made from a hand-dyed, ribbed T-shirt. "I hand-dye most of my fabrics, as it is necessary to tone down colors for miniatures. The greatest challenge facing the miniaturist in costuming is finding fabric whose color and patterns are compatible with the one-inch scale. I couldn't find a plaid small enough for Jaymie's shorts, so I hand-painted the plaid on a solid fabric. For his sandals I used florist's tape, which I painted navy blue. I keep a supply of vintage kid gloves on hand for shoes, but I felt the tape worked better for the openwork of the sandals."

For *Jaymie* and other portrait miniatures, Bellous makes seven separate china paint firings to achieve a lifelike appearance. Her preoccupation with creating realistic miniatures has prompted Bellous to start her own doll mold company with Penni-Jo Jonas of Penni Bears. "Over the years I noticed certain areas in commercial mold-making that could be improved," Bellous says. "I thought, Wouldn't it be nice to have molds that did not need so much sculpting to make them look like real people? For example, I found hands were often clublike and not to scale, and faces often had what I call a 'dolly' look. I wanted to create molds with more detail, including fired-on jewelry and shoes with such niceties as shoelaces and bows." At the present time Bellous is producing about twenty-five dolls a month, taking care of two small children, and starting a new business venture. In spite of all these time-consuming activities, each doll she makes is a miniature model of perfection, destined to be displayed as a cherished keepsake. While Bellous's dolls are the smallest dolls in this chapter, they are made with the same attention to detail that characterizes the best portrait dolls. They can share the stage with larger dolls in revealing the essence of personality.

Plate 23
Photograph of
Jaymie Bellous

Figures from
Literature

 In interpreting characters from literature, the dollmaker faces the challenge of

fulfilling a reader's fantasy, yet surprising and enriching it at the same time. There

are often visual inspirations (or intrusions, depending on the point of view of

the artist) in the original work—sometimes very defined illustrations, sometimes

merely suggestions of physical appearance. If the work has been dramatized, the

dollmaker must also decide whether or not to incorporate the interpretation of the

character made by a particular performing artist. The characters in this chapter are

among the best of this type in that they both satisfy our expectations and give us

new insights. Whether they are familiar characters like Charles Dickens's Scrooge,

Plate 24
Helen Kish,
Victoriana,
22 in. (55.9 cm), 1983

or obscure ones like Oliver Goldsmith's Aminabad, these figures from literature

have been created with a strong, distinctive, and personal vision of the artists, each of whom has seized the opportunity to collaborate, silently, with the original creators. And who would not want the chance to execute the visions of William Shakespeare, Charles Dickens, or Antoine de Saint-Exupéry?

Some of the best-loved characters of children's books have become three-dimensional felt playthings, albeit for collectors rather than children themselves, thanks to the imaginative interpretations of R. John Wright. He and his wife Susan now head up a thriving toymaking workshop, R. John Wright Dolls, in Cambridge, New York. R. John Wright Dolls has produced editions of many of Disney's characters, giving sturdy, tactile life to the well-known animated figures. From traditional figures such as Snow White and the Seven Dwarfs and Little Red Riding Hood to classics like Hans Brinker, Christopher Robin, and Winnie-the-Pooh, Wright's dolls exude the playful lore of nursery storybooks.

The Wrights define themselves as toymakers, and they have admittedly been influenced by toymakers of the early twentieth century like Käthe Kruse, the Italian company Lenci, and the German company Steiff, whose pieces first led them to dollmaking. The Wrights distinguish themselves from doll artists who create one-of-a-kinds or very small editions, defining their challenge as one of designing pieces that can be produced to consistently high levels of craftsmanship by the members of their workshop. "It's not that hard to make a good prototype," they assert. "The hard part is maintaining the level of quality throughout large production."

The Little Prince (plate 25), based on the French story *Le Petit Prince* by Antoine de Saint-Exupéry, was made in 1983 by John Wright. A relatively early piece, it is universally admired and longed for by collectors. Wright began producing pieces on his own with Susan in the late 1970s. *The Little Prince* was created in 1983 in an edition of 250 for The Toy Shoppe in Midlothian, Vir-

Plate 25
R. John Wright,
The Little Prince,
17 in. (43.2 cm), 1983

ginia, whose owners, Barrie and Danny Shapiro, are strong supporters and promoters of dolls and toys of high artistic quality. Wright clearly remembers his reasons for selecting the Little Prince as a character. "I knew that it would be a very important doll to many people," he explains, "since Saint-Exupéry's fable is dearly loved for its message of gentle optimism and goodwill. Secondly, as far as I could tell, no one had yet attempted to make a doll of this enchanting character, and for that reason alone I would be breaking new ground." His molded-felt creation so strongly embodies that message of goodwill and gentle optimism that it appears to have remained the only three-dimensional rendition of this character to date.

Wright also recognized, however, the dilemma of every artist who decides to interpret a character from literature. "The challenge I faced," he muses, "was in keeping the doll simple enough so that my interpretation would not intrude on the various perceptions held by readers of the book who, like myself, had only the sketchy and whimsical illustrations to refer to." Wright's triumph has been in transforming Saint-Exupéry's airy drawings into a piece of warm and solid whimsy.

Far from whimsical is the tragic heroine of John Fowles's novel *The French Lieutenant's Woman*; she is rendered in porcelain as *Victoriana* (plate 24) by the versatile artist Helen Kish. The widely acclaimed 1969 novel, which takes place in late nineteenth-century England, gained even greater fame in 1981 when made into a film starring Meryl Streep and Jeremy Irons. Kish chose to portray the title character as she was played by Meryl Streep, with the result being immediate public recognition for her enigmatic figure.

"I couldn't get that film out of my head," the artist recalls. "The main character of *The French Lieutenant's Woman* haunted me until I finished sculpting a likeness in clay. The piece was an exorcism of sorts." Created in 1983 in an edition of fifteen, the porcelain sculpture pleased its creator: "I captured exactly what I wanted, just the right emotional response."

More than a decade after she created *Victoriana*, Kish still wants to evoke an emotional response from the public. "I am still striving to reach a technical balance in my work," she says, "but this is important only to the extent that technical flaws interfere with the meaning of the work. I hope to evoke some response that comes straight from the spirit, or soul, of the observer to connect with my work, and therefore, myself."

Kish is primarily known for her work in porcelain, although she also works now in what she terms "more immediate media," such as direct-modeled stoneware and porcelain, in which she wants to create pieces that will "reflect my interior landscape to an extent that I have not been capable of sharing up to now." She has designed (often anonymously) for manufacturers such as Dakin, and direct-mail companies, such as The Franklin Mint and the Hamilton Collection. Her own firm, Kish and Company, was formed in 1991; it produces vinyl limited editions of her designs, featuring primarily realistic, daintily proportioned little girls. Regarding both her commercial work and her artistic pieces, she says: "My inspiration has come from the world around me and the world inside of me."

The twenty-two-inch-high *Victoriana* is fully modeled porcelain to the waist, with jointed arms. The lower body and thighs are made of ultrasuede, and the porcelain lower legs are jointed with the cloth upper legs. The toes are pointed. The wig is human hair, and the garment is a white dressing gown covered by a deep green knitted shawl. What is most striking about this creation, though, is the finely modeled face, which strongly resembles Meryl Streep's. In her haunting expression Kish has achieved the ambiguous essence of this complex character, who has been loved and abandoned, emerging broken in the eyes of the world, yet somehow strong within herself. The novel itself posits an ambiguous ending, which is aptly reflected in Kish's figure.

There is nothing ambiguous about *Cowslips* (plate 26) by Maggie Finch and her daughter, Marta Finch-Kozlosky. These two women work independently as dollmakers but also collaborate under the name of Transcendence. Taking as their inspiration a love sonnet by the twentieth-century American poet Edna St. Vincent Millay, they are undoubtedly the first to give form to this lovelorn maiden, who opens her heart to her lover, saying:

> Not in a silver casket cool with pearls
> Or rich with red corundum or with blue,
> Locked, and the key withheld, as other girls
> Have given their loves, I give my love to you;
> Not in a lovers' knot, not in a ring
> Worked in such fashion, and the legend plain—
> Semper fidelis, where a secret spring
> Kennels a drop of mischief for the brain;
> Love in the open hand, no thing but that,
> Ungemmed, unhidden, wishing not to hurt,
> As one should bring you cowslips in a hat

Swung from the hand, or apples in her skirt,
I bring you, calling out as children do:
"Look what I have!—And these are all for you."

The sonnet is a particular favorite of Finch's from Edna St. Vincent Millay's book, *Fatal Interview.* "Since I am also a poet myself, I have always loved Millay's poetry," Finch explains. "I collected all her books as they came out; she was my role model. As I grew older and fell more deeply in love, I found that book, in particular, astounding. To have written so many perfect sonnets. . . ."

When Finch's daughter, who was living in Lyons, France, was looking for a love poem to read to an international women's group at a Valentine's Day luncheon, she asked her mother if she had a favorite; it was only natural that Finch recite this sonnet. After Finch-Kozlosky read it to the group, the poem lay quietly in her mind, beneath the surface somewhere, for a long time. When it next emerged, it was—much to her surprise—in the form of a young woman's head, which she was sculpting from Sculpey.

"I don't have any preconceived notions of what I'm sculpting before I start," Finch-Kozlosky says. "I like to have the head speak to me and tell me who it is." In this case, the artist relates, she heard the woman speaking Millay's sonnet. "As I was working I saw she had a country air, a sort of come-hither look. She is coming with the flowers in her hat and apples in her skirt, honoring her love so simply."

With great timidity and trepidation, Finch-Kozlosky presented the head to her mother the next summer, at their family camp in Maine. "I really felt I was walking on eggshells," she confesses. "I knew this poem was very important to her and I didn't want to presume my interpretation on hers. So I said, 'I did a doll that reminds me of something that's close to your heart, so please tell me if it disrupts your memories and we don't have to use it.'"

She needn't have worried. "It was just astonishing!" remembers Finch. "This poem has such intense meaning to me personally, and when I saw the face, I thought how uncanny it was that Marta had so beautifully caught the feeling of total giving, the openness and complete lack of duplicity the poem expresses."

Plate 26

Maggie Finch
and Marta Finch-
Kozlosky,
Cowslips,
16 in. (40.7 cm), 1992

Plate 27
Kathryn Walmsley,
The Princess,
14 in. (35.6 cm), 1992
(Photo: Courtesy of
Kathryn Walmsley)

Then, following their tradition, Finch assembled the Sculpey head, hands, and feet on a cloth-covered wire armature and created the costume. Usually, the mother and daughter work independently on their tasks. This time, however, vacationing together, they were able to collaborate in a much more immediate way. As Finch-Kozlosky was creating the hands, Finch was going through scrap baskets of old fabrics, putting together the pieces that would clothe *Cowslips*. She scrubbed the fabrics and set them to dry in the sun. Both artists recall their collaboration on *Cowslips* as a particularly resonant experience. "For there we were," says Finch-Kozlosky, "creating this figure in Maine, not very far from the seaside town of Camden, where Edna St. Vincent Millay, the poet herself, was raised."

The open and giving nature of Transcendence's young country maid is a stark contrast to the aged princess in Kathryn Walmsley's (see "Characters") interpretation of *The Princess and the Pea* (plate 27). "She represents for me the idea of waiting for things to happen, not taking charge of your own destiny," says Walmsley. "If you do that, you might wait a long time for something to happen—hence the princess's age and pose." Reminded that the princess in the actual fairytale simply wanders into her future mother-in-law's test, Walmsley admits: "Well, I guess I took some liberties with the concept. I was able to manipulate that fairytale into a concept that was important to me, and I wrote a new story in my mind. But," she adds happily, "nobody's ever the least bit confused when they look at that piece. They know just what's going on."

The artist believes that the best of her pieces are symbolic of things in her own life—"even if others don't see the symbolism." She uses fairy tales and familiar subjects as "jumping-off points, because they help express my ideas and get a response—people get it right away. And that's my objective as an artist: to find a way to express ideas through this medium and get a response." In addition to fairy tales, Walmsley looks to old advertising art, clowns, and children for inspiration. Sometimes political and social situations give birth to new figures. For example, during the 1992 Los Angeles riots, she made a piece consisting of two little girls, one black, one white, dressed in black-and-white checked fabrics, playing together on a black-and-white tile floor, on a turntable.

Making *The Princess* involved the most elaborate positioning and the most Cernit parts Walmsley had ever before used. The head, shoulder plate, arms, and legs are all sculpted in Cernit; she has a cloth body with wire armature, glass eyes, and a mohair wig. All the textiles used, including her gown, are antique. The technical challenges presented by this piece were primarily of an engineering nature, Walmsley reports, such as creating the antiqued copper pea vine and the handmade bed, which is antiqued in gold and knocks down like a real bed.

While she takes part in some doll shows, Walmsley does most of her exhibiting at art shows. "I came to dolls this way," she explains, "having studied at the Tyler School of Art in Philadelphia and the Boston Museum School. My artistic work has coalesced in dollmaking, and I enjoy art shows because there my dolls are perceived as art."

British artist Jane Davies found her young character *Aminabad* (plate 28) one evening at the theater. "I simply went out with my husband, John, to enjoy a play—Oliver Goldsmith's Restoration comedy, *She Stoops to Conquer*. I've always loved Restoration plays; the period is so elegant, and I have more of an affinity with it than with any other," she reflects. "I just love the architecture of that time, the fashion, the wit. . . . In any case, as soon as the child playing Aminabad walked onto the stage, I said to John, 'That's my next doll.'"

Davies specializes in very small porcelain dolls, reflecting her belief that we feel particularly close to beautiful objects that can be held in one hand. She likes

to refer to the work of the late ceramicist Hans Coper, whose widow said, soon after his death: "With some of his pots, if you take them in your hand and see what it is you hold, then it is impossible to be unhappy."

Aminabad, at four and a half inches high, is consistent with the size of most of Davies's work. He is all porcelain, with nine joints. Like all of Davies's dolls, he has luminous eyes that appear to be of glass, but are actually painted. The dollmaker builds up five or six layers of color to achieve this effect. In the play, Aminabad diverts the attention of the audience during scene changes by playing his hurdy-gurdy. Davies made the wood-and-brass instrument, too. "The handle turns," she says, "but sadly, it plays no tune."

This figure is based entirely on the child Davies saw on stage; the artist made no attempt to further interpret Goldsmith's character. She remembers reading the play during college, but had never seen it before, so came to it with an open mind. "I very much like making black children," she says simply, and she was immediately attracted to the young actor playing the role. She did, however, take great liberties with the costume. "Making *Aminabad'*s costume was the first time I'd ever entirely invented a historical costume. Before this, all my costumes have been either Victorian or very modern, as these are the kinds of children I tend to make. I didn't want to base *Aminabad'*s clothing on anything actual—I wanted to be more creative."

The experience was most rewarding for the artist: "I realized I didn't have to be so realistic. Making the costume really sparked off where I am now," she says. "I'm trying to be more creative, rather than taking such painstaking efforts to be real."

Just as Jane Davies based *Aminabad* on an actual actor interpreting the character, so did Nancy Walters look to P. L. Travers's illustrations of Mary Poppins in creating *East Wind on Cherry Tree Lane* (plate 29). Walters' paperclay figure succinctly captures the original angular character envisioned by her creator long before Walt Disney studios and the actress Julie Andrews produced their now universally known portrayal of the magical English nanny.

Walters set out with a purpose when she took on the creation of *East Wind*

Plate 29
Nancy Walters,
*East Wind on
Cherry Tree Lane*,
20 in. (50.8 cm), 1993

on *Cherry Tree Lane.* "She filled a technical need as well as being a favorite character," the dollmaker reports. "I felt that my work was becoming a little static, and wanted to get some more movement in a few pieces. I wanted to do a more elongated figure than I had been doing, and I wanted to interpret from a rather sketchy drawing into three dimensions." At the time, the artist was making what she refers to as "rewritten fairy tales"—putting her own twist on fairy-tale characters, as well as on the literary likes of Washington Irving's Ichabod Crane and Rip Van Winkle.

Walters's one-of-a-kind pieces tend to have a very strong personal vision, usually rendered humorously. Her 1991 *Little Bo Peep,* for example, wears the traditional costume, but has a kind and elderly, line-etched face which peers at the sheep through wire-rimmed glasses. "I normally don't work from drawings or paintings," Walters admits, "but when I started thumbing through the Poppins books and saw the drawing of Mary when she first came to the Banks's house, blown in on the East Wind, I realized that was just the type of movement challenge I was looking for. I adored the Mary Poppins series as a child—it was just the right kind of lightweight magic and fantasy I would have liked in my own life. I actually reread them all with great enjoyment about a dozen years ago when my kids were reading them." By going back to the original renderings of Mary Poppins and bypassing the film interpretations, Walters found, to her surprise, that she failed to meet many people's expectations of the character. "I was quite surprised after completing the book of the Travers version," the dollmaker says, "that so many people didn't know the book, only the Disney movie. I saw the movie when I was in college, and although I loved most aspects of it, Julie Andrews certainly wasn't the Mary Poppins I knew." *East Wind on Cherry Tree Lane* is a piece in which originator and interpreter have successfully met; it is a fine collaboration of P. L. Travers's original version, rendered with Nancy Walters's strong personal signature.

Texas dollmaker Roxanne Becker's creation of *Rapunzel* (plate 30) was also the result of a technical challenge. In Becker's case, however, the challenge posed severe limitations of time and materials. Becker made the figure in response to an invitation to participate in the 1992 *Dollmaker's Magic* exhibition, a display of cloth dolls sponsored by a fabric company, which required the use of its fabric, along with the incorporation of several specific textile-working techniques. It was Becker's second invitation; in 1991 she had created *Viking Woman* for the previous year's exhibition. "I had a lot of fun doing the *Viking Woman,* because I'm almost entirely Norwegian," says the artist.

Becker runs her own business of designing and manufacturing cloth doll patterns, called My Sister and I. She finds special joy in making her own one-of-a-kind pieces. "Although I enjoy designing personable dolls that home-sewers can relate to and want to create themselves," she explains, "I find a great deal of pleasure exploring my creative abilities when creating just one-of-a-kind dolls, without having to consider whether ten thousand people can find comparable materials and without needing to keep the directions simple and clear."

She initially decided on *Rapunzel* as the subject of her rare foray into one-of-a-kind creation for a purely technical reason: "I had used unraveled dyed manila rope for the hair on the *Viking Woman,* and I just loved that rope. The doll that came to mind where I could make the best use of rope hair was *Rapunzel.*" Like the *Viking Woman, Rapunzel* had a sculpted muslin face painted with gesso and acrylics to achieve the texture of a painted wood sculpture. She wears a long peach shift with the hem trimmed in prairie points of aqua with pearl-studded lace trim. A quilted, cream-colored pastel paisley surcoat covers the shift; quilted sleeves and a matching quilted cape lined in purple match the surcoat. Her head is encircled by a modified wimple of aqua chiffon attached to a circlet of twined pearls and flowers. On her feet she wears dyed purple ultrasuede boots.

"I wanted to create the impression of the lushness of fairy tales," muses Becker. "I wanted to make *Rapunzel* look romantic. While I researched medieval costumes, I only wanted to give the impression of an accurate costume; I really played with it and adapted it as I went. Most of all I didn't want to cover up her hair!"

Plate 30
Roxanne Becker,
Rapunzel,
23½ in. (59.7 cm),
1992

Plate 31
Susan Dunham,
Othello,
17 in. (43.2 cm), 1988

Since Becker doesn't feel she has the opportunity to fully express herself in her daily work, she had strong feelings about what she wanted to evoke with *Rapunzel*. "I grew up being an avid reader," she says. "I love storybook characters that are intended to uplift. I want to create things that are beautiful, with a grace. There's enough around to depress people. I want to uplift, and where the *Viking Woman* was courageous and majestic, I see *Rapunzel* as idealized womanhood."

If Rapunzel is idealized womanhood, Shakespeare's Othello may be seen as idealized manhood, carried to a tragic extreme. When Susan Dunham set out to create the "swarthy Moor," as he was called in Elizabethan times, she was moved by the power of the character. "After reading the play," the Oregon artist recounts, "I was on fire with the passion to create this tragic figure of a man, one that 'loved not wisely but too well.'"

The birth of *Othello* (plate 31) came when Dunham was asked to create a souvenir doll for a regional doll conference in 1988. The task would eventually require making 375 pieces of the figure, an idea Dunham found of no interest whatsoever. When the subject of Othello arose, however, she started to change her mind. "The idea of having a powerful adult male for a conference souvenir was controversial," she says, "and . . . seemed delicious to me, a challenge I could not deny . . . to produce such a controversial subject and still make it acceptable to the majority of conference-goers."

Othello has been interpreted countless times, on stage, in film, in dance, in painting, and in sculpture. John Darcy Noble, curator emeritus of the Toy Collection at the Museum of the City of New York, extolled Dunham's sculptural interpretation in a 1990 article in *Contemporary Doll* magazine. "Most often he is portrayed as a young man in the prime of his youth and beauty," Noble wrote. "She visualized an older man, not at all beautiful in the classic sense but possessed of a spare, wiry strength that is saved from brutishness by the intelligence and sensitivity with which he is informed." The original artist's proof of *Othello* is shown here. The piece is modeled in porcelain to below the navel, with the slip tinted to produce the Moor's dark skin. His black beard and mustache, as well as his paler eyebrows, have also been modeled.

Dunham has been making original dolls since 1978, and she is known for her broad range of subject matter and style—which has led to the judgment by some that she has "no identity of art." The artist rejects this criticism: "I define this as works that look like they all have the same mother, all easily recognizable. It is not possible for me to submit to this idea, as the joy of freely creating that which pleases me is too precious an identity and pursuit to abandon." The result is a body of work that encompasses small children representing Mother Goose rhymes, portraits of the Nez Percé Indians, fashion figures reflecting the early part of the nineteenth century, and powerful dramatic figures like King Lear and Othello, which clearly demonstrate the artist's training in classical sculpture. In taking on the portrayal of Othello, the principal character of a play illustrating, as Dunham sees it, "the struggle between good and evil, the gambit of human emotions—passion, jealousy, hate, and envy, love and the honest virtues of tenderness," the artist has put her classical training at the service of classical themes.

While Othello is not a common subject for dollmakers, the Shakespearean plays in general are an often-used source. The most magical among them is certainly *A Midsummer Night's Dream*, with its fanciful cast of mortal, fairy, and animal characters. The play is perfectly suited to the talents of Linda Kertzman, who has made a specialty of fantasy. Her creation of *Titania and Bottom* (plate 32) touchingly evokes one of the humorous yet magical moments of this nocturnal forest fancy.

This is not the first time Kertzman has turned to her favorite Shakespearean play as a subject for her dolls. She has previously created Puck, Young Oberon, and a version of Titania as a young child. Even her fantasy piece, *The Fairy Queen* (see "Fantasies"), was inspired by the idea of Titania with her attendants. "In school I loved English and drama, and I performed in a lot of Shakespeare's plays. I always wanted to do some of these characters as dolls," she says. She was not inspired to create *Titania and Bottom*, however, until she discovered a beautiful illustration of the pair in an old children's book. "I knew then that I had to do them," she remembers. "I couldn't wait to get started." While the piece was inspired by the illustration, the actual pose of Kertzman's fairy queen

Plate 32
Linda Kertzman,
Titania and Bottom,
21 in. (53.3 cm), 1990
(Photo: Courtesy of
Linda Kertzman)

and carpenter-turned-donkey is different. "It's the feeling of the illustration I wanted to capture," explains the artist.

The feeling Kertzman has captured is Titania's blind adoration for Bottom, the result of a spell put on her by her angry lover Oberon. Bottom, on the other hand, "is confused," laughs Kertzman, "first about being turned into an ass! And second, about why Titania, queen of the fairies, has fallen in love with him! He is sitting on a piece of driftwood and dressed in a leather vest and wool pants." The artist used sheep's wool for his hair, while Titania is dressed in corn husks and has silk wings and long blond mohair. The piece is a mixture of Sculpey and Cernit, and Kertzman loves it so much that she won't sell it.

"Old children's books give me a lot of ideas," the dollmaker confesses. "I love them and am always buying them in antiques shops." When she herself was a child, her mother used to read her old German fairy tales, and Kertzman found, when she started dollmaking, that she wanted to bring to life the "beautiful, innocent children and fairies of those storybooks." In *Titania and Bottom* she has created an image of the romantic pair that harmoniously blends her own vision with those of earlier visual interpreters of Shakespeare's couple.

Old German fairy tales were also a strong influence on Jocelyn Mostrom's (see "Holiday Inspirations") innovative corn-husk rendition of *Hansel and Gretel* (plate 33). Mostrom spent her childhood in a house on the edge of the woods. "It was always a mysterious place," she says, "and you could easily imagine going into the woods, getting lost (which I did!), and finding a candy house, like the one in Hansel and Gretel. I think that's why that particular story always had such a strong mystique for me. It's very much wound up in my childhood."

The artist has made—and taught workshops in which others make—numerous other characters from fairy tales and nursery rhymes, like Cinderella, Little Bo Peep, and Little Red Riding Hood. She feels that "they take you back to your childhood. They always appeal to people." But *Hansel and Gretel* had a double draw for her; not only did the characters play a strong role in her childhood, but creating them gave her a chance to indulge her love of costuming and accessory making. She immersed herself in research on regional German costuming in order to make Hansel's and Gretel's Black Forest garb. "I wanted them to be believable German children," she says, "believable, but just beyond reach—just like the candy house." In creating fairy-tale characters she often turns to a variety of illustrated books of fairy tales to examine what other artists have seen in the story. "Then I go back and rethink the whole thing," she says.

What is most unusual about these delicate children is their medium:

Mostrom is one of a very few artists working in corn husks to create realistic figures. She describes *Hansel and Gretel* as her most challenging and time-consuming type of doll. Their faces, bodies, limbs, and costumes are all of corn husk, and the children are just seven and one half and eight inches high. "The head and limbs are done in a controlled drying process, layering glue and corn husk over a period of several weeks, and controlling the drying with dental tools so that there is no shrinking and shriveling. A single split in an outer layer can ruin a doll, so it is imperative to select only supple, soft, yet strong husks—of which there are very few in a given bale of husks." She makes the accessories in Sculpey, while the hair is flax, rayon braid, and trim. The shoes are corn husk with brass trim. Finally, the dolls are treated to seal the husk from moisture and dust.

In spite of her unusual medium, Mostrom's goals are not different from those of other dollmakers. "I want to create a feeling, a cherished moment in time, the fleeting moment brought to life. The medium, with its unique assets and drawbacks, is at once my biggest ally and my constant challenge."

Actor-turned-dollmaker Jeff Redford grew up hearing Charles Dickens's *A Christmas Carol* read by his English grandmother every Christmas. "It was my favorite Christmas story," he says. Knowing the tale so well, Redford has a very strong, very personal understanding of it and, most importantly, of the character of Scrooge. "He represents people's ability to change," he asserts. "Here is somebody who is caught in a web of stinginess, who is stingy with *himself*. He is a very sad man who goes through an experience that completely changes him, and is able to make a 180-degree turnaround. He is able to wake up the next morning open to himself."

A professional actor for the past ten years, Redford finds many actors have played Scrooge "one-dimensionally, they just see him as a mean man." But in the 1951 film *Scrooge*, the title role was played by Alistair Sim in an interpretation that enriched Redford's own understanding of and feeling for Dickens's story. "He was a very innovative actor and, in this case, the part and the man melded. What makes him so incredible in the role is the way he plays the inner stinginess of the character." In his Cernit figure of *Scrooge* (plate 34), Redford chose to create an inner portrait of Alistair Sim as Scrooge.

Redford captures *Scrooge* in his nightshirt and robe, when he sees Marley's ghost for the first time, a moment of fear, with a meanness of emotion that is still in the man. He has not yet undergone the cathartic experience that brings about the morning awakening, Redford's favorite scene of the film.

Scrooge is the product of a very young dollmaking career. Redford has only been making dolls since 1992, and like many more experienced dollmakers, he earns his living in other ways. He is currently a calligrapher for Los Angeles County. Playing with clay in his free time, he started making little figures and decided he needed to learn more technique, so he enrolled in dollmaking courses taught by Jack Johnston, a dollmaker himself who, in addition to teaching, has helped bring his students' work to the attention of the public.

Redford says his goal is short and sweet: "To ever improve in every respect the figures that I sculpt!" He would like to create other film and literary characters, such as Buster Keaton and Charlie Chaplin and, at the other end of the spectrum, someone like Shakespeare's Richard III. In creating his *Scrooge* as a figure that represents the possibility of change, Redford has turned the standard interpretation of the antithesis of Christmas on its head.

Holiday Inspirations

The artists who make holiday dolls are nostalgia buffs, hooked on childhood memories of Christmases long ago, sentimental valentines, homemade Halloween costumes, and Saint Patrick's Day and Fourth-of-July parades. Their dolls are tangible reminders of the past, often unfolding a rich Old World heritage.

Of all the holidays, the most fondly remembered is Christmas, with the figure of Santa Claus the focus of dollmaking efforts. Whether it's a vision of an early Saint Nicholas or the modern-day image of Santa Claus, the "gift giver" has captured the imagination of some of today's most talented artists.

The popularizing of Saint Nicholas began in nineteenth-century Europe as adults slowly came to regard children as children rather than miniature adults. The stern German Belsnickle ("Nicholas in fur") personified the ambivalence toward

Plate 35
Virginia Killmore,
Quilted Father Christmas,
20 in. (50.8 cm), 1994

playtime and obligation. An elderly figure whose white, blue, brown, gray, or occasionally red-hooded robes hid a thin, almost gaunt figure, he inspired fear from his switches as well as joy from his fruit and toys. The Russian Father Frost's image, while less stern, appeared as an elderly, bent-over figure who clutched his wooden staff as he welcomed the winter season. The French Père Noël leaned on a cane and wore long, hooded robes with wooden sabots peeking out from under the hem. He shouldered the heavy weight of the traditional French woven grape basket filled with dolls, toys, and a small evergreen tree.

Modern dollmakers can choose to portray a "gift giver" who dates from as far back as the fourth century, and some contemporary artists have spent entire careers depicting Father Christmas in all his guises. One of Lois Clarkson's favorite Santa figures has always been Père Noël. Inspired by turn-of-the-century postcards, she fashions her Père Noëls in traditional garb and heaps their baskets with antique dolls and toys. Years ago at an exhibit of Clarkson's dolls a French collector rushed over to her booth, admiring the Père Noël figure. Peeking under the cape, she searched for painted stars. Disappointed at not finding any, she mentioned to Clarkson that when she grew up in France, she spent Christmas on her grandfather's farm outside of Paris. Her grandfather told her that Père Noël had a long blue cape, and the inside of the cape was sprinkled with stars. The farmhouse had a massive walk-in fireplace, and on Christmas Eve she would look up the huge chimney and see the stars, whereupon her grandfather would say, "Look! There's Père Noël. I can see the stars under his cape!" After Clarkson heard that delightful tale, she always painted a shimmer of stars on the linings of Père Noël's capes.

Clarkson's *Père Noël* (plate 36) is made of Super Sculpey with hand-blown glass eyes, porcelain teeth, and a mohair/sheep's wool beard. His robe is made from vintage fabric, and he wears sabots of wood and leather. All of his toys and accessories are antiques—he carries a French donkey-racing game in which the players would place the wooden donkeys on a slanted surface, tap with the wooden mallet and wager which donkey would "race" to the finish line first. Around the turn of the century, many toys and ornaments were made in Germany, so Père Noël also carries German Putz animals, cardboard houses, and silver ornaments as well as a German straw-stuffed dog with a mouth that opens when you pat him on the back. All of these toys seem to spill over from the traditional grape-picking basket on his back.

When Clarkson first started making Santa figures, she depicted Belsnickles (the Pennsylvania Dutch Santas). Then her mother presented her with a large, old cardboard box that she had found in the attic. Inside were the 1940s-style train set and Christmas village from Clarkson's childhood. "As I unwrapped each piece," Clarkson remembers, "the feelings of excitement and anticipation of those early Christmases were very real again. There was my Rudolph the Red-nosed Reindeer, my fishing pond that I used to fill with water and float celluloid ducks in, the large cardboard tunnel for the train to disappear in and reappear, with its light shining a path around a large oval in a darkened room. And there were also some old Santas dressed in red flannel. I wanted to recreate these Santas and capture the magic again."

Clarkson envisioned recreating the joys of Christmas past with a variety of Santa figures, including the Santa Claus of her childhood (also known as the Coca-Cola Santa from the image pictured in 1940s advertising).

The depiction of the jolly man from the North Pole derived from older Christmas traditions based on the legends of Saint Nicholas. The 1823 poem by Clement Moore, "A Visit from Saint Nicholas," followed by Thomas Nast's 1860s series of Santa Claus sketches in *Harper's Weekly Magazine,* set the stage for the modern characterization of the Santa figure. By the mid-twentieth century the Norman Rockwell image of an international Santa Claus who distributed gifts to children around the world was firmly entrenched as a living legend.

Beth Cameron, working out of her picturesque studio in Oakmont, Pennsylvania, fashions appealing Santa figures that celebrate the warmth of the Christmas spirit. Her first Santa, made in the early 1970s, was a cloth

Plate 36
Lois Clarkson,
Père Noël,
40 in. (101.6 cm), 1994

European-style "gift giver" based on a store figure she had seen and couldn't afford. She said to herself, "I can make that," little realizing that what was to evolve into a long career of dollmaking had just begun. Her present-day Cernit Santas are roly-poly and red-cheeked, with expressive features that embody the fondest recollections of the kindly old gentleman. Cameron seeks to convey the wonder of Christmas as seen through the eyes of a grown-up who wishes to be a child again. Her Santa figures—while exceedingly complex, with myriad antique and handmade accessories—seem homespun in feeling. She likes to portray Santas at work, surrounded by toys for their sacks. "My favorite Santas can be said to reflect the work ethic," Cameron muses. "After all, what I do is to make things. I spent my life in a workshop. For me the making is as important as the finished product. All the gathering I do, all the time spent making the piece is analogous to the building up to the excitement of Christmas Eve."

Cameron conjures up details for sheer delight, often inserting little surprises in her work. "I'll decorate the inside of a jacket; put a little pocket containing a toy in the lining of the back of the jacket (where no one would think to look), just to keep the new owners on their toes. Often costuming and accessorizing takes longer than sculpting the piece itself," Cameron reveals.

Cameron's tender portrayals are meant to become important Christmas traditions to be taken out each year as part of the holiday celebration. She wants each Santa to look as if he had been caught in midstep entering her living room. To achieve her goal, Cameron eschews doll stands, concentrating on the stance of the figure, including the way the arms are held and the position of her feet. Her face lights up as she recalls a scene in the Broadway show, *Fiddler on the Roof*, which she claims oddly enough greatly affected the making of her Santa figures. "When the father sings 'Tradition,' he lumbers onto the stage in his heavy boots; but as soon as he starts to dance, he moves with the grace of a much lighter man. I want the same sense of movement in my Santa figures." As Cameron works, her Santas become so real to her that she can almost hear the sleigh bells jingle.

While Cameron was working on the Tiffany Christmas window displays for the Boston store in the early 1990s, she felt a recurring urge to make a special Santa for each of her two daughters, Kate and Rachel. They had to be the most wonderful Santas she had ever made, and very personal. While Rachel's Santa was finished in what Cameron felt was a timely manner, Kate's Santa evolved slowly, over a period of three years. "I just couldn't get it right. I had such high expectations for it," Cameron remembers. "I wanted the face to embody the kind spirit of the holiday, to be the face of love that every parent has for their children. Finally, I made a decision. I told my daughters (who were beginning to wonder if the doll was ever going to be completed), 'This is it!' I didn't put a mustache on him because I was afraid it would cover too much of his expression."

Cameron had kept several of Rachel's and Kate's dresses from when they were little. Now they could be recycled as frocks for the dolls nestled in Santa's arms, while material from Kate's school jumper looked just right as Santa's shirt. She delighted in using locks of hair saved from her own childhood days for the hair of one of the dolls. Even Cameron, who admits to being a perfectionist, agrees that *Kate's Santa* (plate 37) fulfills all of her family's expectations and will always be one of the highlights of Christmas.

Like Beth Cameron, Mary Alice Byerly of Grosse Pointe, Michigan, has always regarded the faces of her Santa figures as the most expressive part of her work. The European Santa figures that she studied in illustrations or came across in various stores seemed stiff, and the jovial modern-day Santas did not appeal to her sensibilities; so in 1989 she decided to try her hand at creating a Saint Nicholas doll, whose face would embody "a gentle wit, wisdom, and kindness without the 'Ho, Ho, Ho' quality of many reproduction Santas."

Although Byerly had always been involved in the arts (as an interior designer with strong sewing skills and a love for crafts projects), it wasn't until her first Santa Claus figure evolved that she became committed to dollmaking. Prior to this first effort, Byerly's only other sculpting experience was making a red-clay elephant (which she painted yellow) as a third-grade art project in her hometown of Rockingham, North Carolina. Of her Saint Nicholas, Byerly recalls, "I started sculpting a porcelain head, hands, and feet in February 1989. Three months later I took the finished piece to a local doll shop to find a moldmaker. Much to my dismay I was told that after firing, my Santa's head would shrink to the size of a large marble. I went back to work and finished another Saint Nicholas with a larger head and a posable cloth body over wire armature." Not only was her "special fella" featured in the November 1989 edition of *Dollcrafter Magazine*, but it also won first prize and best of division in the theme category and second prize for original sculpture in the 1989 Michigan Doll Makers Guild Competition. Encouraged by the awards, Byerly decided to pursue dollmaking as a career. Although Byerly has created many kinds of dolls, including fairy-tale characters, elves, an automated doll (the Christmas Tapper), gnomelike Merry Makers, and a series of black character dolls, she

always returns to the Santa Claus theme. "Santa Claus is universally loved," Byerly explains. "Santa's name, clothes, and even his appearance vary from country to country and even from one century to another; but these superficial differences cannot disguise the spirit of love that I believe is Santa Claus. We never become so old that Saint Nick is not alive in our hearts—the spirit of giving and of Christmas never dies."

A pair of antique snowshoes provided the inspiration for *Snowshoe Santa* (plate 38). When Byerly found them in her family's cabin in northern Michigan, she was intrigued by the intricate weaving of the catgut, and began to picture how they would look in miniature. "Since myth has Santa coming from the land of snow, I saw him stopping to collect a tree on the way to feed his reindeer, wearing snowshoes to help him make his way through the forest." One of the most exciting moments in dollmaking, according to Byerly, is creating a new theme for the Santa figures. "It's exhilarating," she explains. "It's like that first ride on a roller coaster—your heart just pounds away."

Snowshoe Santa wears a handmade wool sweater, hat, and scarf. His belted vest coat of rugged suede tinkles with Norwegian brass bells. The suede mittens are trimmed in fox fur, matching the fur on the llama mukluks, which snugly fit into the leather-laced snowshoes. Byerly is particularly proud of the custom-tailored bushy mohair wig, beard, brows, and mustache that embody the spirit of a woodsman.

Plate 38
Mary Alice Byerly,
Snowshoe Santa,
21 in. (53.3 cm), 1993

Mary Alice Byerly's love for antiques is shared by fellow dollmaker Virginia Killmore of Syracuse, New York, who makes Santa figures from the past. Killmore is inspired by antique postcards of Father Christmas, vintage fabrics, old toys, and American folk dolls. Her Santas are famous for their painted cloth faces that resemble the printed and painted cloth faces on dolls that were made both at home and in fledgling factories in late nineteenth-century America. "I work from old chromographs and postcards," Killmore says. "I look for Santas with friendlier expressions than those of the old German Belsnickles. Christmas is a wonderful time for most children, and I just cannot imagine Santa not having a kind face."

Killmore traces her dollmaking career to the days when, as a young girl,

Plate 37
Beth Cameron,
Kate's Santa,
16 in. (40.6 cm), 1992

Holiday Inspirations 🌿 75

she designed countless outfits for her Barbie dolls. "I never remember actually playing with Barbies, but I was consumed with making costumes and miniature accessories." After graduating from Syracuse University with a degree in fine arts and education, she experimented with a variety of crafts, including quilt-making, lacemaking, sewing, weaving, and miniatures. As a young mother she looked for a business she could conduct at home. One of her friends suggested she try making dolls, based on the American folk dolls that seemed to be widely popular at craft shows. Killmore was intrigued by the idea and began reading books on dolls and visiting doll museums, as she searched for the way to make her dolls. "I remember reading Wendy Lavitt's *American Folk Dolls* and being fascinated with the picture of the Funk Family, a group of cloth dolls that had obviously been made by children with more enthusiasm than skill. The dolls had long, skinny heads and were kind of ugly, but to me they were beautiful. Their naivete appealed to me and inspired me to try my hand at making character dolls." Her first cloth dolls, enlivened by accompanying short stories or ditties, sold out at the craft shows Killmore entered, and she looked for ways to improve her work. The idea of combining paint and fabric excited her, as she loved painting but wanted to also work in cloth. "So much of women's work in the past was in cloth," she explains. "Women with little or no artistic training created objects of beauty, driven by their creative urges and the love of their families. If my dolls can be recognized as an art form, not only will they pay homage to these unsung women, but, perhaps, they will bring the work of other talented women to light."

When Killmore started making *Quilted Father Christmas* (plate 35), she had visualized what he would look like when finished. She began with the jack-in-the-box, experimenting with wood grains while making its base. "I love my work because it allows me to dabble in so many media," she muses. "With the jester, a marionette based on an antique print, I was challenged by my desire to have him appear loose-jointed and floppy. When one works on a small scale, fabrics tend to resist draping and flowing naturally (the way they do on a human form); so, I used wire and weights to achieve the desired effect for the marionette and the jack-in-the-box. Actually, the jester and the little girl in Santa's lap were more time-consuming than the main figure. It took several attempts to paint her face, and the clothing for her doll was an exercise in miniature detail. I admit to 'torturing' all of the toys and dolls, so they will look old—I have all kinds of tricks up my sleeve for making a brand-new item appear to be one hundred years old!"

For the Santa figure, Killmore covered the wire-armature body with fiberfill to create an appearance of muscle tissue. She then wrapped muslin around the torso and limbs for the look of skin. When it came time for costuming, Killmore rummaged through her vast store of antique textiles for the perfect crazy quilt. "It is always a challenge to decide what section of a quilt can be used to best advantage on the coat," she reveals. "I want certain embroideries to show up in strategic spots, but crazy quilts are exceedingly fragile, preventing a lot of handling. I never like to cut perfect quilts, so I'm always juggling between worn areas and beautiful embroideries."

Before Killmore positions her Santa onto the sled, tricycle, or chair that she often employs as a prop, she works on the hair and the beard by curling every strand on a dowel and applying them individually, to provide a full beard that is distinctively appealing. As she tucks the last toy into place, she is already thinking of the next Santa and the toys in his pack.

In the last few years an increasing number of doll artists have portrayed Santa Claus as an African-American "gift giver," either as the Kwanzaa Father Christmas in colorful African robes or as the traditional red-robed Santa figure. Many of these artists speak of their desire to portray holiday figures that are more meaningful to black children than the European Santa figure. Beverly Roessel of Burlington, Washington, delights in creating large black Santas carrying both black and white toy clowns, dolls, jack-in-the-boxes, and toy soldiers, as shown in *The Gift Giver* (plate 39). Because it is a time-consuming process to make each doll by hand with-out the aid of molds, Roessel only produces seven or eight Santas a year. "My figures are quite complex, and I sculpt the head, hands, and shoes of the 'gift givers' as well as all the toys using a natural stone clay," she notes. "Before costuming the dolls, I also hand-dye the fabrics to achieve just the right antique-looking red and green. I then add bits of recycled leather, fur, and silk trim."

Not surprisingly, Roessel is a fan of "interesting faces," subscribing to

Plate 39
Beverly Roessel,
The Gift Giver,
19 in. (48.3 cm), 1993

Ebony magazine as a source for her subjects. "I cut out clippings for reference from advertisements and stories," Roessel explains, "and I seem to always pick the smiling ones." Her dollmaking career began inadvertently when the orthodontist for whom she worked as an assistant brought back a German Santa figure from a trip. Roessel remembers, "I knew I could never afford such a doll, so I decided to try and make one."

When Roessel works on a Santa figure, she is always concerned with the treatment of the beard and hair, believing them to create an important visual impression. She notes, "I am lucky to be near several sheep farms, where I can pick out any sheep I want to be sheared. I usually select a breed known as the Lincoln sheep, because their wool is soft and curly. The sheep is sheared right in front of me. After the washing, drying, and combing processes, it is recycled into the beards and hair of my 'gift givers.'"

Angels, as visions of ethereal splendor and symbols of the Christmas holidays, have fascinated doll artists from medieval times to the present. Angels have decorated Christmas trees, participated in nativity scenes, and stood on their own as prized ornamental objects. For Jocelyn Mostrom ("Figures from Literature") the holidays are not complete without her corn-husk angels. Each Christmas a shower of corn-husk beauties covers the branches of Mostrom's Edwardian-style Christmas tree. The angels are delicate creatures, rising out of clouds of flowing husks, wearing haloes and holding garlands of dried flowers. To look at Mostrom's elegant creations, it is hard to believe that they were once mere shafts in bales of Mexican corn husks. During the onerous process of preparing the husks for dollmaking, Mostrom must cut through the steel bands surrounding the heavy bales, sort and process the husks, and finally, dye them. In spite of these difficulties, Mostrom prefers corn husk to all other media, explaining, "Husks are so exciting. Each one has its own unique characteristics. Some are rippled from pressing against the kernels underneath. Even after they have been soaked and dyed, they still retain their ripple patterns, making them ideal candidates for doll skirts. I select the very smooth, thin husks for faces and skin. Each doll has its own requirements, necessitating a lot of sorting and searching."

Mostrom admits that angels are high on her list of personal favorites, even though they are the hardest to make. "With each angel," Mostrom says, "I try to make a more perfect one, a more delicate and expressive one. The *Christmas Angel* (plate 40) is large for a corn-husk doll and required the use of several of my prize eleven-inch-long husks. These particular husks are very wide and white,

and seldom turn up in a bale of husks. The face and hands also called for special husks—supple, yet strong, with low ridges." While some of Mostrom's dolls have porcelain heads, the *Christmas Angel*'s face is made of corn husks. Its porcelain look is achieved by muted glazing.

The hardest task is producing a face without seams or splits. To achieve this goal she has developed a slow pressure-drying technique that replicates, through several stages of hand-sculpting, the three-dimensional characteristics of the face. "The husks demand the virtue of patience," explains Mostrom, who compares making a corn-husk doll to making an apple-head doll. "If you let nature dry the doll, it wrinkles and shrivels. It is necessary to build up the face layer by layer, allowing many hours for drying before adding another layer." After the head has been attached to the wire armature, Mostrom paints the features with acrylics. She prefers a soft palette that expresses the dreamlike world of her angels.

Mostrom estimates the *Christmas Angel* represents forty-five hours of work, most of them spent on the face and hands. To make the billowing gown, Mostrom worked the corn husks until they resembled fine antique fabric. The finished doll illustrates how far Mostrom has journeyed from the primitive art form of Native American and pioneer corn-husk crafting.

Linda Horn, like Jocelyn Mostrom, designs sophisticated corn-husk dolls that are a far cry from the simple figures of the Native Americans and pioneer settlers. She delights in complex, fantastic creations, which she constructs with layers of detail. Living amid the rolling hills of Pennsylvania, Horn finds on-going inspiration in the farms around her. For generations the Horn family has farmed in Rose Valley, Pennsylvania, planting field corn in the early spring and harvesting in the cool, crisp days of October. When Linda Solomon married John Horn, she joined the family in hand-cutting the ripened stalks and loading them on wagons to take to the barn. As they husked each ear, Horn marveled at the beauty of the sun-bleached husks and the rich, brown corn silk, and wondered how they could be used. In 1976 Horn started making simple dolls out of corn husks, slowly improving her techniques as she experimented with dyeing, layering, and trimming, gradually transforming her figures into elaborately gowned Victorian brides and ladies of fashion. She began combing out the corn-silk hair, creating delicate braids and curls intertwined with corn-husk ribbons, bows, and flowers. Her most recent work reflects the magic of the corn husks swaying in the fields. Fairies, appearing singly and in fantasy groupings, are surrounded by trailing vines and garlanded by flowers.

When Horn is about to begin a new piece, she often walks the fields, stopping to touch the dried husks hanging from tall stalks, allowing her imagination to envision forms and details suggested by the husks and corn silk. "After I handle the husks in my workroom," Horn explains, "the figure starts to take shape. What appears to be a pile of corn husks to the casual observer, in my mind is already filled with some measure of life, as I see the outline of an elegant lady or a fairy in a fantasy setting." At this stage Horn makes a rough sketch to flesh out the figure she is visualizing and to help determine the position of various elements. "My sketches never go beyond basic concepts of shape," Horn notes, "because I continue to design and refine the figure as I work. To build the figure I start with a framework, often of clay, that forms a base on which I fashion the form." The corn husks are carefully chosen, soaked in water to make them pliable, and hand-dyed using cloth dyes (a process that can take up to a week). As the figure evolves, Horn adds elements to the design, fashioning leaves, ribbons, rosettes, and bows of corn husks along with other natural materials, such as pepper berries and moss. She observes the tradition of faceless dolls drawn from Native American corn-husk figures, except for her Santa Claus dolls, which appeared too scary without faces. As Horn assembles the doll, she starts with the head and works toward the feet, tying the shredded husks together. She finds that because she is a "detail person," no element is too small to escape her attention as she strives to turn the figures of her imagination into reality.

Plate 41
Linda Horn,
Heart Fairy,
9 in. (22.9 cm), 1994

The *Heart Fairy* (plate 41), an enchanting valentine creation, transcends the historical boundaries of time and style. A fantasy figure, it inspired Horn to blend myriad combinations of natural materials, textures, colors, and forms. The shades of pink, rose, mauve, and lilac lend a romantic air to a fanciful costume that is set off by a leafy green hat resembling an upturned plant stem. A sprinkling of "stardust" glitters from hair to slippers, while finely spun gold threads weave tiny gossamer angel wings. To complete the scene, vines of hearts cascade from the fairy's hands to the moss-covered ground, planted with hearts that appear to be growing in a valentine garden.

The dolls of Susanna Oroyan have been called true originals, the products of a creative mind that always runs on overtime. A self-taught doll artist, she states, "I am a maker. I am a synthesizer and an organizer of materials, experiences, and impressions. I have a compulsion to do this. I am not really a doll artist. It just happens that what I mostly make, the result of the compulsion, are things that people sometimes call dolls." Oroyan is happiest when involved in several projects at once. As a writer of books and magazine articles about the doll field, a teacher of dollmaking, a lecturer, and an artist, she constantly juggles her time. Even though she regards herself as more of a sculptor than a doll artist, her innovative dolls have had a significant impact on the doll world. Many of Oroyan's dolls reflect her love for "bits and pieces." She confesses, "My mind is in a constant state of writhing chaos—always one mass of seething color, form, and engineering problems. Bits coming together, falling apart. Most days I have to make a major effort to turn it off, and keep it turned off, to get something actually done." When speaking of herself, Oroyan's sense of humor is refreshing. She refers to herself as "a curious, questioning old child" and thinks of her dolls as her toys.

It is not surprising, then, that a playfulness accompanies most of Oroyan's work. Her figures slouch, perch, jump, dance, and invite one to smile and share the joke—none of her people can be accused of "just standing around." Literary allusions abound in Oroyan's dolls, probably stemming from her education (she has a master's degree in English and did postgraduate work in linguistics). Although she had experimented with fabric dolls in the late 1960s, it wasn't until 1971, when Oroyan happened upon Jean Ray Laury's book, *Dollmaking: A Creative Approach*, that she began making dolls in earnest. Previously, her only contact with dolls had been limited to her childhood passion for taking them apart to see how they worked. In 1975 Oroyan was introduced to Sculpey and began experimenting with the character figures for which she is now famous.

Oroyan's most popular group of dolls is the Mulliner family series, to which *Minerva Mulliner in Halloween Costume* (plate 42) belongs. The series is a portrait of eccentric personalities. Oroyan comments with a mischievous smile, "The Mulliners all come out of two really badly made disintegrating impression molds, and each is individually sculpted to maintain a family resemblance and to be at the same time a unique persona. They enjoy typically British ancestors with a family tree dating from 'Mull of the Mill,' circa 630 B.C." As increasing numbers of fans fall under the sway of the Mulliners, the dolls are regarded almost as cult figures, with collectors vying for the newest addition to the "family." Oroyan adds with a knowing nod, "*Minerva Mulliner in Halloween Costume* is a big fan of dressing up for Halloween. The owner also collects tiny things for Halloween to add to Minerva's setting. Like most of the Mulliners, Minerva is a collector interactive doll—which means that the owners and I have great times telling stories about her and essentially 'playing dolls' on a sort of sophisticated grown-up level—about as grown-up as anyone who plays dolls can get, that is!"

Throughout Faith Wick's long career, which began in the 1970s, she has made many Halloween figures, from scarecrows to witches and goblins. She maintains that her fascination with witches stemmed from her encounters with old women from Europe, the grandmothers of the children in the town where she grew up in Minnesota. Dressed in black, with bent backs and toothless mouths, these women resembled witches and impressed Wick with their spooky

Plate 42
Susanna Oroyan,
Minerva Mulliner in
Halloween Costume,
18 in. (45.7 cm), 1993
(Photo: Courtesy of
W. Donald Smith)

appearance. In later years they manifested themselves in her witch dolls. Figures of the imagination became an integral part of her life in the early 1970s, when she and her husband bought Fairyland Park, a four-acre park in Minnesota filled with life-size cement figures of fairy-tale characters. She threw herself into repairing and repainting the sculptures, but found she most enjoyed designing and making new characters for the park. After the park was sold in 1975, Wick started making smaller versions, first in clay and later in the clay compound polyform.

Wick regards herself as a pioneer, noting that there were few original doll artists when she started exhibiting her dolls, and that she was often the only doll artist at shows where her work was displayed. At many of these shows Wick offered sculpting seminars, which turned out to be an effective way to introduce the idea of contemporary doll art to large audiences. At a seminar in 1978, the president of Effanbee Doll Company saw Wick sculpting and was impressed enough to ask her to submit some designs to him. As a result, the Effanbee Craftsman Corner was established with Faith Wick Originals as its first line. Since then Wick's dolls have been commercially produced by several companies and have reached collectors all over the world. One of her most well received lines, Faith Wick's Children's Costume Party for Dollspart Supply Company, featured porcelain children dressed as characters such as Cinderella and a scarecrow.

As one of the first commercially successful doll artists, Wick blazed trails for those who followed. She was the first doll artist to use vinyl as a medium for serious work. "In 1985 the notion that vinyl was collectible art was way ahead of its time," Wick notes, "and most collectors were not willing to spend one hundred to two hundred dollars for vinyl creations. But the word was out that porcelain was not the only medium for doll artists."

Wick's latest works, including *The Scarecrow* (plate 43), are in resin, a medium she has adopted because it duplicates exactly her original sculpture. "I like not having to worry about losing size or detail with resin as I did with porcelain," she explains. With resin, Wick can design the most detailed accessories for her dolls and be assured that its replica will be as she conceived it.

Fourth-of-July celebrations encourage doll artists to figuratively shout "Hip, Hip, Hurrah!" in a swirl of red, white, and blue. Artists find inspirations in local Fourth-of-July parades among the flag-waving children who cheer their favorite floats. For Janie Ashcraft, growing up in a small German community in southeastern Missouri, holidays were always important events that enlivened a quiet, rural lifestyle. Christmas was a very hectic but special time. Ashcraft re-

Plate 43
Faith Wick,
The Scarecrow,
16 in. (40.7 cm), 1994

members her grandfather as a central figure. "My Grandpa was the very epitome of the traditional elf—short, fat, and jolly! When I began making dolls that celebrate the holidays, I often found him showing up in my Santa sculptures."

Ashcraft credits the "Captain Kangaroo" television program with providing the inspiration for her first attempts at sculpture. "Captain Kangaroo" did a show on dolls, specifically wax dolls," laughs Ashcraft. "I immediately thought, hey, I can do that! My mother had paraffin wax (used for canning) and my sister had crayons. I came up with a flesh-colored face. I can't remember ever finishing the doll, but I remember the fun I had in the effort." Ashcraft recalls loving art as a child, which led to an interest in portraiture. While she wasn't able to acquire formal training, she managed to take some classes in portrait painting in both oils and pastels. Art and dolls took backstage to becoming a farmer's wife, with painting and sculpture being replaced by driving a tractor, shoveling grain, and cooking for hired hands. Even though there was little time for creative endeavors, Ashcraft's interest remained. Becoming the mother of two children gave her inspiration to return to portraiture, awakening a desire to create dolls that resembled her children. Once again, sculpting became a part of Ashcraft's life.

Ashcraft started *Fourth of July* (plate 44) immediately after she had finished a doll celebrating the Easter holidays. She knew she wanted the subject to be a little boy with a mischievous air. Ashcraft remembers finding the antique "Quick Draw McGraw" toy years earlier, and knew it would fit into the concept of a cowboy theme she was slowly forming. "I found the chaps, vest, and hat at an old trading post, one of those places that sells all fifty states' souvenirs and cliché Indian items," continues Ashcraft. "I could not make this a 'real' Fourth-of-July piece without having fireworks and the American flag. Most importantly I wanted his face to glisten in anticipation as he waits for his favorite holiday to arrive!"

Ashcraft began *Fourth of July* with a "skull" that had a central ball of foil as its core. She then sculpted over the foil, using a mixture of Super Sculpey and Cernit. After inserting the eyes and completing the dental work, she finished the face, sculpting in Cernit. Ashcraft placed foam over the wire-armature body and fashioned the hands out of Cernit. Although she keeps a file of photographs of children and often refers to them while working, she believes *Fourth of July* resembles her nephew, Brian. "Everyone in my family calls the doll 'Brian,'" she mentions with a smile. "Actually you often see family resemblances in the dolls of artists at doll shows all the time. Certainly in my dolls, my family shows up all the time."

The picturesque images of the Fourth of July appeal to Jodi and Richard Creager, artists whose work reminds observers of Norman Rockwell. Their love for Americana is revealed in humorous miniature sculptures of characters found in small towns throughout America. The Creagers are a unique husband-and-wife team, and they collaborate on designs from which they distill a combination of their separate ideas. Their aim, to reach a common goal by separate paths, assures a freshness in the work that excites and challenges them. The Creagers share a passion for history and folklore, spending days in the library researching their subjects. While Jodi Creager pores over costume and design books, Richard Creager studies technical manuals, seeking information to create the realistic details that distinguish their work.

"We each have our own visual images of what a particular character should look like," Richard Creager says. "We sit down with two separate points of view and begin to work our way toward a common ground through extensive discussion and lots of sketches. Once we have arrived at an image that fulfills both of our ideas, we begin the necessary research. We always strive to assure that the character is properly portrayed and is accompanied by appropriate accessories. This is the point where we each begin our separate work on the character."

Jodi Creager begins each piece by sculpting the head and hands out of Super Sculpey, which she paints by hand, using transparent tints to achieve a lifelike translucency. After she constructs the body out of heavy canvas and paints the eyes, Richard Creager sculpts the legs and feet. His background in machinery and industrial photography proves useful in drafting patterns and building armatures. While he fashions the shoes and the accessories, Jodi Creager makes the clothing out of patterns they have both designed. Both artists are pleased that their own individuality shines through their joint effort. Richard Creager notes, "I share Jodi's devotion to the work, and always strive to put as much of myself into each piece as she does. A good part of my spirit goes into each doll."

Richard Creager's interest in art surfaced in his childhood. His mother encouraged his art projects and taught him ways of being creative with what was at hand. His father, a railroad engineer, fostered in his son an intense interest in machinery and the way things work. Since college Creager's many interests have led him over the years to jobs working as a mechanic, machinist, photographer, artist, and teacher. Jodi Creager regards her husband as a Renaissance man whose diverse skills have contributed to the success of their collaborations. She notes, "Richard creates doll settings that speak volumes about the dolls. To figure something out on paper and then make it work by using tools and his learned skills is one of the greatest joys in Richard's life."

Jodi Creager, like her husband, traces her involvement in art to her school days, when she would visit her grandparents' house after school. She remembers sitting for hours on her grandfather's lap, watching him sketch. A creative man, he was a set artist for Universal Studios from the 1920s to the 1940s. Creager is equally enthusiastic about her grandmother, saying, "She had a wonderful and slightly wicked sense of humor—she had me looking for fairies under leaves and flower blossoms, and many times, I swear, I saw them. My grandmother gave me my first doll, a china head doll that was hers when she was a little girl." Creager's mother taught her to sew, and even though Creager resented at the time being separated from her baseball mitt, she now thanks her mother for her prescience. As a teenager she started painting, drawn to the character faces that would appear years later in her dolls.

Fourth of July (plate 45) challenged the artist not only in creating a doll that can stand securely on stilts, but also in achieving an expression of pure joy in the little boy's face and pride in his accomplishment. "We envisioned him walking (on the stilts his grandpa made for him) the entire length of his home-town's Fourth-of-July parade. . . . He even decorated the stilts all by himself," Jodi Creager explains. "Both Richard and I are true 'Red, White, and Bluers.' We take great pride in our country, and it gives us great joy to be able to create a piece so close to our heart."

At holiday time women, particularly wives and mothers, are the movers behind the scenes—they cook, bake, make costumes, and decorate until they are often ready to drop from exhaustion. One woman who empathizes through her one-of-a-kind dolls is Jane Cather. After years of giving away to family and friends the cloth dolls she made, she formed a company of one, naming it "Made by Night." The title aptly refers to the hours stolen for dollmaking: She had to wait until after the children were in bed, the show-quality Skye terriers she bred were in the kennel, and the household chores were finished. Now a grandmother living in Carmel Valley, California, Cather says nothing has changed except she works "night and day." Like many families of dollmakers,

Plate 45
Jodi and Richard
Creager,
Fourth of July,
17 in. (43.2 cm), 1994

her husband and children claim she is obsessed with dollmaking, a belief that Cather shares. She says, "I work completely alone. Sometimes I stare at the work in progress for literally hours without moving. I will often try hundreds of combinations before choosing. It is me and the work—the work and me. Everything else is gone—this is difficult to do to your family."

Cather, a distant relative of the novelist Willa Cather, was born in Lincoln, Nebraska, to a family of artists "of one kind or another." She moved as a child to the "backwoods" of New Canaan, Connecticut, and she met her husband while she was still in high school. As a young mother she satisfied her artistic inclination by painting dog portraits, doing needlepoint, and making cloth dolls. Like many successful doll artists, Cather had an established background in art as a commercial artist before she ventured into dollmaking. As a lover of antiques, Cather had always loved American folk dolls, and chose to create her own very personal interpretations based on nineteenth-century cloth dolls. In 1986 Cather and her family moved to Carmel Valley, California, where she maintains a studio in her home. She finds it more difficult in the West to find antique accessories and unusual fabrics, and she is forced to rely on friends who send her their finds. She still incorporates a moon and a star in her logo in honor of mothers everywhere.

Cather began *Martha, an American Flag Doll* (plate 46) by drawing it on paper in her sewing room, which is filled with dolls, tiny accessories, ribbons, and bolts of colorful fabrics. After tracing one of her standard body patterns onto cotton material, she cut and sewed it together. If *Martha* could speak, she would have a story to tell, for Cather typically creates the story before fashioning the doll. Martha's story is inscribed in ink on the hem of her petticoat. Behind the penned-on, irreverent "one-liners" are volumes of life histories that Cather has gathered, full of the foibles and quirks of humankind.

When Jane Cather reflects upon the body of work, her thoughtful commentary reveals her storytelling gifts. She concludes, "All of my days have been threaded together with the thoughts, hopes, plans, ideas, feelings, and knowledge of many women. The messages have come from the women on your street and mine. They are women who have trouble with their hair, the direction of their lives, and those who enjoy success and deal with pain. They are women we know. They are us."

Plate 46
Jane Cather,
Martha, An American Flag Doll,
12 in. (30.5 cm), 1994

Reflections of Cultural Diversity

 The diverse artists in this chapter are spiritually connected to each other by their reverence for humanity in all its forms and their passionate curiosity about different lifestyles. They express a longtime fascination with other cultures and delight in replicating traditional costumes. Most of all, they desire to create dolls that will reflect their own emotional search for meaning and beauty in a changing world.

Many of these artists delight in portraying people from "faraway places with strange sounding names," while others find their subjects closer to home. All of the artists eschew stereotyping and render their dolls with a sensitivity that places them in a category above the ubiquitous tourist dolls we are used to seeing.

On the North American continent Mary Ellen Frank, a lifelong Alaskan, is renowned for her Inuit and Tlingit dolls. The daughter of a bush pilot from Idaho

Plate 47
Lawan Angelique,
Nigerian Earth Mother,
10 in. (25.4 cm), 1994

and a Manitoba-born nurse, she has collected and costumed dolls since childhood. After studying Inuit dollmaking with Dolly Spencer, a legendary dollmaker, at the Alaska State Museum, she left her job as a research economist and apprenticed in Tennessee for four months in 1989 with Akira Blount (see "Fantasies"). Although she had studied portrait drawing and painting, Frank's previous art experience was largely in theater set and costume design, with a background in fabric and clothing arts. After committing to a professional dollmaking career, Frank advanced her skills by studying fur and leather tanning, Aleut bentwood hunting hat construction, Northwest Coast design, and Northwest Coast bentwood box and bowl construction.

Mary Ellen Frank's dolls are portraits of actual individuals or people she finds in historical collections and books. She believes in identifying her subjects whenever possible, forever linking the image with the name. Before Frank models a doll, she secures permission from the individual, and in exchange offers the subject a doll. When she occasionally finds a picture of a person who can't be located, Frank blends two people's images together. For her portraits Frank often consults the Juneau photo repository, where photographs and negatives date back to the early 1800s. Fascinated by "the stories in elderly faces," she gravitates toward dignified older subjects, finding beauty in the character lines of age.

Frank begins by working in polyform (a clay compound), sculpting a head and oven-firing it. She then carves the head by referring to both the photograph and the three-dimensional polyform studies. The heads are carved from either Alaskan yellow cedar or Alaskan paper birch, obtained from friends who are clearing land or cutting firewood. After the wood has dried for at least half a year, Frank starts to carve, usually working on three wooden portrait dolls at a time, finishing them in about two months. She also makes dolls from the original polyform studies. She attaches the dolls' limbs with buttons for natural posing, thereby achieving more lifelike dolls. Frank notes that she costumes her dolls from traditional Inuit designs: "My clothing is made from Alaskan leathers and furs. I use fish, ermine, muskrat, small beaver, fox, deer, and elk skin, wolverine tail, often the scraps off fur crafters' floors. I have had to learn to tan and have tanned Arctic ground squirrel, beaver, and fish (halibut and cod) for use in rain gear. Sometimes I leave the head and tail with the pelt, incorporating them into the parka hood or into ermine head mittens. I do this to recognize the contribution of the animal, which is consistent with Inuit practices in clothing design. I sew by hand, using bladed needles and artificial sinew. I like to take turns, interweaving the clothing construction with the carving to relieve the intensity of the latter work. I can take the leather and fur hand-sewing with me outdoors, when I go fishing, sit in the sun, or visit a friend."

Berta (plate 48) is a commissioned doll made for Diane Mayer of Juneau, Alaska; the artist made her after sculpting a polyform clay head using photos of Mayer's grandmother and an Inuit woman who resembled the grandmother. The head is carved out of Alaska paper birch with a polyfill-stuffed pima-cotton body jointed at the shoulders and hips. Her striking head of hair is made from Icelandic sheep's wool, which is naturally three shades of black, white, and gray. After conditioning and combing the raw hair, Frank braided and glued it onto the wood head. The parka *Berta* wears is a modified dress parka that features decorative ermine "walrus tusks." It is made from Arctic ground squirrel, a short speckled fur preferred for the "dress parka." (For a full-size parka, many squirrel furs are sewn together.) The parka ruff is mink, and the rest of the clothing is made from deer skin and Alaskan furs.

The Native American dolls of Michele Malpica embody the dignity and proud tribal traditions found in Mary Ellen Frank's creations. Working in the New Hampshire countryside, high on top of Isinglass Mountain, she sculpts her dolls because of her desire to form a "link" with Native American cultures. "I try to create a passing moment," Malpica explains, "a glimpse of faces past that reflect pride and sadness— ethereal, powerful faces that make people respond." Malpica claims that ideas for dolls sometimes arrive in dreams, rich in rainbows of colors and textures. After the initial concept has captured Malpica's imagination, completing the doll can take up to two months of work. Malpica is a stickler for accuracy, often collecting materials and accessories from Native American suppliers. Her studio is brimming with remnants, furs, and exotic pieces of the paraphernalia she is constantly gathering. Although Malpica studied sculpture at the studio of Augustus Saint-Gaudens in Cornish, New Hampshire, she regards herself as a self-taught artist. Malpica works in Cernit for the heads and hands, which she attaches to wire-armature bodies. If the heads don't please her in the early stages of sculpting, she discards them, believing they must "breathe" from

Plate 49
Michele Malpica,
Father and Son,
26 in. (66 cm), 1993

the start if they are going to embody her spirit. She avows, "My work is an extension of myself—it is a look into my soul."

"For *Father and Son* (plate 49) I began by making a warrior face that I envisioned having a Mohawk headdress. I blended the Cernit clay using both flesh and brown to create a warm color that wasn't too dark. This process took several hours, as the clay is blended in a pasta machine which must be checked often to make sure the finished piece appears evenly colored, without streaks. As I finished the head, it became evident that this dignified and proud face was not fierce enough to be a warrior. He appeared to me to be more of a hunter, with his piercing black eyes gazing toward the distant horizon. From that perception came the idea of a hunter and his son on their first journey."

Malpica cut out suede deerskin hides that she painted with symbols of the hunt and adorned with beads and fur remnants. The son wears a fur headdress,

Plate 50
Michael Langton,
Turtle Shaman,
24 in. (61 cm), 1992

while the father sports turkey plumage. Intent upon replicating authentic jewelry and accessories, she skillfully incorporated Navaho loomwork, Crow beads, bones, dentalia, and turquoise nuggets into their costumes. They are "dressed for success," reflecting their honored status as providers for the tribe. Malpica adds, "I used smaller-scale fur for the son, so he would not be out of proportion to his father. I tried to reveal the strong bond between father and son— I think I captured that in their faces. The little boy is imitating his father, but he has a child's face and a softer expression." Malpica concludes, "They seem to step out of the woods, not speaking a word, poised for the hunt as they look out over the fields and meadow."

Turtle Shaman (plate 50) is a testament of Michael Langton's affinity for Native American culture (see "Portraits of Real People"). Originally, Langton was commissioned to create a bronze sculpture commemorating the five hundredth anniversary of Columbus's voyage. As he began researching the history of Christopher Columbus's explorations, he grew uneasy. "I discovered I had a profound feeling of regret," he explains, "for what was lost as a result of the western expansion in the New World. There was no way I could portray this anniversary in any heroic terms, so I canceled the Columbus piece, and instead developed the Turtle Shaman."

The myth of Turtle Island, shared by several Native American tribes, describes the creation of North America from a sea of water. It tells how a great tortoise rose from the water, his shell becoming dry land, which brought forth a tree, which, in turn, brought forth humanity. "As part of the creation myth," Langton reveals, "I felt the turtle was appropriate to illustrate the fall of the Indian culture." For the skull in the shaman's hand Langton used the skull of a giant snapping turtle that he had found years before the project. At first Langton was afraid the skull was too large for the scale of the twenty-four-inch doll. However, while attending the NIADA convention in New Orleans in 1991, he wandered into a Ripley's Believe-It-Or-Not museum, where he was astonished to see a North American snapping turtle that had the same size head as the skull he was planning to incorporate in his piece. Langton regarded his serendipitous viewing of the snapping turtle as a sign to use the skull and decided the shaman would hold it rather than wear it as a mask. He carved a pipe out of red marble and incised a turtle into the bowl of the pipe. Langton saved the front claws of the snapping turtle for the necklace that hangs around the shaman's neck.

Turtle Shaman is composed of about sixty-five parts, and thus it can assume a multitude of realistic poses. A master of the mechanics of jointing, Langton receives as many accolades from woodworkers as he does from fellow doll-makers (*Turtle Shaman* appears on the back cover of the July/August 1992 issue of *Fine Woodworking*).

Marilyn Phillippi grew up in rural western Pennsylvania, an only child for fourteen years who spent most of her time entertaining herself. She remembers, "I always had a vivid imagination, which my parents encouraged by supplying me with lots of paper, paint, clay, books, music, and a beautiful forest just outside the back door to dream in. I made my first doll when I was three or four. I bunched two pieces of navy blue crepe into balls and connected them, aided by a very large darning needle threaded with black button thread. My mother kept my less-than-perfect creation in her button jar for the longest time. Over the years I learned to sew, knit, crochet, tat, and work in clay—all of which became useful in dollmaking. Some years ago I was making very intricate clay wind chimes and I found myself sculpting little heads. I made slab-formed bottles and used the heads as stoppers. I guess my fascination with dollmaking started then but didn't resurface for another ten years." When Phillippi started making dolls a few years ago, she sculpted the heads, hands, and feet from poly-clay and attached them to padded wire-armature bodies. The first dolls she made were very detailed. Phillippi recalls, "It was a challenge to work so intricately, but now I'm leaning toward simplicity. I once took a figure-drawing class in which the instructor stressed capturing gesture using a minimum of lines—I guess that's what I'm attempting with my dolls now." Like many artists, Phillippi experiments with various media. Recently she has discovered Paperclay, admiring its similarity to fabric. "I'm excited," she confesses, "about the possibilities of combining fabric and Paperclay in my dolls. I've begun making jointed fabric bodies that can be moved and therefore posed."

The head, hands, and feet of the *Himalayan Fluteman* (plate 51) are made of Super Sculpey, tinted with acrylics attached to a padded wire armature. As Phillippi sculpted the head she let it evolve. "When I make a head, I find that if I don't try to force a particular face to happen, but just kind of feel my way along, a character shows itself, as if by magic," Phillippi notes. Most of the fabric in the *Himalayan Fluteman*'s costume is antique—the blue sleeves of his shirt are silk from Phillippi's great-grandmother's sewing basket, and the saffron-colored vest was salvaged from an old Chinese hanging. The flute is carved bamboo, and the black beads hanging from it are made of rose petals. "When I was sculpting the hands," Phillippi notes, "I had to stop quite a few times, hold my hands in the correct position for flute playing while looking in a mirror, reverse the image in my mind, then try to keep it all straight while I worked. It was a little confusing and amusing at the same time." She concludes, "I just hope the viewer sees a simple man dressed in tattered finery, happy to make beautiful music to a Tibetan sky."

Janis Harris lives on the outskirts of Auckland, one of New Zealand's largest cities, in the midst of breathtaking scenery. Here she has been making original dolls since the mid-1980s. A native of New Zealand, she grew up on a sheep and cattle ranch on the North Island. Her schoolmates included a few European descendants like herself, but most were Maori children whose Polynesian ancestors had settled in New Zealand in the fourteenth century, four hundred years before the first Europeans arrived. Her childhood experiences amid the Maori instilled a deep appreciation for their legends and handicrafts. As a child Harris developed a love of sewing (made more enticing by the forbidden fruit of her mother's treadle sewing machine) that eventually led to a dressmaking career before she discovered dollmaking.

After a brief fling with making reproduction dolls, Harris attempted her first original doll; not surprisingly, it was a Maori figure. Annoyed by the uninspiring tourist dolls that were simply "brown plastic *white dolls*," she was convinced she could make sensitive portraits that reflected the beautiful Polynesian features and coloring of the Maori people. Instead of the crude clothing found on tourist dolls, she fashioned true-to-life, miniature replicas of pre-European ethnic costumes. Harris is a perfectionist in matters of authenticity, insisting on using time-consuming processes to insure accuracy. She was determined to capture the delicate skin tones of Polynesian people rather than use brown porcelain, which she felt was too dark. By trial and error she found that four separate firings of the hand-painted porcelain heads and limbs could achieve a luminous, creamy skin tone. Harris also painstakingly replicates the elaborate *mokos*, or facial tattoos, of adult Maoris. She substitutes synthetic wigs for human hair out of respect for Maori customs and sensibilities. She explains, "While I prefer using human hair on my non-Maori figures, I don't want to offend their belief that the human head is sacred." In costuming the dolls Harris creates miniature replicas of historic clothing. The most spectacular garment in a Maori tribesman's wardrobe is a cloak that is handwoven from flax and adorned with feathers. It is regarded

Plate 51
Marilyn Phillippi,
Himalayan Fluteman,
14 in. (35.6 cm), 1993

as a status symbol, often taking six months to complete, that only wealthy Maoris can afford. For Harris's miniature versions she commissions loom-woven fiber copies that she adorns with dyed cotton trimmings and feathers. Harris feels that the Maori spirit in her dolls is augmented by the contributions of Maori craftspeople, who fashion clothing, create authentic jewelry using traditional implements, and make a variety of accessories.

Wiremu and Marama (plate 52) represents a well-to-do Maori family. Wiremu is a proud warrior; he carries a *patu* (carved wooden fighting club), which he uses in hand-to-hand combat and in ceremonial dances. He also wears a *tiki* (a neck ornament), carved in bone. In one ear he has a shark's tooth and in the other a jade *(pounamu)* pendant. Marama wears a handwoven cloak with black tassels over a handmade flax shirt known as a *piu-piu*. Her *tiki* is carved in *pounamu*. The baby is naked, as custom dictates, with a leather body.

Harris thinks of New Zealand in Maori terms, calling it "the land of the long white cloud." Of the many dolls she makes, the Maori dolls hold a special fascination, for through them she tells the story of her country and its people.

Many doll artists choose African subjects. Doll artists who have made their mark in character dolls as well as more traditional dolls are inspired by the majesty and poignancy of African subjects. Jodi and Richard Creager (see "Holiday Inspirations") are typical of artists who wish to expand their horizons. *Selephi*, "the African Woman" (plate 53), in Super Sculpey, represents the Creagers' first African portrait. "Our inspiration for her," Jodi Creager relates, "came from a lovely black-and-white photograph of an American woman dressed in African traditional clothing. We thought she should be recreated in a much older, regal version. To us she appeared to be a strong-willed, fiercely proud woman sitting for her royal portrait." The dignity of *Selephi* appealed to the Creagers, who have always revered the beauty found in older subjects. By entering into the life of *Selephi*, the Creagers make an emotional commitment that is a very important part of the dollmaking experience. "There are so many wonderful people in the world who we never have the pleasure of meeting or getting to

Plate 52
Janis Harris,
Wiremu and Marama,
34 in. (86.4 cm) and
31 in. (78.7 cm), 1994

Plate 53
Jodi and Richard
Creager,
Selephi,
14 in. (35.6 cm), 1993

know," Jodi Creager explains. "It is a unique pleasure for a doll artist to create characters and imagine them to be long-time friends or neighbors—people you might like to chat with for hours over the backyard fence. Richard and I often see old friends and realize new ones in our creations."

Lawan Angelique is one of a small number of African-American artists in the contemporary doll field. Her colorful needle-art sculptures celebrate ethnic diversity and cross an invisible line between folk art and fine art. "My cloth dolls seem to attract an unusual kind of doll enthusiast," Angelique notes. "Many have never bought a doll before, and a lot are men."

Nigerian Earth Mother (plate 47), the third fabric sculpture in a series of black Madonnas, personifies Mother Earth—from the garden-inspired pattern of her dress to her contemplative expression that silently asks, "Will this child survive?" Angelique chose a hand-blocked, resist-dyed fabric from Nigeria for the traditional dress and draped it in many folds, letting it almost envelop the piece. The African Madonna wears a brass Nigerian fertility bell and rings as bracelets. Other beads and coins also come from Africa. The doll's mysterious expression can be attributed to a needle-sculpture technique developed by Angelique that emphasizes abstract rather than realistic features. "I sculpt the head and torso with surgical stockinette," Angelique explains, "and then cover it with cotton knit. (I use cotton knit because it paints well and feels nice.) It is a two-step process in which I exaggerate the features on the stockinette base, so that they are not lost when I cover them with the cotton-knit layer. For my colored dolls I paint over black knit fabric, using thin layers of acrylic and textile paints in a wet-on-wet impressionist style. The dolls are painted black as opposed to brown. I try to imbue my dolls with an air of mystery and a certain allure: to do this I let the viewer's imagination finish the face."

Angelique grew up in Washington, D.C., and remembers a childhood in which art played a central role. She says with a smile, "At that time the schools had great programs for children and the arts. (My claim to fame is that I saw the Mona Lisa before I was twelve.) My mother, an illustrator, attended Howard University and met Dad there. Our house was filled with music, art, theater, and politics. I spent most of my time painting and model-making. I learned needle arts from my grandmother. In college I soon rebelled against a structured pro-gram and began to take whatever appealed to me: from fine arts to design, to theater arts—the perfect education for dollmaking!"

In 1988 Angelique made her first doll for her son. The experience led her to begin making dolls with the intention of having a business by 1990. As a woman of color from a racially mixed family and as a partner in a mixed mar-riage, Angelique thought it important that her children see dolls in a variety of colors, and thus, her ethnic dolls were born. "When we lived in Hawaii, the beauty of racially mixed children was all around us, and it became apparent to me that I should commit myself to creating dolls that represent children of color. Of course, I ended up doing a lot of other dolls, too. One of my favorite dolls is an Irish goddess, who is part of a series of dolls I have made involving sacred art." Angelique's interest in sacred art, which includes her series of Madonnas, intensified as she studied women's mythology. The beauty and power of her female figures reflect her desire to show them in a strong light. Angelique also plays with visual and historical contrasts, dressing a black African girl with tribal scars in a white Victorian dress or choosing a flaming red wig for an

African Medusa priestess in traditional African costume. "This is what I love about dollmaking!" she joyfully explains. "There are no rules—it is a very open art. I can challenge myself with each piece I make, so I never get bored."

For artists who make African dolls, current events often play a role in the selection process. When Lisa Lichtenfels was glancing through a newspaper in the kitchen of her home in Springfield, Massachusetts, a photograph of a Somalian native waiting at a food airlift site caught her eye. Lichtenfels recalls, "The image was from the shoulders up, and it occurred to me that he'd make a magnificent full-figured sculpture. Apart from researching his background, capturing the facial expression proved the most challenging aspect of the project. There were many conflicting emotions in his face at one time—it was the type of face that is a treasure to find, and one that demands the utmost from the artist."

Lichtenfels's soft-sculpture figures always start with a series of drawings of the figure from every angle. Her approach was honed by years of working as a Disney animator, when she used to make at least ten drawings for every second of visual time. After finishing a skeletal overlay on tracing paper, Lichtenfels makes a three-dimensional aluminum skeleton. Her prodigious knowledge of anatomy (she has fainted at more autopsies than she cares to remember) serves her well in a laborious process in which she 'builds' muscles and tendons by sewing synthetic quilt batting to the skeleton, and then covers it with layers of nylon stockings. Although nylon is extremely difficult to manipulate, Lichtenfels appreciates its versatility, especially its propensity to simulate the smoothness of a baby's face or replicate the wrinkled visage of old age. "Working with nylon takes a long time, but that time becomes a meditation, forcing me to dig deeper in the character I am creating," Lichtenfels muses. To achieve a lifelike glow in the "skin," she paints each of the several layers of nylon stockings a different shade, allowing the light to create translucent effects, as it permeates the "skin." Because the minute thread filaments must be hidden from sight, Lichtenfels can spend two days on a single seam. Such painstakingness makes it impossible to create more than ten dolls a year.

Somali Man (plate 54) is distinguished by the indomitable living spirit that emanates from the work. A feeling of calm patience contrasts with the force of his personality. The resulting tension catches the viewer off guard, which is precisely Lichtenfels's aim.

Although they work in different media, Lisa Lichtenfels and Brigitte Deval (see "Women of the Imagination") have both been described in similar terms; as doll artists intent on portraying the soul of their subjects. A captivating spirituality pervades their work, so much so that their vision has defined their individual art forms, setting a high standard for others to follow. Deval, an artist's artist, inspires the use of superlatives from her peers in a field that is known for its critical eye. A fellow Bavarian, Peter Wolf, was one of the first artists to recognize Deval's talent, calling her work "classical." He introduced her to John Noble, who was then the curator of the Doll and Toy Collection at the Museum of the City of New York. From the moment Noble saw Deval's dolls, he was captivated by her riveting portraits. Over the years his appreciation of Deval's work deepened. Recently, he compared Deval to such famous portrait artists as Goya and Gainsborough, noting the ability of these artists to strip away superficial aspects of their subjects' personalities to reveal "the true identity, the secret soul."

Deval, a native of Germany who moved to Siena, Italy, in 1974, credits her multicultural heritage with inspiring her interest in making dolls of many lands. Her artistic talent was obvious as a young child (at six she fashioned her first *stock puppe*, which are dolls modeled over sticks and bottles). Deval's father, a famous portrait photographer, encouraged these early artistic endeavors. Deval found her signature medium, wax-over-ceramic, at the beginning of her career in the late 1960s, and she has spent the last twenty-five years perfecting her techniques. Deval, who is fluent in three languages, explains, "I prefer a wax-over-ceramic mixture to wax-over-porcelain, because I am confident that my recipe will outlive me by hundreds of years. Unlike pure porcelain, ceramic absorbs wax and does not have the tendency to chip. The wax imparts a subtle glow to the skin."

After Deval's move to Tuscany, occasioned by her marriage, her dollmaking efforts intensified. Over the years she has created a network of artisans worldwide who are devoted to creating the handcrafted accessories Deval demands for her dolls. Glass eyes are made by an eighty-five-year-old Roman craftsman, who follows Deval's detailed instructions regarding size and color. A weaver in Florence is called upon to create special silks for dresses, while a hosier in Romania hand-knits stockings. Deval has a local Tuscan cobbler make the shoes that she personally designs, and relies upon a German wigmaker to fashion custom-made wigs of human hair or mohair.

Deval's *Afghanistan Child* (plate 55), like all of her work, is personal and intimate. The child seems pensive rather than active, thereby instilling a compatible feeling in the observer. Deval claims she purposely avoids using strong facial expressions, but rather aims for a more ambiguous state: "My dolls appear to be on the verge of emotion." *Afghanistan Child* exudes a quiet air of mystery. We are not quite sure of his heritage. The face is very dark and Indian-looking. "Maybe he is a nomad," suggests Deval. His delicate features seem androgynous, implying a universality of childhood beauty. Deval created the *Afghanistan Child* from the same mold as a Caucasian girl holding puppets. "It does not matter where I begin," she notes, "for the dolls are completely different in the end." Deval is not interested in strict costume accuracy, but rather in creating a mood. Here, she uses fabrics from Afghanistan, while selecting jewelry from Afghanistan and Pakistan.

Like Brigitte Deval, Christa Canzio left her native Germany for Italy on the occasion of her marriage. She gave up her position as an art instructor, and by her own account became "somewhat of a bored housewife." Inspired by the great works of art around her, Canzio decided to try sculpting on her own, in the form of dolls. As doll-making classes were unheard of in Italy, Canzio learned her craft in unusual ways. She worked with master craftsmen—restorers, potters, and experts in stucco— absorbing information in both contemporary and antique approaches that helped her devise special surfaces and firing techniques. At first, Canzio made stuffed-cloth bodies, which proved too weak for supporting the torsos, so she developed underlying wire armatures. "At times," Canzio recalls, "I had periods when all my experimenting with different techniques seemed fruitless, and I thought I might just give up—but my husband loved my dolls and encouraged me to go on. Costuming proved to be the easiest part of the process. Since I had learned sewing from my mother when I was a small child, I did not find it daunting to create original costumes. In fact, it is my greatest pleasure to make miniature clothing that represents different countries and periods."

When Canzio returned to Augsburg after a few years in Italy, she was finally able to set up her own studio and collect the trinkets and fabrics she needed for costuming. "I found antique silks from India, silver jewelry from Morocco, miniature pottery from Peru, and many books on foreign costumes," she adds. As Canzio began to exhibit in Europe, her immediate success prompted her husband, Renzo, to join forces in a joint dollmaking effort. Today they work

Plate 55
Brigitte Deval,
Afghanistan Child,
25 in. (63.5 cm), 1994

together on various projects, traveling less because their dollmaking keeps them at home.

Mi-Zhoui (plate 56) reflects Canzio's fascination with Mongolia. "Years ago I saw an exhibition about Mongolian works of art," she reveals. "I was so taken with their mysterious culture that I read every book and saw every film about Mongolia that I came across. Renzo and I began a series of a Mongolian family: the powerful *Dschingis-Khan*, the ancient *Pao*, patriarch of the family, and *Mi-Zhoui*, the youngest daughter, with her baby. As I worked on *Mi-Zhoui*, I concentrated on making her face reflect a serene happiness. I pictured her walking over the silent Mongolian prairies in the gentle summer wind. I envisioned her traveling to her grandmother's, anticipating the joy her visit would bring." Canzio describes *Mi-Zhoui* as a hand-sculpted clay figurine. Her wig is made from human hair, the long tresses wrapped up in decorative sheaths. The baby's wig is hand-braided mohair. They are both dressed in typical elaborate Mongolian silk garments, and they wear silver jewelry. *Mi-Zhoui* is a limited edition of twenty-five pieces.

Jacques Dorier's stated goal—"To create objects of everlasting beauty and comfort; dolls that soothe the soul and act as a peaceful refuge from the hectic modern world"—is grounded in an ancient craft that came into existence more than three centuries ago in Japan. Originally Washi paper dolls were made as teaching aids to show children proper ways to dress. Once simple and flat, these dolls evolved from their utilitarian nature into the slender three-dimensional figures that today are considered a sophisticated art form. Every part of the doll is folded and shaped by hand with Washi papers, whose exquisite textures and patterns resemble oriental textiles.

Dorier's Washi paper dolls, made out of the exquisite Japanese papers that come in a dazzling array of colors, textures, and patterns, are objects of lasting beauty. While some of Dorier's dolls epitomize traditional characters from the Kabuki theater, others, although always depicted in a Japanese framework, are fanciful creations from his imagination. All of his dolls bespeak Dorier's fascination for stylized decoration and intricate patterning.

Dorier started making papier-mâché dolls in 1978, the year he left the small medieval French town Manosque, in his native Provence, to come to the

United States. "Even then," Dorier recalls, "I had an interest in paper. When I chanced upon a book about Washi papermaking at the museum shop of the Boston Museum, I knew that someday I would like to attempt Washi doll-making. At the time, it was very difficult to obtain Washi papers, so I put the idea on the back burner. In 1982 a course in Washi dollmaking was offered by a Japanese dollmaker, Sachiko Wendel, in Cambridge, Massachusetts, and I rushed to sign up. After the course ended, I continued to study with Sachiko on a private basis until I had completed thirty dolls. Each one represented mastering a single technique, another 'secret' revealed, to add to my growing palette of skills. I have never given away or sold those first dolls, keeping them in my collection as talismans." Since 1986 Dorier has continued to make traditional paper dolls, while at the same time developing his own style and creating an original series of dolls inspired by the Japanese Kabuki theater and Japanese prints, "Ukiyo-e," which were the main art forms during the Edo period in Japan (1603–1868). Using only simple tools (glue, scissors, tweezers, floral tape, and a paper-crumpling tool), Dorier transforms sheets of paper into an exciting cast of warriors and courtesans.

Yoshitsune (plate 57) depicts an actor from the Kabuki theater who portrays a twelfth-century Samurai warrior. He is a study in contrasts. In one hand he grips a baton, indicating his rank; in the other hand he holds a peony. These symbolic gestures suggest that an appreciation of nature tempers the fierceness of his warrior side. "It is a moment in time, a typical pose, that is often defined in Kabuki theater," Dorier says. Like a Kabuki actor in costume, *Yoshitsune* has a white face without features, and depends on conveying an emotional message by his body language. Dorier notes that the posing of the doll is the most critical phase of the dollmaking process, calling it "the moment when life is born."

Yoshitsune's costume, an elaborate construction of layered papers, represents weeks of work. The ornately patterned coat of the Samurai warrior glitters with Japanese symbols. The green and blue hexagonal patterning contains double meanings: the scales of the turtle and the colors of the sea. The iris, a symbol of knighthood, is one of the most revered flowers in the Japanese lexicon. Underneath the coat, the red suit of armor contains metallic and colored "plates of armor" that Dorier wove through the red paper.

Dorier sees an exciting future for his creations using Washi papers, one that will incorporate foreign designs into a traditional medium. "I am starting to create dolls that are more abstract, that are my own inventions," Dorier explains. "I layer patterns, combining them in ways that you would never see in

traditional Washi dolls." He is now creating fictitious characters from an imaginary world, which allow him to mix styles and cultural references freely. While his new dolls are still made from paper, the faces, hands, and feet are composed of Paperclay. From afar, faces appear to be traditional, but up close, one can see facial features that have been painstakingly sculpted.

Dan Fletcher, an American dancer turned dollmaker, also regards himself as an innovator in the world of Japanese Washi paper dolls. Fletcher has turned his considerable artistic talent and energy from dancing to exploring Japanese culture as seen through Washi dollmaking. Fletcher was lured by the beautiful patterns in the Washi papers, patterns that are created by silkscreens, woodblocks, and stencils. "I am fascinated with patterns, and want to start my own paper company to create a silkscreen process that will allow me to express exactly what I want . . . that will let me make a doll that is entirely mine," Fletcher says. "Right now people who are making handprinted papers in Japan are economically pressed to produce papers that are of good stock with interesting patterns. Often, the better the pattern, the cheaper the paper. In Japan one has to spend 125 to 150 dollars for the best-quality paper, and in America, of course, paper is more expensive."

Fletcher also uses silk crepe crushed paper, *chirimen momigami*, to achieve interesting textures. He took lessons for six months with an eighty-four-year-old master of *chirimen momigami* to learn the art, and believes he is the only man outside of Japan who has this skill.

When asked about the most important aspects of Washi-paper dollmaking, Fletcher breaks down the components into three basic elements: texture and pattern, pose, and story. "The choice of texture is key to movement, as it dictates viewer involvement," Fletcher explains. "It can be smooth as silk or a heavy, ponderous fabric. I like breaking the line by finding the drape of the fabric that is most exciting. By distorting the pattern, by letting the viewer see only a piece of the pattern, I prompt the viewer to finish the pattern with his own eye." Fletcher feels that story and pose are interrelated as the story dictates the pose. "By 'story' I mean the sense of something that has just happened or is about to happen," Fletcher notes.

In *The Courtesan* (plate 58), the story reveals the male figure, a merchant, who is crouched on one knee, about to take the hand of the courtesan. Originally

Fletcher planned to show the hands interlocking. He accidentally jostled the dolls; the hands came apart, and he decided to leave them almost touching, as he felt this pose added to the sense of movement. Before Fletcher started making the rudimentary forms that are the base for his dolls, he pored over woodblock prints and pictures of the Kabuki theater. The female figure, representing a courtesan of the highest class, wears an *obi* (sash) of *momigami* and carries a towel, which, along with her hairdo, identifies her as a courtesan.

Fletcher's childhood in Southern California gave little indication of his artistic talents. Occasionally he joined his father in lapidary projects, but it wasn't until after an unsuccessful freshman year as an engineering major that Fletcher turned to dance—at the suggestion of a friend who told Fletcher he had terrible posture and ought to do something about it. Fletcher became a dancer, moved to New York City, and joined the American Dance Machine as a performer and an instructor. On a trip to Japan with the dance company in 1984, Fletcher happened upon a Washi-paper doll in a crafts store in Tokyo that he thought was not only unusual but beautiful. In his own words, he became "obsessed" with the idea of making his own dolls out of Washi paper. He bought the doll, studied it in his Tokyo apartment, found an instructional book in English on Washi papermaking, purchased some Washi paper, and proceeded to make a doll head. This rudimentary effort began an eight-year journey into Washi dollmaking, as Fletcher studied with the most respected Washi dollmakers in Japan. To this day Fletcher marvels at the generosity of his teachers, who transcended cultural differences and language problems to impart their secrets to an American visitor. In 1987 Fletcher received the supreme compliment of an invitation to exhibit his dolls with those of thirty-six Japanese dollmakers at the Takashimaya Department Store in Osaka. An observer is tempted to note that the cross-cultural relationship between Dan Fletcher and the Japanese is as beautiful as the dolls he creates.

Harry Perzyk, a California artist originally from Indonesia, compares his multicultural dolls to a rainbow. Each doll represents an individual who Perzyk transforms into a synthesis of cultural mores, folkways, mythological tales, and religious values that he hopes will express the structure of a particular society. Saketo was a well-known *ronin* (a masterless samurai) who lived in the early nineteenth century at the end of the shogunate of Ieyasu Tokugawa (the last Japanese shogun). As the shogunate's social structure crumbled, the populace of Japan suffered at the hands of government officials. Perzyk views Saketo as a kind of Japanese Robin Hood who fought for the rights of the common man. "While he never stole from the rich to give to the poor," Perzyk notes, "he literally cut, slashed, and killed to accomplish his goal. My biggest challenge was to carve *righteousness* into the soft porcelain head. I carved and destroyed eight heads before I was satisfied!"

In costuming *Saketo* (plate 59) Perzyk chose the finest silk fabrics, including a silk brocade made on a triple-jacquard loom. "These fabrics are not available in America," he explains, "so I buy all my fabrics in Japan, and even commission special silks to be hand-dyed and woven for me. One might wonder why I use such expensive fabric and go to all this extra trouble, but I am not satisfied unless every detail is true to the spirit of the historical figure. I simply can't dress a wealthy samurai in fabric from the dime store! For *Saketo,* some of the fabrics were new and some were loomed in the 1920s and 1930s."

Before Perzyk made *Saketo,* he submerged himself in the history of Japan. He visited the country, read everything he could about the samurai warriors, and saw the grand palaces of the period, as he tried to become, in his words, "for one fleeting moment, Saketo."

Perzyk came to dollmaking after years of being a master tailor in Los Angeles and Lake Tahoe. His list of clients reads like the Who's Who list for the entertainment industry, from Taylor Caldwell and Sammy Davis, Jr., to Donna Summer. In the 1970s Perzyk traveled around the world with Taylor Caldwell as her personal dressmaker. "It was an unbelievably elegant life on the cruise ship," Perzyk reminisces, "and I loved making her evening dresses. I don't go around the world anymore, but in making a doll collector happy with a special piece I experience the same type of joy that I used to get from making an elaborate gown!"

Contemporary
Children

Dolls representing children abound. The form of a child is the most traditional a doll can take; certainly, dolls created as playthings almost always represent children. And, too often, the dolls portrayed as children have a superficial charm; they are rendered as sweet, artificially innocent creatures, whose appeal is to the lowest common denominator of sentimentality. In fact, these do appeal, and broadly; over and over again dolls in the form of children prove to be more popular than any others.

The artist who chooses to portray a child faces the challenge of moving beyond this easy image. The dollmakers featured in this chapter succeed at creating figures that do far more than simply tug at our heartstrings. These artists reach deeply into themselves to give shape and substance to something more than a

Plate 60
Uta Brauser,
Home Boys,
22 in. (55.9 cm) and
26½ in. (67.3 cm), 1994

111

Plate 61
Malou Ancelin,
Girl with Her Doll,
17½ in. (44.5 cm),
1992

nostalgic rendering. They work at technical innovations that will form a more authentic expression. Whether striving to re-create their own inner selves or to give life to qualities they see in other children, in choosing young people as a subject, artists are often trying to give a voice to those who cannot yet articulately express themselves, yet whose very presence can be so eloquent.

The French artist Malou Ancelin says her dolls are the opposite of nostalgic: "I try to look at everything and to translate it all through the penetrating vision of my childhood. It is an emotional, intimate, and very personal quest, to bring forth the raw emotions of childhood, to preserve them as treasures, to give birth again to childhood's power of wonder and imagination and, in so doing, to find again the original intensity of that time of life."

Born in 1947 and raised in the countryside of Charente in southwestern France, Malou spent her childhood in a creative atmosphere. "It was a fairy-tale childhood," she says. "In the summer we played under cherry trees; in the winter school closed on the days when the boar·hunts were on. I lived in the midst of wonderful aromas of all kinds: fabrics—cotton, taffetas, woolens—that my father's truck transported to the farms nearby, jams and cakes that came from the kitchen where my grandmother, aunt, and maid worked. Then there were the sounds—I was rocked to dreamland by the music of my two older sisters' piano lessons." Her mother was a teacher and taught her children not only reading and arithmetic, but also how to garden, to watch the bird migrations, and to record their thoughts, feelings, and observations in private journals. School was a one-room schoolhouse with twenty pupils. While Malou's words and images approach the sentimental, her creations themselves are far from it. Her chosen medium—kid leather—and her technical realism save her dolls from what could, in other hands, be sentimental. Instead her pieces are at once painterly and sculptural, and very contemporary.

Her techniques have evolved over the years. Today she pours the resin heads from molds taken from clay models. She then covers the heads with glue and encases them with leather. She sets in glass eyes, and paints the other features. The faces are protected with a layer of wax, and sprayed with a waterproof base. The bodies are modeled, sculpted, and encased in kid leather.

Malou's *Girl with Her Doll* (plate 61), made in 1992, is more than a little pouty. When viewed from certain angles she is even a bit angry, and almost suspicious of her surroundings. Still, she holds her doll, however carelessly. In this creation, Malou captures the essence of a difficult age. The charm and simplicity of the smocked dress, one a much younger child could wear, are in opposition to the girl's wary expression. Her casual treatment of her doll is a clear image of the ambivalence of her age. She is almost ready to let her go, but not quite.

Always articulate, introspective, and creative, Malou also has a simple sense of her artistic purpose. "My dolls are the many little girls that I was. I make dolls because they are soft to the touch, pretty to look at, and smell good. I make dolls because, when I have completed one, and I sit her down, opposite me, face to face, she on her chair and I on mine, I am not sure which one of us is more surprised. I make dolls for that moment."

In Israel, Edna Dali also finds the moment of completion a surprising one. "Although I know more or less what kind of a character I have sculpted, it always astonishes me when I finish the painting and put on the hair," she admits. Best known for her fragile-looking young women dressed in antique fabrics, she also makes the occasional child. *Daphne* (plate 62), wearing antique printed velvet, is a sixteen-and-a-half-inch girl inspired by the artist's three-year-old next-door neighbor. "She's a very pretty, very clever girl," says Dali, "and a rather sturdy child. She is not as delicate as the older dolls I create."

Plate 62
Edna Dali,
Daphne,
16½ in. (42 cm), 1994

Much of Dali's inspiration comes from the fabrics and other treasures
she is constantly looking out for. She first makes a doll's face, starting with the
hand-blown glass eyes, and usually has a fabric in mind as she sculpts from the
translucent Fimo that is her medium. While she never knows how the face painting will turn out, "I usually keep the fabric by my worktable as I am painting
the face," she notes. *Daphne*'s light hand-painted freckles delicately echo the coral
print of the forest-green velvet she wears. Beneath her dress she has on a slip
and pantalettes, all of antique fabrics, and kid-leather shoes. *Daphne* has a wired-
armature torso covered with cloth, and a Fimo shoulderplate, forearms, and
lower legs. Her crystal glass eyes are gray; her other features are hand-painted.

Although she was born and raised in Israel, and lives there now, Dali's
dollmaking began when she lived with her family in Brookline, Massachusetts,

in 1983. Her husband, at the park one afternoon with the children, struck up a conversation with the husband of another Israeli woman, Anna Avigail Brahms (see "Women of the Imagination"). Brahms, already an acclaimed doll artist, invited Dali to see her dolls. "I was fascinated and fell in love with them," Dali says. Because Dali had always enjoyed a variety of arts and crafts, and had a special love for antique fabrics and accessories, she eventually began to help Brahms with the sewing for her dolls. She absorbed much of the experienced artist's doll-making technique, and after about a year, decided to try making her own dolls.

While Dali's creations have a strong individual grace and presence, a hint of the early influence of the legendary Brahms is also there. Dali herself sees the clear delineation of this influence: "Certainly I have been influenced by her, but I am more realistic. Avigail is more dreamlike, more imaginative. I have my feet more on the ground." While both dollmakers rely on their love for antique textiles and accessories for inspiration, Dali's figures and their costumes are characterized more by elegance and Brahms's more by a fleeting sense of romance. Dali looks more to the heavier velvets, satins, and beaded silks. Her figures, while evoking a dreamlike magic, have a weightier presence than those of Brahms.

In a very different vein, Idaho artist Hal Payne's depiction of childhood seen here is a light-hearted, seemingly historical vignette of youngsters at play. The versatile artist calls this work *The Great American Button Box Wars* (plate 63). The piece incorporates nine six-inch dolls in a giant-sized button box, all interacting in highly individual ways. ("Do you like my self-portrait?" laughs the artist. "It's the little guy on the left, lifting the girl's skirt.")

Payne is hard to pinpoint or categorize as an artist. His vast range of subjects brings an almost hard edge to his children; they are endlessly charming, but their charm comes from their wiry frames, their knobby knees and elbows, their mischievous grins, often surrounded by freckles. They are always active, always lively, always engaged in some outrageous activity. Payne is a technical master of the odd balance: children playing leapfrog, Jack and Jill tumbling down the hill with their pail of water, Old King Cole and his fiddlers three, attached in such a way as to create the illusion of motion.

Payne's creations go far beyond children and nursery rhymes. He has interpreted Romeo and Juliet, a young Pan and a Civil War soldier in wood, gnomelike figures he called Knobolds in Sculpey and Plasticine, and dignified, ceremoniously dressed Native American braves and maidens in resin. The artist explains that his use of different media expresses various aspects of his personality, with works in wood generally expressing the more serious side of him, the resins giving vent to his humor and fantasy, and the stoneware pieces, which he has used for less active, single figures representing children, reflecting a gentler nature. He is continuously exploring different media and subject. "I bore easily," he notes. "Once I've mastered a skill or concept, I move on. My work is in a constant state of transition." He characterizes himself as "unpredictable."

While children are only one of the versatile dollmaker's subjects, the root of his inspiration for all his work lies in childhood. "I want to re-create," he says, "if just for a moment, that time when we were all children, and the world was filled with delightful wonder—a time when reality and fantasy were one."

German-born Uta Brauser also has a feel for reality and fantasy, but in her work there is a strong separation between the two. She made her reputation in the late 1980s with her stylized white-porcelain female figures in elaborate Baroque costumes and her theatrical marionettes. Today she is equally well, if not better, known for her very urban contemporary African-American street kids with what has become known as "attitude."

Raised in an artistic family in Munich, Brauser lived in Italy for seven years before moving to New York City in 1993. In 1990 she began creating black dolls—very specifically, she says, representations of black people in Western culture. "I have a very special sympathy for black people," says Brauser. "I lived with a Nigerian man for four years, and I find black people very beautiful." Initially she focused on black men because, given her European upbringing, she was most familiar with them. "Only male Africans come to Europe to study," she explains, "The women are not emancipated, they stay home. So I never saw very many black women. Now I have both sexes as friends."

She began by making portraits of her black male friends, working in Cernit, ceramic, or porcelain painted with acrylics. "I wanted to make a contemporary statement," she says, "about black people in the Western world, so I started with statements about music. I feel that black people have been able to communicate so much through music, to make important political statements through rap, for example." Once Brauser began researching black culture, she learned more than she ever expected. "Books opened my eyes about the whole issue of Africans in the United States and Europe. I saw a lot more than I first wanted to see, and I got in a lot deeper than I ever planned."

Finding her black male figures somewhat threatening, people began to ask the artist to create children. She had a lot of friends with children, and found it easy to oblige—though she has not given up making her black males, just as she continues to create her Renaissance-era dolls and marionettes. The children, like the three *Home Boys* shown (plate 60), are very realistic, expressive urban kids. Their outfits, from the baggy jeans showing off the Calvin Klein undershorts to the oversized layered shirts, accurately capture contemporary street fashions. Brauser gives each doll individual attention, but feels that it is her body of work that is more important than any one piece. "You can't make a statement about black culture with one doll," she asserts. "You can add piece by piece to make a statement; the whole body of work becomes the statement."

Lorna Miller, who was born in the Bahamas, is clear and straightforward about her artistic purpose: "My goal is to show the black child in his and her incredible beauty and splendor." Her one-of-a-kind dolls, which she has been sculpting from Super Sculpey and Cernit since 1991, win notice for their intense, sparkling expressions, which often feature realistic tongues and teeth.

Miller came to the United States in 1980 from her home in Nassau, in the Bahamas, to attend the California College of Arts and Crafts in Oakland. After receiving her degree in 1984, she put her artistic skills aside to earn a living. But in 1990, visiting a friend in Hamburg, Germany, she saw her first handcrafted dolls in a shop and experienced one of those moments that changes a life. "It was the light-bulb thing," she says. Miller knew she had discovered what she was meant to do—something both emotionally meaningful and suited to her talents.

She soon saw that there were few dolls representing realistic black children, and that this was something she could create. Her methods are instinctive: "The dolls tell me what kind of expressions they want. I don't work from photos, usually, I just make them up. My fingers just dictate where to go."

Ysah (plate 64), who is playing cat's cradle, is typical of Miller's creations. Her children are always remarked upon for the level of detail in their sculpting, which includes their realistic toes and open mouths, like *Ysah* has. "The inside

Plate 64
Lorna Miller,
Ysah,
20 in. (50.8 cm), 1994

Plates 65

Carol Trobe,

Standing Tot in

Pink Undershirt and

Saggy Diaper,

12½ in. (31.8 cm), 1994

of the mouth is all painted," the artist explains. "I do the music under the tongue, and the tongues have little tastebuds." The teeth are sculpted from Fimo, glazed, and inserted into the mouth in strips. The human hair is glued on piece by piece.

There is nothing subtle about Miller's work. Her dolls almost attack the viewer with the strength of their expression and attitude. They are what one might call "in your face" with their emotions, be they joyful, angry, stubborn, or mischievous. *Ysah* is one of the happier ones. "I made her on one of my 'up' days," the artist explains. "I was feeling really happy that day." As for the grinning child's name and game, Miller says *Ysah* came from her own imagination. "I don't even think about names until the last minute. I made this one up, and I love it because it's kind of funky. She's playing cat's cradle because it's a kid's game, which I never really knew how to play. I was the one who always got my hand tangled up in it. *Ysah*'s really happy because she knows how to do it. I was too frustrated."

Frustration led Illinois artist Carol Trobe to make her first doll. "During one very hot summer," the artist relates, "when my youngest was a year old, and I was close to pulling my hair out, I picked up some clay and began to sculpt portraits of my two girls. This led to the thought of making dolls for them. One thing led to another, and before any of us could believe it, I was totally absorbed by dollmaking."

Trobe's *Standing Tot in Pink Undershirt and Saggy Diaper* (plates 65) must be seen in the round to be truly appreciated. Trobe describes her earlier work as "pieced" dolls in that, like many dolls, they have heads, arms, and legs sculpted of Cernit, on cloth bodies. But the entire Tot is sculpted from Cernit, the result of a self-imposed artistic challenge. "Some of the ideas I was exploring in my head would not work in a pieced doll," she explains. "For instance, a natural tummy peeking out from under a shirt, or a portion of baby bottom. I knew I was ready to move on to sculpting the entire figure, but needed to develop some new techniques and resolve the technical problems that Cernit presented."

Although Trobe originally experimented with moldmaking and cast composition, when she found Cernit, she recognized it as her medium. "I have stayed with Cernit, enjoying the spontaneity that this medium allows, as well as its lovely translucent fleshlike quality," she reflects.

Trobe has been interested in art since early childhood, and remembers "forever drawing and cutting out paper people" even as a preschooler. Her personal and professional life always revolved around art, as she pursued studies in portraiture and illustration, then built a career in paper conservation. "During these years, though, my desire to pursue a more personal form of expression was ever present, waiting for the right opportunity and form," Trobe says. "Having daughters brought dolls back into my life. I loved dolls as a girl, and shopping for them now became a revelation. I was astonished at the number of beautiful dolls being created. That I have become a doll artist seems now to be a logical blending of my interests in portraiture, illustration, and sculpture."

Trobe is known for her one-of-a-kind dolls illustrating the various complex emotions of childhood. She has created pieces like *Mine!*—an angry red-headed girl protecting her doll from a predatory child—and *Trouble*, another unhappy girl with arms folded across her chest and the signs of a chocolate spill on her dress and shoes. "Living with and loving children," says the artist, "even at their soggy-diapered and snotty worst, has filled my memory with unlimited doll ideas. I feel that these memories are ready to claim their place in the rather crazy world of dolls."

Like Carol Trobe's *Standing Tot in Pink Undershirt and Saggy Diaper,* the little girl made by the French artist who calls herself Héloise is also the result of a self-imposed artistic challenge. For most of her dollmaking career, Héloise has depicted ethereal young girls on the edge of womanhood, with resin heads and limbs on cloth bodies. In creating *La Petite Fille Debout* (Little Girl Standing) (plate 66), which is an edition limited to eight pieces, Héloise has not only turned to childhood as a theme, but has also met a technical goal: that of sculpting the entire doll of resin. The difficulty of this endeavor, explains the artist, lies in the fact that the doll must be hollow and several molds must be made: one of the head and the bust, one of the arms, one of the knees. Then all of these must be joined together with resin. To meet this challenge, Héloise sculpted the entire girl, unclothed, from clay, then cut the sculpture at the hips and elbows to make the molds.

La Petite Fille's softly rounded face and body are a clear departure from the longer, leaner forms Héloise has mastered. Yet the piece retains the romantic aura she is known for, this time in the form of a child. "In the past I often tried to make a childish face," confesses the artist. "But bit by bit, the face would always change into an older one, without my wishing it to do so. It is very important for me to be open to what is born without my knowledge—that is, without my permission." When creating a doll, Héloise begins with a ball of clay and, bit by bit, a face, a shape begins to form. *La Petite Fille Debout* came from her memories of her own daughter, Celine, as a child. "I was charmed by her mannerisms, the positions her body—her arms and legs—would assume, which were awkward but natural to her. I feel very proud that I have somehow managed, in this sculpture, to reproduce the charm of a little girl's body."

The girl's dress is of a fabric bought by Héloise many years ago, simply because she was struck by the beauty of its color and texture. When she completed the little girl, she realized the fabric would be perfect for a dress that exists, as she explains, "only to bring out the charm of the childish body."

Héloise believes that this doll marks an important stage in her artistic evolution. "I have renounced the traditional idea of an articulate doll," she says, "to go further toward something that is still called a doll, but which is actually closer to a sculpture, and which is a form of art in itself."

Kansas artist Charlene Westling says, "I like to think I have a feel for children, for what they are saying with their eyes and body language. Perhaps this is influenced by the few years I worked with learning-disabled children in our school district. From so many different backgrounds, mixed heritages, affluence, or poverty—their attitudes and problems were always unique. Their eyes reflected their hurt or their joy, and were often more revealing than their speech. Consequently the eyes seem of vital importance in bringing to life the dolls I do." The eyes of Westling's dolls are skillfully painted to hint at the depth of potential and feeling within. Her children do not have the exuberance of Lorna Miller's, nor the ethereal quality of Héloise's or Edna Dali's. Their presence is sturdy and quiet, yet they seem to embody the old saying that "still waters run deep." They clearly convey that there is a lot going on beneath the surface.

Westling's educational background was in music, painting, and drawing, and as a child she had a creative mother who taught her and her siblings to sew, knit, and make paper dolls. Westling recalls that making and playing with paper dolls was her favorite activity. When she first began making dolls, in the early 1980s, she worked in porcelain. "The warmth and flexibility of cloth held an appeal for me, though," she recalls. After much experimentation she developed her current style, in which she makes the entire body of composition, then covers it with cloth, and paints with oils the textured surface, like an oil portrait, "developing intensity of expression with each application of paint," she explains.

Plate 66
Héloise,
La Petite Fille Debout,
15½ in. (39.4 cm), 1994

Ben (plate 67) is a small black boy, "playing at being a real baseball player," says Westling. "When beginning to sculpt a new head, my immediate goal is to capture an emotion in a dimensional portrait that can be developed into something time might hold dear." While she does determine whether she is making a girl or boy, and of what age and race, she likes to follow her instincts, experimenting as she creates. Many of her dolls represent earlier eras, though she never plans this, either. As she sculpts, the piece takes on its own being. "They become distinct personalities as they emerge, and indicate to me what name they wish, their period in time and the most appropriate style of clothing for them," Westling explains. "My endeavor has been to develop a style that would enable me to create beauty of expression, posture, and color, which will evoke a feeling and a response in a viewer's mind."

German artist Gabriele Lipp is fascinated by the transparency of children. "Children's faces are so open, you can read them. Adults can hide their thoughts, but children haven't learned this yet," says Lipp. "I made only children for a long time, because I find them so fascinating. Then I began making old people, too. They can be even more fascinating, because their life is written in their faces." Lipp has become internationally known for her small cloth figures, which usually represent these two poles of life she finds most compelling as subjects. "The most difficult people to make are those between the ages of twenty and fifty," she states. "I cannot find anything in their faces."

The dollmaker remembers her own childhood in Bavaria as a very special time of her life, which is evoked in the Bavarian-costumed dolls that are well represented in her repertoire. "I like to remember the days when I was a little girl in my village, surrounded by high mountains. I had wonderful free summers in our woods and meadows, and went barefoot to school. I had strong winters, with a lot of snow, and went skiing and tobogganing. These times come out in my Bavarian dolls."

In spite of her strong attachment to her childhood (she often appears at doll shows in Bavarian costume), the artist also feels an intense bond with native peoples of various nations. "I believe that I was an Indian in my past life. It is in my heart, and wants to come out. Sometimes it seems I am expressing a memory of this past life in my dolls." Her *Bolivian Girl with Brother* (plate 68) is one such piece that comes from these mysterious depths.

The young pair is typical of Lipp's style. Their skin is made from stockinette, which covers a wire skeleton built up with cotton wool and thread. Lipp makes all the costumes, sewing the dresses and knitting the sweaters, jackets, and stockings. The head is also cotton wool covered with fabric. "I build the face—eyes, nose, mouth, cheeks, and chin—with the needle," explains the dollmaker. "I sew them." Then she models the features until she is satisfied, and hardens the face with what she calls "a special tonic." When it is half-dry, she paints the face with acrylic paints. The mohair wigs are also made by the dollmaker. "The most difficult part is certainly the face!" she explains. "But it's also my favorite part of the work. If I am sad, my dolls are sad, and when I'm happy, their faces laugh and they do funny things. Some dollmakers say that they let themselves be surprised by their work," says Lipp, "but my dolls are in my mind, and most of them turn out to be just as they were in my imagination."

Far from Lipp's European studio, in Downingtown, Pennsylvania, one-time teacher Maggie Iacono also creates cloth dolls. Iacono's all-felt creations, known as Maggie Made, have clearly grown out of the felt-dollmaking tradition that includes the historical (and contemporary) Italian Lenci dolls as well as the work of R. John Wright (see "Figures from Literature"). But Iacono has taken the body construction of felt dolls a step further in developing an eleven-piece body with wooden-ball joints at the shoulders, elbows, hips, knees, and ankles. The artist's inspiration for making an articulated felt body came from the English dollmakers Lynne and Michael Roche, whose porcelain-bodied children are similarly jointed for realistic posability.

"When I create one of my dolls I try to pull together a feeling of warmth, a sense of style, and a personality that sets a mood," says Iacono. "I hope the collector will be drawn to hold, reposition, and ponder over each piece. The ball-jointed body allows the flexibility to bring the doll to life."

The warmth of the dolls comes as much from their carefully designed felt clothing as from their molded three-dimensional faces and sturdy bodies. Iacono's costuming stands out in a field noted for beautiful clothing. *Noah's Ark* (plate 69), which has the 1994 face all of Maggie Made's pieces bore that year (she makes a new face each year), wears a one-of-a-kind costume depicting the Biblical story. "The dress has

Plate 68

Gabriele Lipp,
Bolivian Girl
with Brother,
9 in. (22.9 cm) and
7 in. (17.8 cm), 1994

been pieced together with many hand-dyed swatches of felt depicting a scene from the story of Noah's Ark," explains Iacono, "with the many animals traveling along pathways, two by two. When I begin to make this type of doll, with appliquéd clothing, I try to think of a theme or scene. In this case, I was trying to think of something circular, that could go around the skirt. When I thought of animals going along a path, I thought of the tale of Noah's Ark."

Iacono creates scenes on her dolls' costumes, and these, she says, are always influenced by the season. In the summer she has done a seashore scene; a winter blizzard inspired a boy dressed in a sky-blue hooded jacket bearing the scene of a snow-covered mountain village. So far, *Noah's Ark* is the only story that inspired a costume, but she is working on telling the story of Little Red Riding Hood on the dress of a girl in a green hood. It seems fitting for the artist to depict children's stories on her very childlike dolls. Such scenes can only enhance their playful aspects. "My dolls should not only bring visual enjoyment, but encourage you to be drawn into their playfulness," says Iacono. "I myself like to play with and pose my dolls as I am creating them, to feel their personality."

Dollmakers throughout the world seem to love playing with their works, even if they are made with adult collectors in mind. "I have discovered that I don't 'make' dolls, but 'play' with dolls," laughs German dollmaker Jutta Kissling. "If we, as adults, permit ourselves to return to playing with dolls, we have had our lives' experiences and achieved a certain distance from our childhood play. From this distance . . . our adult playing becomes a play of interpretations. We recognize what we have already encountered before, what we have experienced, and react with sweet melancholy or joy." Kissling's serene, all-porcelain creations have a pristine calmness and dignity that embody this detached distance she describes. Yet they are not cold; their perfection entices the observer, without urging, to touch, to pose, and to play.

Kissling, who left behind the security of the secretarial profession for the independence of "playing" with her dolls, knew from the start that she was creating dolls for adults, and immediately began crafting her pieces entirely from porcelain. She wanted her dolls to have a totally modeled body, with no sudden changes from hard to soft materials, no seams or cloth darts to hide, and the ability to stand on their own two legs without support. The socket heads turn, the arms can move from front to back, and the dolls can sit with legs spread, but they cannot bend their limbs, since Kissling wanted movement, but was not willing to make any compromises concerning her materials, not even to incorporate ball joints or hinges into the body. She also paints all of her dolls' eyes, having tried glass eyes and rejected them as a "foreign substance."

Leonie and *Linni* (plate 70), two 1994 creations, are typical of her work in their simple black-and-white clothing, plain hairstyles, and half-serious expressions. "I wish to only hint at the facial expression and body positioning," the artist explains, "not to determine it, so that there is always room for a change, for interpretation, for 'play.' I try to harmonize clothes and hairstyles in shape and color. I also want to use good material for the clothes—so-called natural fibers like cotton, silk, and linen. But the finish has to be as plain and simple as possible. As I love the color black, it is the leitmotif through all my collections of the past few years. The simplicity and color scheme of the clothes are an important part of my 'handwriting.'"

Kissling's dolls are all children "of a certain age." She is not interested in the very young, but looks to model dolls that represent the human being in the process of developing individuality. "I want to show the first signs of their personalities, when they start showing their difference from others. They don't invite cuddling any more, they don't reach out their arms toward the viewer with that touching gesture of 'please, take me.' On the contrary, they wish to be taken seriously, and I try to express this with their faces and body language, keeping a balance between expression and abstraction."

The dolls of Japanese artist Kazuyo Oshima, while created in the medium of cloth, have a similar simplicity and dignity to those of Jutta Kissling; certainly, they too strike a graceful balance between expression and abstraction. "It seems to me," says the artist, "that a doll

Plate 69
Maggie Iacono,
Noah's Ark,
16 in. (40.7 cm), 1994

Plate 70
Jutta Kissling,
Leonie and *Linni*,
19½ in. (49.5 cm), 1994
(Photo: Courtesy of
Jutta Kissling)

has a kind of immaculate existence, which is inaccessible to a human being." Oshima, who has lived in Paris since 1976, studied painting at the University of Fine Arts in Tokyo. She began to develop her own technique of dollmaking when she came to France, and began exhibiting her dolls in the early 1980s.

Her 1994 *Portrait of a Young Japanese Girl* (plate 71) is all cotton covered with silk. The girl sits casually in a wooden chair, holding a small dog, which the artist also sculpted. Bare-armed and barefoot, the girl has an air of abandon and dreaminess; she could be just awakening or on her way to sleep. Her hair, which appears to be human hair, is actually silk, as well. While the doll is not a portrait, her attitude and expression were inspired by Oshima's own daughter.

Oshima works slowly and meticulously, completing no more than five or six dolls a year. Some of them are actual portraits of her daughter, Junwa, at different ages and with different attitudes, based on memories, observations, and photographs, and always bear Junwa's name. For others, like *Portrait of a Young Japanese Girl*, Oshima looks for inspiration in her own collection of photos. While not all of her creations represent Japanese girls, they do all have a serious and introspective quality. The artist believes a doll has its own existence, which comes to life through the creator's hands. "A doll is not a simple copy of the human figure," she says. "From her beginnings as an amorphous idea matched with a lump of fabric, she takes on form and life through a series of snips and seams." The artist's goal is to capture a moment of life as well as an aesthetic balance in a piece.

For Oshima, a doll always begins with the face and the expression, but her passion is what she calls "the form, the sculpture of the doll." Although she has had a long-time interest in nineteenth-century French clothing, she believes the clothing is the least important aspect of the doll, and exists only to bring out the sculpture itself. She has turned more and more to transparent fabrics that allow the entire sculpture of the body to be seen.

A vision of a doll matures for a long time in Oshima's mind before she begins to form it; the element of chance rarely plays a part in her work. Her aim is always to achieve a harmony of proportions together with a truthful expression. She explains: "A small body is born in my hands, a personality emerges, and surprises me, her creator! But, rather than imprinting my vision on her, I listen to her dream and try to bring it to life. I accept her claim to existence; she permits no negligence on my part."

Rotraut Schrott's *Little Lady Ready for a Walk* (plate 72) is a thoroughly modern little girl whose carefully modeled face reveals her maker's expertise in

Plate 72
Rotraut Schrott,
*Little Lady Ready
for a Walk,*
33½ in. (85.1 cm), 1994
(Photo: Courtesy of
Rotraut Schrott)

Plate 71
Kazuyo Oshima,
*Portrait of a Young
Japanese Girl,*
14½ in. (36.8 cm), 1994
(Photo: Courtesy of
Kazuyo Oshima)

portraiture. Schrott, one of the best-known German doll artists, is equally adept at sculpting from a real child and from her own imagination. *Little Lady,* a one-of-a-kind Cernit doll, comes from a memory of her own childhood. "I remember when I was a little girl I spent a lot of time looking in the mirror, or dancing in front of it, wearing whatever clothes of my mother's and grand-mother's I could find," the artist recalls. "So I had the idea to sculpt such a little girl, who is very satisfied with her own reflection." *Little Lady Ready for a Walk* wears a modern denim dress with a generous amount of bright yellow petticoat showing, paired with her grandmother's old velvet hat and pocketbook.

Contemporary Children ❧ 129

The vanity of little girls, which she set out to express in this piece, is something Schrott has noted in many of the youngsters she continually studies as her research. "Little girls can be very funny, adorable, and like little women—very vain!" she laughs. "I noticed this in my own daughter, too, when she was a little girl. It was my particular challenge, with this doll, to sculpt the self-satisfied expression on her face, that says, 'Oh, I am a pretty girl!'"

Schrott's dollmaking evolved naturally from her artistic background. She learned to draw and paint from her father, Ludwig Adam, a well-respected German painter, and later, as a wife and mother, designed clothing for her family. When her children grew older, she took a course in dollmaking and discovered immediately that she had found her life's work. From the moment of her first appearance at a major exhibition in Munich in 1982 she attracted major attention and began winning awards all over the world. A number of her dolls have been reproduced in porcelain and vinyl editions by the American company GADCO, and she has inspired successful dollmakers in many countries.

The artist's own inspiration comes from the real-life children she studies so carefully and from the portraits of children by the Old Masters, in particular Rembrandt, Botticelli, Velázquez, and Murillo. "Their portraits of children, with this lovely, soft, sensitive, and very expressive painting, let me dream and muse on the mystery of life. All this I would like to convey in my children." Schrott always begins with a very strong idea of what she is creating, and she is happiest when sculpting a face. "I am very relaxed, very happy, and very concentrated on bringing the expression into the face," she reflects. "At these moments, all other thoughts leave me."

Many dolls beautifully depict real children. Yet there is one indisputable master when it comes to this genre: the French artist Anne Mitrani. The movement of emotion that she captures on the faces of her dolls gives them the appearance of having been caught in a candid photo, and photographs of her creations are often mistaken for photos of actual children. In spite of their realistic appearance, Mitrani's one-of-a-kind Fimo dolls come entirely from her own inner vision. "Sometimes I have a very precise idea of what I would like to make," she says, "but often it's as if the character leads me into a better direction. Then the work is long and difficult. But then sometimes, it is clear and simple."

Though known primarily for children, the French artist has made a variety of characters, both men and women, old and young. Like other dollmakers who concentrate on children, Mitrani is drawn to the intensity of their feelings and their transparency. The mother of two teenage daughters, she finds that her memories of them as children are often hidden in her dolls and give them some of their more amusing aspects.

Creative endeavors always played a large part in Mitrani's life; she studied at a school for theater design in Paris and went on to work on stage sets and scenery. But for Mitrani, as for Edna Dali, it was a chance meeting with doll artist Anna Avigail Brahms (see "Women of the Imagination") while Brahms lived briefly in Paris in the late 1970s and early 1980s that led her to dollmaking.

Brahms, for whose dolls Mitrani made the clothing, gave the French artist her first glimpse of Fimo and its possibilities for sculpting. After Brahms left for the United States, Mitrani began her own dollmaking in earnest. Her dolls slowly evolved from rather pensive beings of various ages into the very realistic, lively, often freckled familiar faces of today's children.

In creating the redheaded *Girl with Braids* (plate 73), Mitrani thought back to a redheaded boy she had made several years earlier, who wore a black tuxedo, bowler hat, and a very colorful T-shirt. Bursting with laughter, the boy expressed, she says, "happiness and a great joy of life. I decided that I wanted to make a girl, also dressed in black, looking as if she had emerged from an American musical. I wanted to express joy and humor, with a very strong contrast between the color of the clothing and the luminous and radiant look on her face. With her face," she continues, "as with each face that I sculpt, I tried to capture an emotion that comes from the inside. I want to grab and hold this privileged moment of emotion as it passes."

Like many masters, Mitrani has been imitated often, but her own work has a strength and a vibrancy that her imitators lack. The artist herself is aware that she walks a fine line between realism and caricature. "The most difficult thing," she reflects, "is to recognize that passing moment of emotion [on the doll's face] when I am working. A few too many minutes of work on a face can take away the doll's soul and expression, and leave it empty, or turn it into a caricature."

Women of the Imagination

 The female form has been a potent inspiration to artists since earliest times. Whether symbols of love, beauty, or wisdom, expressions of an artist's self-exploration or exercises in aesthetics, representations of women in art have been executed in an amazingly broad range of interpretations. In fashioning the female form as a doll, artists come from worlds as far apart as fashion design and wood-carving, music and family therapy. The figures that result are as cool and elegant as Antonette Cely's *Lucille* (plate 81) and Robert Tonner's *Model 1991* (plate 85), or as warm and loose as Marla Florio's *Babushkas* (plate 80) and Gretchen Lima's *Rasha* (plate 82).

Brigitte Deval, one of dollmaking's contemporary legends (see "Reflections of Cultural Diversity"), brings a strong inner spirituality to all her creations, be they

Plate 74
Nancy Wiley,
Carnivale,
25 in. (63.5 cm), 1993

133

women, children, or unusual characters. *Lady in Green Velvet* (plate 75) is a romantic figure of Gothic sensibility whose appearance takes on a different cast, depending upon the angle from which she is viewed. A delicate yet towering presence, she is ethereal and enticing, with an almost wicked edge. Deval admits she wanted to create this mood in her doll: "I had it in mind from the start to make a Gothic-style lady," she says.

The *Lady*'s long velvet gown, with an underside of two-toned silk, was made quickly by Deval's two seamstresses, who live fifteen miles away from the dollmaker's home in Siena, Italy, and execute all of her costumes from the dollmaker's designs. While many dollmakers insist that the integrity of their pieces lies in making every element, including clothing and accessories, themselves, Deval shrugs off what she is not interested in. "I am not a decorator, I am not a costume-maker," she says simply. "For me, my doll is not an object to decorate, it is the object itself that is important." As a result she occasionally creates a special doll for a fabric she has found, but just as often, she has the dress made before the doll.

Like most of Deval's dolls, *Lady in Green Velvet* is wax-over-ceramic, with the resulting translucent glow of human skin. The haunting elegance and mystery of this figure cannot be explained by technique or inspiration; the piece has emerged from an artistic hand and spirit and is a classic, timeless creation.

One rarely conceives of wood as an elegant medium. The stereotypical image of wooden figures is of stiff, somewhat primitive pieces with a strong folk tradition. Ken Von Essen's elegant wooden women belie this image. Carved from jelutong, basswood, or Alaska cedar, the long-limbed ladies often represent ballerinas and peddlers. Von Essen, who has a strong interest in the human form, admits that he especially likes the elongated, graceful look of a dancer's body. "Ballerinas are such magnificent creatures," he says. "They're so graceful and so fragile."

In creating *Paris Babe* (plate 76), Von Essen achieved grace, but fragility is not a word that comes to mind when looking at this doll. She is perhaps best described as having a graceful strength. Von Essen sculpted her especially for a 1991 exhibition of dolls at the Musée des Arts Décoratifs, a division of the Louvre in Paris. "I wanted to create my own stereotype of a modern young Parisian," he explains. "She has the attributes of many young people everywhere. She is creative, intelligent, pretty, and goal-oriented. Yet she remains happy and carefree."

The artist often seeks to develop and display a range of harmonious emotions in one character, but his real interest is in the shape and form of the piece. "I used to find the head most challenging and exciting; however, that's not always the case any longer," he says. "The hands, of course, are equally difficult, but I find myself getting emotional over a knee or a foot, and especially the area about the base of the neck and the shoulders." Most of his dolls have rotating steel-spring joints at the hips, shoulders, and head, and friction joints, which move in one direction only, at the ankles, elbows, and knees.

Von Essen, a systems engineer for Hughes Aircraft by day, traces his love for wood carving back to his maternal grandfather, a wood-carver who died when the doll-maker was three, but whose memory, and carvings, were a strong presence throughout his childhood. As an adult, Von Essen found a mentor in the wood sculptor Rudolf Vargas and studied with him for more than a decade. In any discussion of his own wood carving, the artist invokes Vargas as his strongest influence, and the source of much of his understanding of wood and sculpture.

As for turning his wood carving talents to dolls, the sculptor credits his wife, Norma Von Essen, for that move. A longtime doll collector, repairer, and costumer, she finally convinced him, in 1982, to try his hand at a doll. (Now Norma does most of the costuming for the dolls; she created the simple contemporary clothing worn by the twenty-four-inch *Paris Babe.*) "I was surprised how much enjoyment I received from that first doll," Von Essen recalls. "I like anatomy and the human form very

Plate 76

Ken Von Essen,
Paris Babe,
24 in. (61 cm), 1991

much; it's a complicated structure that continues to amaze me. Dollmaking is an art form that allows me to experiment and develop my skills in that area."

Helen Facto brings a variety of professions to her dollmaking. She has been a medical photographer, dressmaker, antique dealer, jewelry manufacturer, professional singer, and medical librarian. She feels that the challenge of making dolls calls upon all the skills and experiences she has acquired in her multifaceted life. "Every new doll makes new demands on my creativity and ingenuity," she reflects. "I once told someone that I must have become a dollmaker because I must love solving problems." *A Letter* (plate 77) is a dramatic porcelain figure; her pose clearly captures a moment of emotional response.

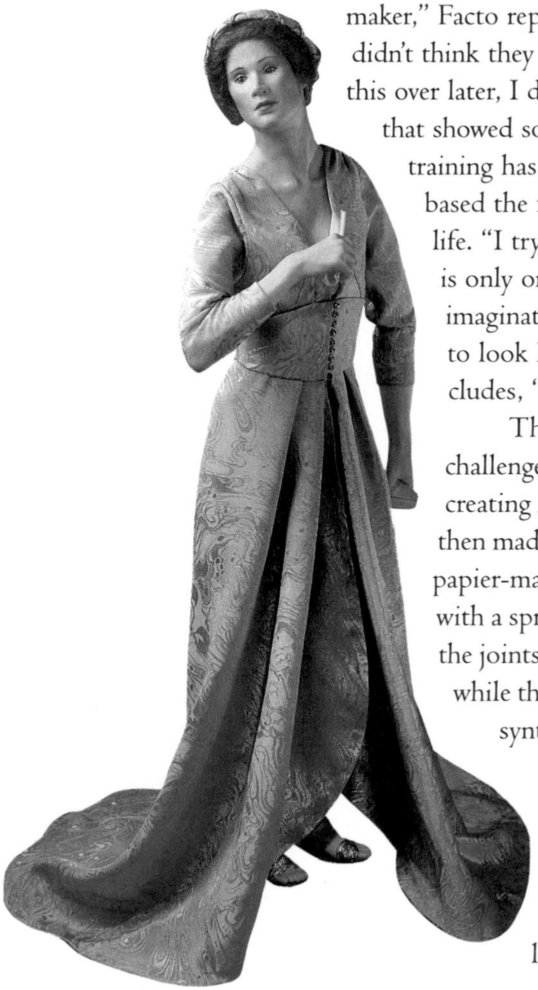

"The idea for this doll came from a question put to me by another dollmaker," Facto reports. "She asked if I ever did 'pretty ladies.' I replied that I didn't think they were very interesting or have much personality. Thinking this over later, I decided that it might be a challenge to do a pretty lady doll that showed some emotion and personality." Facto, whose only formal art training has been the study of sculpture with the teacher Anna Koh, based the face of her "pretty lady" on a portrait sculpture she did from life. "I try to stay as close as possible to sculpture from life, and this is only one step removed," she says. "Faces should never come from imagination—something will be lacking, and they have a tendency to look like the sculptor. Maybe some people can do it," she concludes, "but I can't."

The Illinois artist works in porcelain, and finds the biggest overall challenge is getting her dolls to stand in the active poses she prefers. In creating *A Letter,* she direct-sculpted porcelain for all the exposed parts, then made the body of armature wire, wood, styrofoam, plaster, and papier-maché. "The doll is initially constructed with shoulder joints held with a spring between the arms to facilitate costuming, and at a later stage the joints are fixed with glue and papier-maché. The hair is dyed mohair, while the costume is an attempt at a 'no-period' gown, and is made of synthetic material. The buttons are fourteen-karat gold."

A Letter immediately raises the question: "What's in the letter?" The doll's pose is so clearly a reaction to whatever is written on the paper that the entire emotional attraction of the piece is focused on this query. The artist deflects this intensity with her usual humor. "Nothing is written on the letter the doll is holding. I leave this up to the viewer's imagina-

Plate 77
Helen Facto,
A Letter,
18 in. (45.7 cm), 1991

tion. My friend that inspired me to make her says it's her January VISA bill, but I like to think it is something more romantic."

Like Helen Facto, Alaska artist Dorothy Hoskins believes in basing her dolls' faces on a real person, or modeling them as a composite of faces she has seen. "I don't do actual portraits," she explains, "but I always use photographs to help me along with the faces." She says that she tries not to let the faces grow purely from her imagination, for she fears that way "they might all look alike." A versatile artist who has created Eskimos, graceful women, and laughing children Hoskins was first known for her miniature dolls, but has also made pieces as large as five feet tall.

Her first mother and baby, an evocative sleeping pair, fell between those two sizes, with the mother measuring twenty inches and the baby five. *A Blue Ribbon* (plate 78) which is made up of a mother with her baby on her lap, and measures about fourteen inches seated, portrays an equally tender moment. Many of Hoskins's pieces are made of Super Sculpey, but both mother and baby pairs were sculpted directly in porcelain.

Plate 78

Dorothy Hoskins, *A Blue Ribbon,* 14 in. (35.6 cm) seated, 1994

Both pairs demonstrate that Hoskins continues to reach her constant goal of inspiring a gentle emotional response to her work. As long ago as 1987, she told writer Ann Bahar in an interview published in *Miniature Collector* magazine, "My greatest desire is to portray tiny, homey moments that strike a responsive chord in others." Today she holds fast to that aim. "I want to have a feeling of relationship in my dolls; I like the interaction."

The dollmaker admits that she rarely has a clear-cut idea of a doll in mind when she begins sculpting. "I might have a vision of a mother and baby together," she says, "and once I get the faces together, they sort of tell me what needs to be going on."

A mother of five girls and grandmother of ten children, Hoskins plans to create one mother and baby pair each year.

"I had some horrific moments with my five girls when they were growing up," she laughs, "but I like to remember the moments that were special. That's what this doll is about. I don't usually make child dolls, but I love this combination. The relationship between the mother and child is what's important here. I think what I wanted to say with this piece is that we don't need a lot in life, just each other," she adds. "With a child, all you really need is your presence and their presence, and any little game—like playing with a ribbon—can become a very special moment."

Martha Armstrong-Hand's porcelain mother-and-child pair also captures a close moment between a parent and young child, but her creation, *Motherhood 1784* (plate 79), represents a colonial couple in 1784, expressing that those emotional bonds have been experienced by families throughout time. This set is one of three in a series entitled Motherhood—Now and Then, in which Armstrong-Hand (herself a mother of four girls) set out to portray a mother and baby of 1784, 1884, and 1984. The same sculpture is used for each pair, with different period costumes identifying the three centuries. As she worked on the joint connecting the adult's head and neck, the foremost thought in the artist's mind was the woman's identity as a mother. "I wanted to be sure she could move her head to look at her child in every situation," she explains.

The German-born artist had a fifteen-year career as a doll designer for Mattel before deciding to create her own porcelain pieces in 1976. Before working for Mattel, she honed her artistic skills sculpting figures for Viewmaster, making puppets for Bob Baker's Marionette Productions in Los Angeles, and creating special effects for George Pal Productions.

Her love for sculpting was born early in her life, Armstrong-Hand recalls. "In nursery school, when I was three, my Montessori teacher asked us to model a snake. Everybody else fashioned a worm, but mine was graduated in size, with a head, a tail, and a pattern on its back." Following a creative childhood, the young artist apprenticed as a wood-carver at the Academy of Arts in Berlin, but she was forced to leave her studies, and her country, under Hitler's rule. After World War II, marriage eventually brought her to California, where she still lives.

Armstrong-Hand was first hired by Mattel in 1963 to design doll faces, including that of the Barbie doll's friend Midge and little sister Skipper. She soon moved on to modeling dolls for the company, and was responsible for many well-known toys of the 1960s and 1970s, such as Kiddles and the Sunshine family. Her awareness of the possibilities of original dollmaking came when she stumbled onto a National Institute of American Doll Artists (NIADA) confer-

Plate 79
Martha
Armstrong-Hand,
Motherhood 1784,
15 in. (38.1 cm), 1984

ence, but she credits her late second husband, David Hand, with avidly encouraging her to pursue her own creations. Since the late 1970s she has designed and executed impeccably made porcelain-bodied children and babies with innovative jointing and sweet, expressive faces.

Renowned by her peers as a technical and artistic master, Armstrong-Hand is also known as one of the most generous of dollmakers, sharing her knowledge and expertise through workshops, classes, and informal teaching sessions. She is clear-eyed about her legendary reputation and her many achievements. "People often look at my creations and say I'm talented," she says. "I just tell them I've been practicing for more than fifty years."

Fabrics are Marla Florio's inspiration. "I grew up in a household surrounded by fabrics," says the Michigan artist. "My mother, Zelda Strecker, was a textile designer, and she had a studio behind our house filled with every art and craft material imaginable. I myself have been actively sewing for about twenty-five years, and have been making fabric dolls since childhood."

Florio's cloth dolls are sophisticated and unmistakably contemporary both in style and aura, yet at the same time they hark back to an earlier era and a simpler, less sophisticated tradition. Their dual identity is largely due to the medium; cloth is one of the oldest materials for dollmaking, and dolls simply constructed from scraps of calico, gingham, or muslin were often homemade by a mother for her child and treasured as the only plaything. But fabric is also a most versatile and malleable medium, which presents a tremendous range of possibilities for the artist who chooses to work with it. Florio's choices of subjects and textiles—the colorful combinations and lively styles she fashions—clearly mark her work as belonging to the late twentieth century.

Florio constructs the bodies from cotton muslin, articulating the limbs with button joints. Once she left the hands soft and undefined; now she wires the fingers, which makes the hands poseable. When the body is complete, she costumes the dolls. She may pair scraps of a vintage Japanese silk kimono with a hand-knit sweater, or quilt a jacket to wear with a hand-knit scarf. Florio's focus in dollmaking is always fashion, rather than facial or figural sculpting. Not until the doll is dressed does she turn her attention to the head and face.

She draws directly on the muslin head with colored pencils, selecting colors that harmonize with the costuming, then stitches the nose and—bringing her quilting technique to making the face—stuffs the nose with fiber to shape it. Finally, she needle-stitches the eyes and lips, adding another bit of dimension to the face. When the features are in place, she stuffs the head and protects the pencil coloring with an acrylic sealer. A doll's hair may be styled from yarn or mohair, or she may wear a hat or scarf, giving Florio the chance to incorporate yet more fabric into her piece.

The artist's subjects trace her life, she admits. "When I moved from Chicago to Michigan my dolls had overstuffed chairs strapped to their backs and they moved, too. When I had my daughter, Emma, my dolls were pregnant, and then they were carrying babies. I am now making toddler dolls—the first child dolls I have ever made." In addition to chronicling her life, though, her pieces

Plate 80
Marla Florio,
Babushkas,
13 in. (33 cm), 1994

are a personal, eclectic exploration of the possibilities of textiles. They are the result of Florio's artistic upbringing, academic training (she has a B.F.A. in fashion and fabric design from the Art Institute of Chicago), and experience as a fashion designer and pattern maker, as well as a quilter. The *Babushkas* (plate 80), with their Old World flavor, are a one-of-a-kind series that shows off the simpler, more traditional aspect of Florio's creative spirit. Each one wears the same costume in different fabrics and colors. "I like making *Babushkas* because I can use so many fabrics," Florio muses. "There are different fabrics for the legs, shirts, sweaters, caps, and scarves. The beading on the edge of the sweaters allows me to add more color and texture to each doll. The colors in their clothing are reflected in the colors in their faces. Each doll has layers and layers of color and textures, which gives her an impression of mood or character."

Antonette Cely's background in film and theatrical costuming is clearly evident in her one-of-a-kind cloth fashion figures. Each one, be it a beauty from the 1940s, like *Lucille* (plate 81), the Egyptian queen *Nefertiti*, or one of her own early favorite creations like *Marie Antoinette*, is magnificently and appropriately garbed in perfectly scaled period clothing. Yet Cely's art goes far beyond costuming. Beneath the elegant fashions are elaborate fabric armatures constructed of copper wire, pipe cleaners, and beads, supplemented by needle-sculpture and stuffing at key points, such as knees, elbows, and collarbones, and the entire skeleton is covered with hand-dyed cotton broadcloth. Face masks are molded in Sculpey and then covered with broadcloth. Professionally experienced as a theatrical makeup artist as well as a costumer, Cely uses the former skill in painting her dolls' faces. The eyes are made of plastic clay, such as Sculpey III, Fimo, or Cernit, then hand-painted and glued in from the back.

"By creating a miniature human in sculpture, using the medium of fabric," Cely reflects, "I find it easier to present my own opinions and hopes and dreams about the human condition." The dollmaker, who continues to work professionally in both theater and film, taking on assignments like making cos-

Plate 81
Antonette Cely,
Lucille,
15 in. (38.1 cm), 1989
(Photo: Courtesy of
Antonette Cely)

tumes for Jamie Lee Curtis for the 1992 film *My Girl*, and often working as an extra or stand-in, likes the challenge of taking on commissioned works, which is how she came to make *Lucille*. The 1940s redhead was commissioned by an Australian collector who has a particular fondness for the fashions of the 1940s, and especially the wearing of gloves during that era. "In order to make real-looking gloves," Cely explains, "I did not give *Lucille* any skin on her hands. The gloves go directly over the skeleton of pipe cleaners and wire that forms her fingers."

Although Cely finds "total creative freedom" in the challenge of a commissioned piece, she does have requirements that must be met before she takes on an assignment. "It must be a subject that I can take an interest in, the doll must fit into my repertoire of work, and the collector must know my work and trust my abilities as a dollmaker." Then, the artist continues, "The person who commissions the doll becomes a playmate of sorts, but more importantly, they set the guidelines I need to follow. These become the rules of the game. The heart of my work is in the challenge of staying within the limits set."

Cely's thrill in the process of fulfilling a commission stems partially from her background of working in theater and film, as part of a team that must meet, with creativity and excellence, stringent requirements of subject, time, and budget. But there is more: the heart of her art is not as much in the finished doll as in the process of creating it. "Somehow," she says, "the finished product does not seem as important as the act of making it often seems. While I am working on a doll, it is like a little love affair. The thrill of getting to know a new person . . . stimulates my creativity throughout the dollmaking process. But once the creative process is finished, so too is the relationship. And (unlike many human love affairs!) I get a genuine thrill knowing that it is now bringing happiness to someone else."

Fabric artist Gretchen Lima also enjoys meeting the challenge of a commission. Where Antonette Cely's work is distinguished by a refined realism, Lima's cloth figures are much looser interpretations of a character's emotional characteristics. "My work is not only an expression of what I see, but what I feel," explains the Wisconsin dollmaker. She believes that when somebody commissions her to create a figure, they are asking for her personal artistic vision of the subject.

Plate 82
Gretchen Lima,
*Rasha, the Crystal
Gazer*,
21 in. (53.3 cm), 1989
(Photo: Courtesy of
Gretchen Lima)

When she creates from her imagination, she looks inside herself, seeking to discover a voice and a message that needs expression. The figure she calls *Rasha, the Crystal Gazer* (plate 82) emerged from just such a deeper part of her being.

"Her creation marks for me the beginning of a voyage toward self-discovery," Lima reflects. "At that time, 1989, I was not conscious of the trip. . . . My life, however, was crumbling around me and I was acutely aware of a feeling of crisis. My father had passed on, my marriage was not working, and I felt as though I was drowning and coming up for the third time. At the same time I was creating mystical, strong, and spiritual women. Looking back, I see now that the very part of me I felt was worn and used up was, in fact, alive and well. That part was struggling for a voice, a message to myself that at the time fell on deaf ears."

Rasha is a twenty-one-inch muslin wall doll with New Zealand wool hair and a handwoven shawl; she is holding a quartz crystal. While some of Lima's dolls have Sculpey faces, *Rasha's* is muslin with painted features. She also wears a fabric headdress and satin boots; metallic and colorful symbols and beads dangle from her belt. Like most of the artist's work, this figure is characterized by spirited colors and textures.

Lima combines natural fibers for the hair and clothing of each doll, sketches the face, and paints it. She makes the jewelry and other accessories for her pieces, and sometimes creates her own fabric. These skills were honed during her years of art studies, which were followed by a decade of teaching arts and crafts to homebound people. Now she devotes all her time to the design and execution of the constantly evolving figures that express her deepest needs and passions.

"After five years of a long pilgrimage through dark and cold caves of my subconscious, I have started listening to that part of myself," Lima says. "I create the messages and give a voice to a girl inside who has patiently waited to be heard."

"Every doll I've made is another face of me, just an expression of how I feel," says Israeli-born Anna Avigail Brahms. The artist, who has lived in Massachusetts since the early 1980s, has few peers in dollmaking, and her intensely romantic creations have inspired many. Brahms's female figures appear to have been formed intuitively from her hands. "I don't think at all when I work," says the artist. "I just get an image of the body . . . I know the person I am going to make and I see the outlines of how she sits or stands."

Brahms's Fimo creations are almost exclusively young women; the *Young Woman Seated* (plate 83) is typical of her style, but is slightly younger than many of her dolls. In her lap, she has a doll (also made by Brahms) and a volume of Shakespeare, two objects that seem to aptly symbolize the threshold she is just crossing, from girlhood to womanhood. "Just a book would have been too serious," says the artist, "and just the doll would have been too childish." Brahms's dolls often have an intangible inspiration, but in this case, she knows that the image came to her as a response to the antique white dress the doll wears, which she found in an antiques shop. "When I saw the dress, it just looked so clean, the lines were so fresh. When I worked on the doll I concentrated on this clean, fresh crispness and the inno-

cent face formed itself for me." Technically, Brahms focused on the figure's posture. "I sculpted her to sit, turned, in this chair."

Brahms works daily in her studio, beginning her morning with a short period of meditation in which she envisions the work she will do that day. "Even when I don't know what I am going to make, just the work itself is very sooth-ing," she explains. "When I have dry spells, I just let my fingers take over and see what happens." When she has a clear image of the doll's face and posture, she begins sculpting. Once she is happy with her sculpture, she fires it, then paints the doll. "This is when the doll comes alive," she says. "When I paint the skin color—this is when I know whether it's good or not." Her dolls' hair comes from angora goats, dyed and made into wigs by wigmaker Susie Goff, and the clothing is usually a mixture of old and new fabrics, often executed to Brahms's designs by dressmaker Ellen Perkins.

Plate 83
Anna Avigail Brahms,
Young Woman Seated,
30 in. (76.2 cm), 1994

Brahms's signature is an ethereal sensuality, achieved by a figure's glowing flesh, full lips, and mass of heavy, luxurious curls. While the external attributes of a Brahms doll have been imitated by many dollmakers, there is no mistaking the original. It is the essence of the artist's own spiritual and artistic nature that comes through the dolls. "When I make a doll, I know if it's true or not," she says. "It must come from the heart."

Nancy Wiley's *Carnivale* (plate 74) has a dramatic and imaginative presence that evokes the eighteenth-century Italian carnivals celebrated in Venice. From the waist up, the porcelain piece is a well-sculpted figure that bears traces of the eighteenth-century Venetian sensibility Wiley (see "Fantasies") set out to achieve. The surprise lies below the waist: the pannier-style skirt is actually an Italianate stage set, where two porcelain marionettes, in period-perfect costumes, perform. "Ever since I was a child, I thought that the pannier-style dresses of that period looked like curtains on either side of a stage," Wiley explains. "So eventually, I guess it was in 1992, I decided to try turning the doll's skirt into a stage set."

The artist's first mentor in the study of dollmaking was her brother, the late William Wiley (see "Beyond Dolls"). A graduate of the Rhode Island School of Design, Nancy Wiley focused on painting and illustration, but spent her early life surrounded by her brother's figurative sculptures and her mother's pursuit of dollmaking as a hobby. After graduating from art school, Wiley lived and collaborated with her brother, turning out projects such as a children's book and window displays for Tiffany. Eventually, in 1989, inspired by Bill's work, she began creating dolls herself.

After her brother's death from AIDS in 1991, a somber note appeared in some of Wiley's dolls, along with a new willingness to explore unconventional dollmaking techniques and other media besides porcelain. One constant that has remained throughout her career, though, is a painterly approach to her craft. Inspired by works of Impressionist portrait artists, Wiley paints her dolls as if they were works on canvas, using oils—an unusual choice for dollmaking—to create shadows in the faces. Before painting the entire porcelain head with oils, she treats the surface with gesso, which produces a textured appearance. Wiley often paints on the dolls' costumes, too, then goes on to create interesting juxtapositions of skin and hair by incorporating rough fibers, such as burlap, string, and straw, for hair.

The textured skin and coarse hair bring a stylized emotion to her work. In the case of the pannier dolls like *Carnivale,* the artist paints the front of the wide underskirt to look like a theater backdrop, then arranges the gathered overskirt to become a curtain.

Wiley has created imaginative pieces, like a *Lobster Lady* and a *Crab Man*, that combine human and crustacean attributes, and the Sculpey *Tasselheads*, a pair united by a knot joining their hair. Her work is always characterized by its textured quality and a strong influence from earlier artistic periods, interpreted with a very contemporary sensibility. She is a strong advocate for promoting dolls as three-dimensional figurative artwork, and has been active in placing the work of doll artists in conventional art gallery settings. "I have a lot of ideas for the medium," she told writer Louise Fecher in 1994 (in "Rendering Magical Visions," *Dolls,* August 1994). "There is really no end to the different ways to create and present dolls as different kinds of art forms. My ultimate goal is to be a respected artist with the freedom to experiment. . . . If I get a really strange idea, why not go ahead and make it into a doll and see what happens?"

Michigan artist Barbara Buysse would undoubtedly concur with this statement. Buysse's work is very different from Wiley's; the medium is cloth, the faces are flat, and the underlying aesthetic is American folk art. But the two artists share a painterly background, which each uses to impart a strong individual style to her work. Even more importantly, the two share the passionate need to stretch, through their work, the concept of what a doll can be. "The artist Milton Avery says that art is about turning corners, and you never know what will be there until you make that turn," says Buysse. "There are those of us that are trying to stretch the envelope of what a doll is. I continually ask myself questions about what I'm doing. I guess the only thing I know for certain is that I'm not comfortable doing the same thing over and over."

Like Nancy Wiley, Buysse is a painter by training. Her interest in dolls goes back more than twenty years, when she began collecting early-American cloth dolls, in particular those with primitive, flat, painted faces. "It was their texture, their feel—a tactile thing—that got to me," she explains. "And the painting, no matter how crude it was, seemed so interesting, with a real hands-on look." She started painting her own dolls in 1973; they had very simple cloth bodies and painted faces.

To earn a living, Buysse turned to family therapy. To help bring out her child patients, who were often quiet and withdrawn, she began to sketch them during therapy, giving them the sketches. Most of the portrait dolls of children that Buysse has made come directly from these sketches, while her highly developed signature style—flat faces that achieve a three-dimensional aspect through many thin layers of paint—is influenced by her love of early-American dolls.

Buysse is well known for her black characters, especially children, which have amazingly lifelike faces. On first sighting, one rarely realizes that the detailed features, lights, and shadows of Buysse's dolls are achieved entirely through the paint. The fabric beneath the paint, which is barely perceptible, lends a warm, solid texture to the painting.

Buysse's fascination with the painting process is leading her to create even more abstract body forms with even more detailed painting. "I think I'm trying to make a marriage between a two-dimensional painting and a three-dimensional object," she reflects. In working on one recent piece, she recounts, "I thought, 'Why am I making these dolls with arms and legs but flat faces?' The only part that is important to me is the painting. So I thought I'd start with a flat form, and just do it as a cloth sculpture."

In *Blue Ball Bouquet* (plate 84), however, she has stayed with a traditional, full-bodied, seated form. "I had an idea that I wanted this doll to have more gesture to her," Buysse says. "I don't know what she evokes—I think she's kind of tentative and confused. Then I had to play with the fabrics a lot for her. I really played with this piece; creating her was almost like doing a painting, in terms of the composition." The painting of the face was also a challenge. "She's just a face that came to me," says the artist. "It really changed as I painted the layers—especially around the nose and mouth. I had a quirky face on her, and it wasn't what I wanted. In the end, the face was a little mysterious to me." A final lighthearted touch comes from the doll's hair, which is made of orange feathers that move gently in the breeze caused by any movement nearby.

Robert Tonner, who makes dolls representing sophisticated fashion models and modern young children, is accustomed to hearing himself described as a "fashion designer turned dollmaker." He is also used to hearing praise for his dolls' classic contemporary clothing. But tasteful and elegant as his creations are, costuming has never been Tonner's focus as a doll artist. His goal has been technical mastery of his medium—be it Sculpey, porcelain, or vinyl—and forging a strong "identity of design" (his term for an artist's signature) for his work.

Since creating his first doll in 1980 (a papier-maché head that he terms "a disaster and almost the end of my career"), Tonner has moved from one-of-a-kind Sculpey creations to small editions of porcelain pieces to vinyl dolls made in his own small factory in Stone Ridge, New York. Along the way he has struggled with the technical demands of each medium, taking inspiration and advice from experienced artists like R. John Wright, Martha Armstrong-Hand, Elizabeth Brandon, and Helen Kish, all of whom he is quick to acknowledge as instrumental in his artistic evolution.

Model 1991 (plate 85) is a key doll for Tonner. "It was one of those breakthrough dolls," the artist explains. "I jumped into it before I was technically ready, and it was a nightmare. But finally, technically, she was leap years ahead of anything I'd done before—and the doll that came after her was leap years ahead of that."

Made in 1991, the elegant all-porcelain figure wearing a tissue-taffeta evening dress does immediately call to mind Tonner's education at the Parsons School of Design and his eight years of experience designing for Bill Blass. But that's just second nature, and not terribly important, to the artist. "I just tried to do a dress that was quiet and dignified, but the dress always comes after the doll," he says. "The sculpture was what this doll was all about. She was the first all-porcelain doll with porcelain joints I made, and really taught me porcelain making." Once he had mastered the skill needed to make this doll, Tonner moved on to another challenge, that of making ball-jointed little girl bodies.

Model 1991 exudes the quiet dignity Tonner was after. "I wanted her to be beautiful, not saccharine-pretty, but with depth to her. I wanted more than just pedestrian-pretty for her. I'm still very happy with her because I felt I made the head I wanted to—that was the first doll I felt that way about."

Among the artists Tonner most admires is Elizabeth Brandon, whose work he describes as "technically astonishing. She creates an idealized form in which nothing is simplified, taking infinite time to work out all details of her dolls prior to sculpting." Brandon, who usually sculpts all-porcelain figures with complex jointing, is interested, above all, in achieving a figure that has a particular range of movement integral to its dramatic purpose. "She does not let the mold dictate the form," explains Tonner. "She determines the form and makes the mold work for what she desires."

Brandon's *Madge Overbee* (plate 86) is unclothed, by the artist's choice. While a fashionable dress was made by Virginia Studyvin, who costumes Brandon's work from her ideas and sketches, the artist prefers to reveal the figure's sculpting and jointing. "I know that others need to see the doll in a wig, clothing, and shoes," she says, "but for me, my whole heart and soul are tied up in the form."

Plate 84

Barbara Buysse,
Blue Ball Bouquet,
16 in. (40.7 cm), 1994
(Photo: Courtesy of
Barbara Buysse)

Plate 85
Robert Tonner,
Model 1991,
21 in. (53.3 cm), 1991

Her wide range of subjects includes sophisticated women like *Madge Overbee*, dramatic characters, young children, and a recent angel inspired by the eighteenth-century wooden and terra-cotta Neapolitan angels on view each Christmas in New York City's Metropolitan Museum of Art. With each creation the self-taught doll-maker starts anew in conceiving a technical form that will integrate the spirit and emotion of her piece with its physical presence. She begins by drawing her concept from several angles, then building a wire armature from which she sculpts with oil-based or water-based clay. She goes on to make waste molds of the original sculpture, then wax casts, followed by the final molds. Each figure's individual method of jointing is determined by the range of motion Brandon is aiming for.

The Kansas artist brings a musician's sensibility and love of expression to her sculpting. An accomplished pianist and violinist, Brandon wrote eloquently about her artistic philosophy in *The Art of the Doll*, published by NIADA in 1992. As a musician, she reflected: "I was concerned with sculpting in sound, presenting a rounded whole in spatial time, a perfection of the moment. There was emotion, movement, and meaning in that ephemeral musical sculpture. Though it was lost as soon as the music ended, it could be rebuilt immediately, and with the variation of my mood, the sculpture could alter slightly. But this was sculpting with too fragile a medium; at my death, nothing would remain."

The discovery of porcelain sculpture gave Brandon the possibility of spiritual expression, and the discovery of jointing her figures allowed her to continually reinterpret them, like playing a musical composition. "By jointed-figure sculpture, I catch and hold a tiny fragment of the universe," she concluded. "The music has become solid, and this is what I want to do during my lifetime."

Plate 86
Elizabeth Brandon,
Madge Overbee,
16½ in. (41.9 cm), 1989

Characters

 Artists who create character dolls regard themselves as sculptors whose work

explores the joys and foibles of the human condition. They emphasize personality

rather than fashionable standards of beauty and are not afraid of strong images.

The mood of character-doll artists can turn on a dime—the same artists who

move us to tears also delight in making us laugh at ourselves with comic figures

whose eccentricities border on the outrageous. Flamboyancy is a virtue in this

realm of "anything goes," although an underlying compassion always accompanies

the use of caricature. Convinced that the lines of age etched in their characters'

faces reflect the achievements and disappointments of a lifetime, artists such as

Robert McKinley and Bill Nelson often present moving statements about society's

view of old age.

Plate 87
Van Craig,
Delilah: Folies 1924,
32 in. (81.3 cm), 1994

153

When speaking of character dolls, artists mention the lack of formal restraints in the field. NIADA doll artist Susanna Oroyan states, "I make characters because of the absolute, total freedom they give me to do whatever I want to do. I can doodle around in the clay, and if something looks interesting—like a long nose or buck teeth—I can pursue it and play around with it and decide who or what it will be as it evolves."

To reveal the essence of personality, an artist must define the attitude of the subject by a skillful rendering of its facial features and body movements. A successful character doll packs an emotional wallop. "A little bit of me is in each of my dolls" is a refrain one often hears from these men and women, who don't hesitate to bare their souls. The results are dolls that connect with people from all walks of life.

As in every field, the world of character dolls has its stars: artists who not only contribute acclaimed work, but who have shaped the field itself. In this sense the term character dolls and the name of the late Robert McKinley are synonymous. His many admirers find his work both amusing and melancholy. McKinley admitted that his dolls possessed an underlying sadness; he once said, "I can't make them smile. They just refuse to smile."

McKinley's most powerful works are men and women of a certain age, many of them elderly ladies whose memories of milestones in their lives mingle with yearnings for their younger selves. The empathy shown in these portraits can be traced to McKinley's love for his grandmother, whose influence remained with him throughout his life. The pull of memories from youth to old age struck a chord that was hard to ignore. Gallery owners where McKinley exhibited his works comment that viewers stood as if they were rooted before McKinley's work, took a few steps to the next piece, only to return again, not wanting to let go of their bittersweet memories.

McKinley also showed an enduring fascination with street people, portraying them with dignity as well as pathos. His most famous series of "bag ladies" appeared in Tiffany's store windows on Fifth Avenue in New York City. The furor they created, including protests and demonstrations, proved that the McKinley "electricity" could move even blasé New Yorkers. This was fine with McKinley, whose greatest desire was to propel art dolls into the consciousness of mainstream America.

Born in the small town of Owensboro, Kentucky, McKinley grew up in Birmingham, Alabama, where he made puppets and dreamed of becoming a fashion illustrator. After he won a scholarship in fashion design to Washington

University in Saint Louis, Missouri, he discovered the lure of city life. Moving to New York in 1971, McKinley worked for many years designing children's clothing while at the same time creating and performing with his puppets. In the mid-1970s, a bad case of stage fright halted what had promised to be a successful career in puppetry. (McKinley performed in many nightclubs and was featured on NBC-TV.) "I hated performing," McKinley once admitted, "and it was too tiring, working full-time and performing nightly." While browsing in a bookstore one rainy weekend at the beach in Long Island, New York, McKinley picked up the first volume of Helen Bullard's *The American Doll Artist.* "I was absolutely fascinated," McKinley recalled. "I didn't know dolls like that existed; I'd never seen any." So began an illustrious career in dollmaking and a rewarding association with Bullard, who later became McKinley's mentor. A quick succession of triumphs, including exhibits in Tiffany's windows in 1981, 1982, and 1983, culminated in his election into NIADA in 1985. For the rest of his career, McKinley let his many interests determine his choice of subjects. "I am never happier than when I'm up to my elbows in whatever medium I am into at the moment," he confessed one day in his studio-apartment. "My subjects range from the ridiculous to the sublime. If my work makes you laugh, great—or cry, great. It is rarely my intent to do either. I just keep trying to get it right—not perfect, just right—and sometimes I come close."

Robert McKinley drew his inspiration for *The Countess of Central Park* (plate 88) from a homeless woman he saw on TV. "She was mad as a hatter, angry, too, but fabulous," McKinley exclaimed. "Her image stayed with me for a long time. Finally, I just had to make her. I worked very quickly. Even though she appears angry and troubled, you can see that at one time she was a fine-looking woman." The once-beautiful shawl, a symbol of better days, was made out of an old sock. "I poked holes in it to give it an old look," he revealed. "Note how she clutches her shawl, almost tenderly, as she stares into an uncertain future." *The Countess of Central Park* was one of the last dolls McKinley made before his death from AIDS in the fall of 1994. The sadness and anger about his own uncertain future were exposed in what many consider one of the most powerful statements of his all-too-short career.

Bill Nelson met Bob McKinley in 1989 at a crossroads in Nelson's career. He had amassed an impressive portfolio as an illustrator, designing posters, record albums, and magazine covers for a client list that reads like the Who's Who of corporate America, and had only recently turned to dollmaking. He had taught himself to sculpt in the early 1980s out of a desire to "attempt the elusive third dimension." At first he made life-sized heads in Plasticine, masks, and ventriloquist dummies. Nelson, wondering whether his dummies could be sold as art, showed them to a manager of a craft show, who thought they would be more favorably received as freestanding sculptures. Nelson's first efforts were the same size as his dummies, forty-two inches high. He was happy with the faces but felt the bodies were a little stiff and awkward. When Nelson met fellow exhibitor Bob McKinley at a show in New York City, he was impressed by the amount of detail McKinley packed into his diminutive women dolls, and admired the flexibility of their bodies. The secret, McKinley revealed, was wire armature. Nelson immediately changed his approach to dollmaking. He substituted Super Sculpey for Plasticine and constructed wire-armature bodies for dolls no more than twenty-three inches high. While his dolls' bodies improved, the heads remained the focal point of Nelson's sculptures. He claims that sculpting the head is the most creative step in the process, so much so that he often works on a few heads at a time.

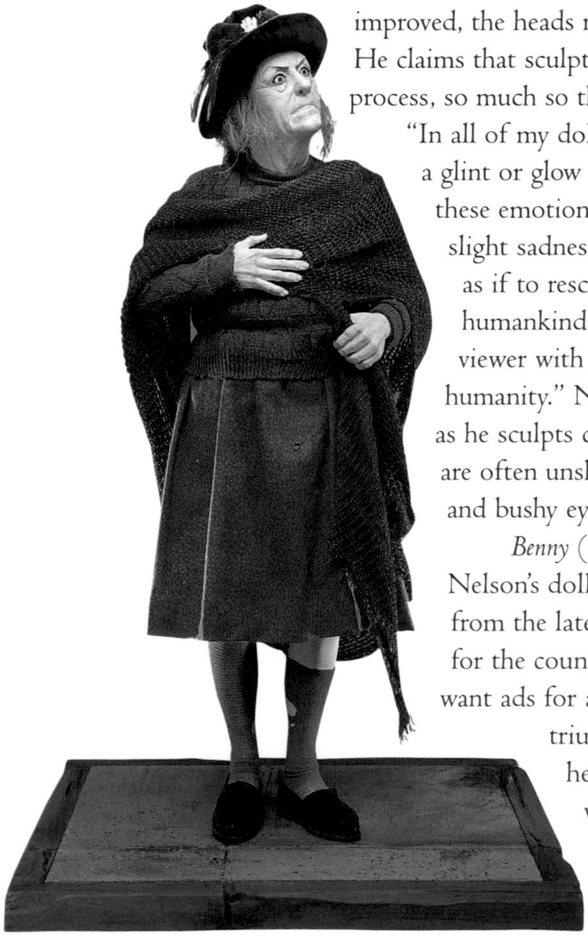

"In all of my dolls I am interested in capturing in their faces a glint or glow of warmth and humor, joy and pathos. Of these emotions, the latter is key—because I believe it is the slight sadness around the eyes that draws us to each other as if to rescue or aid. It is this desire to help that ennobles humankind," he elaborates. "So, too, my dolls draw the viewer with their implied vulnerability, their bottomless humanity." Nelson eschews the unlined features of youth as he sculpts character lines in the faces of his dolls, who are often unshaven older gentlemen with receding hairlines and bushy eyebrows.

Benny (plate 89) follows the humanistic tradition of Nelson's dolls. "My original idea was to create a gentleman from the late 1930s who, while down on his luck, is not out for the count," he explains. "I pictured him looking in the want ads for a job; trying real hard to hold it together and triumph over adversity. While I was sculpting the head, I was working on the shoes; and once they were complete, I couldn't bring myself to scuff them up. I was faced with a dilemma: If his shoes looked unscuffed, then his clothes shouldn't look worn either. So, I thought

Plate 88
Robert McKinley,
*The Countess of
Central Park,*
17 in. (43.2 cm), 1994

about it and came up with this solution: I have a slightly sad man bearing the weight of the world in those soulful eyes, yet dressed impeccably. What about the want ads? I just turned the page to the comics. How do I justify the dichotomy? I guess it was a sad day in the funnies!"

For most of her career Beth Cameron has been involved with portraying older gentlemen, often in the guise of Santa Claus (see "Holiday Inspirations"), and she is considered a master of creating older faces that bespeak tenderness and caring. At the time she began work on *The Velveteen Rabbit* (plate 90), Cameron was concentrating on African American figures, prompted by her annoyance at stereotypical dolls she saw advertised in various magazines. "I said to myself," Cameron reveals, "that if I were an African American, I wouldn't want to be portrayed in this manner. I was convinced that I could do better, that I could make black dolls that were typical of anyone." During this period, at one of the antique doll shows she frequents on the lookout for props and accessories, Cameron found a velveteen rabbit, whose scruffy appearance she couldn't resist. "It must have been serendipity, because soon afterward I discovered an old copy of the storybook, *The Velveteen Rabbit,* and I *knew* I had the 'anchors' for this piece that was slowly taking shape in my head. After looking at the rabbit again, I found him too stiff—so, I took most of the sawdust out of him. His patchy fur was just perfect: obviously a child had already 'loved' the fur off!"

Before Cameron picks up a tool, she conceptualizes the scene: "I knew I wanted a peaceful figure, one sitting to avoid the problem of a doll stand; so I thought he should be reading. I pictured a Sunday evening with a grandfather reading to his half-asleep granddaughter. He still wore his 'Sunday best,' but had taken his tie off and put on his slippers. When his granddaughter requested a story, he put aside his newspaper (headlined Portland, Maine, 1944) and his pipe. At first I had a different head on the grandfather—he was looking directly up, but then I wanted him to be half-asleep, as grandfathers often are as the stories lull them into a drowsy state; so I switched the head at the eleventh hour, and the whole piece came together!" Cameron finishes with a satisfied smile.

As Cameron works, she plans each detail with an eye to establishing the emotional credibility of the scene. In *The Velveteen Rabbit,* she so carefully sculpted the grandfather's feet that even the corns on his feet press against the soft slippers she made herself. While she found the little girl's crocheted slippers at an antique doll show, she hand-knitted the grandfather's sweater-vest. Between the search and discovery phase and the actual time spent working on

Plate 89
Bill Nelson,
Benny,
15 in. (38.1 cm), 1993
(Photo: Courtesy of
Bill Nelson)

Plate 90
Beth Cameron,
The Velveteen Rabbit,
15 in. (38.1 cm), 1992

the piece, *The Velveteen Rabbit* evolved over a year. When it was finished, it met Cameron's main objective of expressing the tender bond between generations.

Happy Birthday Grandma (plate 91), by NIADA artist June Goodnow, also celebrates the special relationship between grandparents and their grandchildren. Goodnow, known for her sensitive portraits of Native Americans, has recently expanded her work to include many ethnic groups. An advertisement in a magazine of a young girl leaning down and hugging an elderly woman provided the inspiration for *Happy Birthday Grandma:* "I was enchanted by the scene," Goodnow remembers. "It reminded me of my relationship with my own grandmother. I'm not really known for my children, but I decided to try it. I wasn't sure how little girls' legs really looked, so I borrowed my neighbor's child to use as a model. With the grandmother figure I had a lot of fun incorporating such touches as her gold tooth and rolled-up stockings. But after she was dressed and the piece basically finished, I felt something was missing. The

question wasn't answered of why the grand-mother was laughing. My sister suggested it was her birthday and set about making a hat for her. Of course, once the hat was on, she had to have a present; so I added a little box that had been given to me by my great aunt, containing a love poem."

The expression of joy on the grand-mother's face is evidence of Goodnow's ability to breathe life into her carving. She believes she inherited her gift for sculpting from her mother, who delighted her children with figu-rines carved out of river clay, bars of soap, and wood. It wasn't until the early 1970s, when she was first married and living on a farm in South Dakota, that Goodnow tried her hand with clay. Her first doll, a portrait of her husband's elderly uncle ("Even then I liked character," she interjects), was in Plasticine, a type of clay that necessitated a plaster mold. After years of experimentation, Goodnow primarily uses Super Sculpey for her figures, taking about a week to make the face and sometimes the hands and feet as well. She fashions the bodies out of cloth before tackling the painstaking job of costuming.

Holly Conrad, an artist from Fredericksburg, Virginia, pores over news-papers and magazines to search for faces that interest her. Eventually, dolls will emerge with heads that are composites of her selections. *Gertrude* (plate 92), however, is derived from a single photograph, sent by her sister, who was aware of Conrad's passion for faces. "My sister had seen this photograph of her friend's grandmother that she thought was right up my alley," Conrad recalls. "She was right. I put aside everything else and went to work on her. Before the head was finished, I knew she was meant to be a lady in red. I remembered I had seen a red-sequined hairband at the dollar store, which I didn't need, so hadn't bought. I hustled down to the store, bought the band, and *Gertrude's* costume was born. I keep a collection of boas and feathers in a drawer in my storeroom, and sure enough a red boa emerged from the jumble. As I worked, her persona evolved: I saw her as a fun-loving lady of the '20s, dressed for an

evening of dancing. Beneath the glittery dress, she is wearing a red, lace-trimmed slip and bloomers with garters to hold up seamed stockings. If you open the little pocketbook *Gertrude* carries, you'll find a lace hankie and her favorite perfume. *Gertrude*'s veined and age-spotted hands have carefully manicured fingernails, and her teeth are the actual artificial teeth used in making human dentures (compliments of my dentist dad)."

In an indirect way Conrad feels her mother contributed to the making of *Gertrude* by her endorsement of the creative arts during Conrad's childhood. "My mother encouraged all seven of her children to put their talents to use by providing a ready supply of arts-and-crafts materials that covered the dining-room table several months out of every year—and Dad tolerated it! She taught me sewing skills at the age of eight, when I began making some of my own clothes." Conrad also notes that as a little girl she was told that one couldn't truly love an inanimate object. She confesses, however, to an undying love for *Gertrude.*

Paula Hemsley can easily understand Conrad's love for *Gertrude,* as she confesses to identical feelings for *It's a Mighty Fine Day, Miss Ruby* (plate 93), a work inspired by a bartender named Henry whom she met in the Cayman Islands. "I started with Henry—I just loved his kind face, in spite of the fact that he is a bartender. When he was completed, I knew he had to have a friend. Thus, Ruby evolved. I always thought of them as friends and pictured them meeting on Miss Ruby's front porch before they went to church—she is seated and waiting. As the work progresses, my dolls take on their personality and become real people to me."

Although Hemsley originally worked in porcelain when she began making dolls in 1978, she switched to wood in the mid-1980s. "Porcelain was easy to work with, but I wanted to make more durable dolls," Hemsley explains. "I don't really like making a doll more than once, and the process of sculpting, making a mold, and only using it once seemed so time-consuming. When I discovered wood, I knew I had found the perfect medium for me. I love the smell of wood, the way it feels, the temperament of the grain." Hemsley's first wooden dolls were painted, but she now stains them with linseed oil and oil paints to bring out the grain. She changed techniques after attending a NIADA conference where she had her dolls critiqued by fellow doll artists. When Pat Brooks saw Hemsley's dolls, she said, "Why go to all the trouble of working in wood, if you are going to cover it over with paint?" Hemsley took her advice and has since been staining her dolls.

Hemsley enjoys dual status as a dollmaker and craftsperson. In 1993 she gained admittance as a juried member to the Pennsylvania Guild of Craftsmen and she also belongs to the Lancaster Woodcarvers Organization. She often chooses basswood, the straight-grained, white wood from the linden tree, because it is easy to carve. Hemsley claims that 80 percent of her work occurs before the first cut, as she "thinks out all the problems." She is particularly concerned with the challenge that movable parts pose, from elbows and shoulders to hips and knees. She begins by drawing the general shape of the figure onto the wood.

Plate 93
Paula Hemsley,
*It's a Mighty Fine Day,
Miss Ruby,*
26 in. (66 cm), 1990
(Photo: Courtesy of *Contemporary Doll Collector/
Scott Publications*

Hemsley uses a band saw for the rough cut and then high-powered grinding tools for details, resorting to a knife for the final touches. After sanding, Hemsley stains the piece with a mixture of linseed oil and oil-based paint before applying a final wax finish.

Nino the Clown (plate 94), a nineteen-inch Cernit doll, is the work of Terry Lynn Eaton, a relative newcomer to the doll-making world. She has recently finished three doll seminars given by Jack Johnson, a professional marketer turned dollmaker and teacher. Graduating artists of his professional course (which may be taken by invitation only) are inducted into the Professional Doll Maker's Art Guild, whose membership benefits include an opportunity to share booths at the American International Toy Fair in New York. It was at the 1994 Toy Fair that Eaton introduced her much-heralded *Nino the Clown* to the doll world.

Eaton, a New Hampshire native, dabbled in arts and crafts for years before she turned to dollmaking. As a child she spent countless hours sketching the seacoast with her mother. Later she studied painting with watercolors with a local artist. When Jack Johnson offered a seminar at a local doll shop, Eaton became enthralled with the possibilities in a field that had heretofore escaped her attention. Before she had finished her first doll in the introductory course, Johnson recognized Eaton's potential as a dollmaker. When asked to join Johnson's professional class, Eaton jumped at the opportunity.

Nino the Clown was inspired by Eaton's lifelong fascination with clowns. "There is something that has always intrigued me about clowns," she notes. "The fact that they can put on makeup and literally change who they are is mind-blowing. Sometimes one can't even tell if they are male or female. This transformation into another 'being' is the core of what I believe makes them so intrinsically attractive—especially to adults. Children love the exaggeration of all that is silly, loving, colorful, and funny in a person." Eaton was interested in creating a doll first and then performing the transformation—that of a "normal" man to a clown by painting on a face. For the clown's makeup she consulted a doll artist friend, Jeff Redford, who was also an actor. Having gone through the necessary schooling to become a clown, Redford advised Eaton on the various styles of clown makeup. "He shared with me secrets of the trade, such as the whited-out top lip, which added to the realism of the piece. I didn't want him to be a cartoon, but rather a portrait of a real clown," Eaton says.

The art of performing before an audience, whether it be in an arena, a theater, or a concert hall, offers an opportunity for doll artists to develop themes of high drama. In *Music, Maestro, Please!* (plate 95), Pat Eagan of San Jose, California, has captured the golden moment when a conductor hears the right notes. When Eagan started the piece, she admits she had no idea what it would turn out to be. "The work came about quite by accident out of a desire to create a face less sweet than those of my previous sculptures. For me, it was a difficult task to refrain from smoothing and straightening each feature. When the small head was completed, it seemed to be saying, 'I hear the perfect sound—yes, that is it!' In my mind the look of satisfaction on that face corresponded to the sound of music."

Eagan embarked on a dollmaking career after many years of working in Chinese brush painting, tole painting, china painting, and portrait painting. She also was involved in ceramics and costume design. These skills came together when she began to make porcelain dolls, eventually teaching classes in porcelain dollmaking. She spent several years as an active member of the International Doll Restoration Artists Association, but eventually tired of repair work and sought "a more fulfilling area of dolls—that of sculpting and creating originals." After experimenting with a variety of clays, Eagan recently settled on polyform clay. She says, "Polyform clay allows me a freedom of expression that contributes to my enjoyment of making dolls and their settings."

Plate 95
Pat Eagan,
Music, Maestro, Please!
17 in. (43.2 cm), 1992

Once Eagan had settled on a personality for her maestro figure, she zeroed in on the costume. The making of a miniature tuxedo presented a challenge. Eagan cut pictures from newspapers and magazines, followed the outlines of her husband's suits, and even visited two tuxedo-rental stores while drafting her pattern. She found the fine wool and silk satin difficult to manipulate in such a small scale. In her desire for authenticity, Eagan included all of the underlinings and linings. She wired the tails to foster a sense of movement and created a windblown hairstyle out of a curly lambskin wig to suggest vigorous action on the part of the maestro. She borrowed a baton from a musician friend and copied it in miniature. Eventually Eagan plans to sculpt a small group of "unorthodox" musicians to accompany the maestro. However, she is thinking of a mostly female ensemble, so she won't have to make many more miniature tuxedos! "Marketing my work is not a high priority for me—however, the response I get when showing my finished pieces to others gives me a lot of satisfaction."

Kathryn Walmsley (see "Figures from Literature") claims she always made and collected dolls. As a child growing up in New Jersey, she designed clothes for herself and her dolls under the tutelage of her grandmother, who had "very high standards for sewing." Walmsley collected textiles, buttons, and lace, and made her first doll, a cloth elf, at the age of thirteen. After taking every art course her high school offered, she attended art school, pursuing courses in design. Her continuing interest in needlework eventually led Walmsley to start a leather clothing business with an emphasis on custom work requiring unique patterns for each design. Walmsley notes, "By the time I became a serious doll artist, pattern making was the same as breathing to me." After marriage to a fellow artist, Walmsley settled in rural Indiana, where she and her husband designed and built their house. While raising two sons, Walmsley continued to experiment with needlework, textile printing, and wood carving. She looked upon her early dollmaking attempts with fondness and eventually decided to return to her roots. "I remember very clearly the exact moment," Walmsley muses. "I was on the last leg of a long car trip with my children, who were three and six. I was feeling a little tired of motherhood after three days in the car, and started wondering about the rest of my life. It was suddenly very clear that the thing to do was to start over again at the beginning—at that magical time when I created my first doll, the cloth elf. I went home and redesigned that doll and successfully sold all the spinoffs. I worked in cloth for a while, and then discovered sculpting! I knew immediately that all my training had been in preparation for dollmaking. I had finally found the outlet for all my interests in one art form." As a student and a designer Walmsley had regarded herself as a technician or a "mimic," who could recreate life in her work. However, she didn't consider herself an artist until dollmaking allowed her to project emotion into her work.

The Suitor (plate 96) represents a commissioned piece for a special friend, who used to supply mohair for Walmsley's dolls from her herd of goats. The circumstances behind the making of the doll are poignant, inspiring the heartfelt emotion that Walmsley captured. "I had always wanted some of Judy's angora goats, thinking we could keep them with our milk goats," she recalls. "One day she called me with the sad news that her husband had died. She no longer could keep the goats, and wanted to trade the goats for a doll. When I made the doll, I decided Judy needed a man in her life, and designed an elegant huntsman for her. Along with his bow and arrow he carries a bouquet of flowers and smiles with a loving expression."

Unlike many artists, Walmsley insists on finishing every doll she starts, even if she doesn't like the particular piece. She regards each doll as an educational opportunity, feeling she learns the most from her mistakes. Until *The Suitor*, all of Walmsley's dolls were composed of heavy cotton-knit body fabric over a wire armature. After Walmsley made her first version of the doll, she wasn't satisfied with the body. She redid the armature, making it stronger, and designed a new technique for making the body. Now, for any doll over twelve inches high, Walmsley makes a cardboard body model and a twelve-to-sixteen-piece muslin body pattern in the desired pose. Walmsley regards *The Suitor* as one of her most important pieces—not only did it thrill her friend but it also marked a change in her work.

High drama and Van Craig are synonymous. His love for the theater and the stars who make it shine is embodied in a cast of flamboyant figures who confront the world with a raised eyebrow. Many of his sculptures resemble famous actresses and actors, a beguiling combination of caricature and portraiture. Craig views himself as a storyteller who transforms famous personalities into vehicles for the labyrinth of his imagination. Glamour synthesized with burlesque has been called the keynote of his work.

Plate 96
Kathryn Walmsley,
The Suitor,
17 in. (43.2 cm), 1992
(Photo: Courtesy of
Kathryn Walmsley)

It appears that Craig has never met a sequin or a bead he doesn't adore; yet his dolls achieve a stark power that bespeak an ordered, although complex, creation. The sculptures breathe an authenticity based on solid research. "When I decide on a figure, I start to gather photographs from books and programs of old movies, shows, and operas from the rich periods of the 1910s and the 1920s, soaking up nuances of the period, from costuming to art and architecture. I often get ideas for costumes by walking around my neighborhood, the theater district in New York, where the most exciting supplies of materials can be found in the old trim shops and fabric warehouses." Craig traces his signature costuming to a childhood love for the elaborate show costumes of the Ice Capades. While rummaging in a thrift shop in the early 1970s, Craig found some figures that were originally used in the creation of the Ice Capades' costumes. They piqued his interest and inspired him to combine costume design with sculpture. His first three-dimensional designs were puppets that appeared in various theater productions. Then in 1982, while performing in a Las Vegas production of *Hello, Dolly!* he sculpted his first face, which led him to add doll-making to his multifaceted career. By 1984, with an exciting inclusion in the first Fine Arts Sculpted Doll Show in Soho, sculpting had become a major commitment. The Dyansen Gallery in New York sponsored Craig's work, providing support for him at a time when few art galleries recognized doll and figurative art. Throughout the 1980s Craig balanced a theatrical career with sculpting. While he performed in a number of Broadway productions, designed costumes and sets, and also worked as an art director and photo stylist in advertising, he always made time for sculpting. The creative energy of the theater became the most important interactive force with his sculpting.

Among the highest accolades doll artists receive are commissions to design window displays for such prestigious stores as Tiffany, Saks Fifth Avenue, and Lord & Taylor. Craig has created windows for all three stores, in New York, San Francisco, and Chicago. He views window display as "the gallery of the 1990s," appreciating the opportunity to let thousands of people enjoy his work. The sculpture featured in this book, *Delilah: Folies 1924* (plate 87), initially was conceived as a piece for the Tiffany windows in Chicago in 1990. When the project was canceled, Craig had already sculpted the figure, but hadn't costumed it. He set the unfinished piece aside on a shelf until 1994, when he was asked to create a work for this book.

The original inspiration for *Delilah: Folies 1924* came from an early 1980s exhibit of romantic and glamorous Hollywood design sponsored by the Costume Institute of the Metropolitan Museum of Art in New York City. "There was a photograph in the program," Craig remembers, "of Glorious Gloria in a silent film in 1919, wearing an unbelievable robe with a peacock train and a headdress of pearls. The idea of a mythical princess, a symbol of Babylonian excess, in a land as mythical as Hollywood, appealed to me." For *Delilah: Folies 1924* Craig pulled out his most treasured vintage costumes and accessories to create a dazzling Art Deco design with black velvet and white rhinestones. "The piece was really boring," he deprecatingly states, "until I included the black-velvet backdrop."

The face, with its bedroom eyes and theatrical makeup, suggests the heady days of young Hollywood and is framed by a glamorous headdress of black peacock-type feathers. The sensuous legs were also a priority for Craig: "I love doing women with big hips and interesting body types—so Delilah represents a departure. I don't do many serious pieces, but I wanted to do her straight—

from slim hips to gorgeous legs." Craig found the pose he had chosen for *Delilah* to present an interesting challenge. "I wanted a raised shoulder with the arm wrapped around the body," he recalls. "The arm actually comes off where the armband is, so I could costume her before adding the arm. To hide the joint I devised the armband—it was a little tricky, but it turned out the way I wanted it to."

E. J. Taylor is, like Craig, the object of great admiration. Both artists, although traveling down very different paths, have reached the pinnacle of their profession through inventive window displays and outstanding sculpture. While Craig highlights the outrageous in his work, Taylor reaches into history to create magical kingdoms. The first dolls he showed to John Noble of the Museum of the City of New York and to Gene Moore, Tiffany's window-display impresario, showed a talent that overwhelmed all who encountered his work.

A shy man who has lived in England since 1979, E. J. Taylor dates his first interest in dollmaking to a puppet show he saw as a child and to the folk dolls that his first- and sixth-grade art teacher displayed in school. Her words always remained with him, and became his mantra as his dollmaking career evolved: "Whatever you do, make it original!" When Taylor attempted his own versions at home, he made them in a time-honored tradition, using what was available on his parents' farm. Using baling wire for armatures, cotton from the medicine cabinet, Elmer's glue, and scraps from his mother's quilting basket, Taylor fashioned a pioneer family, enjoying the process of inventing and solving problems as he went along. For his first piece he saturated the head with glue and molded the features as it hardened. Taylor remembers shredding the fibers of his mother's worn-out nylon stockings to use for hair. The inventiveness he displayed as a child would eventually become a noted signature of his later work. However, Taylor's dollmaking efforts were not "what was expected of a boy of my age," and he gave it up until after high school.

In college Taylor experimented with sculpting and creating marionettes out of wood putty, using techniques he learned from a book in the library. In the late 1960s Taylor studied fashion design at the prestigious Parsons School of Design in New York City. "The skills I learned at Parsons would later be invaluable in dollmaking," Taylor says. "My sense of form, structure, and drapery comes from those years." Although Taylor worked in costume after his training at Parsons, he recalls, "the doll thing kept coming back and wouldn't go away." A friend suggested he call Gene Moore, the designer of Tiffany's windows, who when he saw Taylor's work commissioned him to create a series of

Plate 97
E. J. Taylor,
Jessie,
28 in. (71.1 cm), 1993
(Photo: Courtesy of
E. J. Taylor)

dolls for Tiffany's windows. In 1980 Taylor branched out into the field of children's books, writing and illustrating a series that not surprisingly was a huge success. While he enjoyed the monetary rewards of this venture, he found that by 1986 he missed dollmaking. "I was always buying the materials, but never using them," he ruefully acknowledges. *Jessie* (plate 97) represented his first doll after a six-year hiatus. Taylor worked intermittently on the head for three or four months, pouring all of his pent-up desire to sculpt again into an intense quest for perfection. He challenged himself by attempting to portray a poignant rendition of a pregnant nineteenth-century African-American woman. "I was so pleased with the head when I fired it," he recalls, "but, then I had to paint it. I hadn't any experience with painting a darker skin tone. I went out and bought every shade of brown, sepia, terra-cotta . . . and I began. As the paint was going on, it was very opaque. One of the things I have always loved about the technique of painting was that you could get these very translucent skin tones. I started around eight in the evening, and I didn't finish until three in the morning. As I worked, I grew more and more panicked, because I was afraid I was ruining this wonderful work, and I kept taking the paint off and starting again. Out of absolute desperation I tried the lighter pink, Caucasian tones, and then I added the brown colors, and all of a sudden it began to work! The pink tones underneath brought forth the highlights I had been seeking."

Taylor put the finished doll on a shelf and didn't think about it until a few months before the 1993 NIADA conference. He wanted to take *Jessie* to NIADA but decided her clothes and body were not right. He reworked the body to make her more pregnant, and recreated her costume. "I felt the head was so powerful, that everything else had to underscore the feeling of nobility and dignity," Taylor says. "To me she is like a tree bearing fruit."

It is Taylor's gift that he can evoke deep emotions from work that exemplifies subtlety and restraint. *Jessie* can be thought of as a portrait that connects us with our humanity, and in that sense it brilliantly achieves one of the most significant aims of the character doll artist.

Fantasies

 To enter the world of fantasy dolls is to step into a magic kingdom inhabited by a beguiling group of personages—from fairies, elves, gnomes, and wizards to a large cast of anthropomorphic creatures. A special breed of doll artists is attracted to this sphere, where few rules or inhibitions stand in the way of the imagination. Fantasy dollmakers are free to create spirits who transcend the human form, ageless sprites not bound by period or style.

Many of the artists in this chapter were blessed with parents who encouraged their children's natural bent for fantasy, who understood their daydreamers, and who provided instruction in a variety of crafts that proved useful in dollmaking. Their parents instilled in them a love of mythology, folklore, poetry, and fairy tales. As the

Plate 98
Linda Kertzman,
The Fairy Queen,
28 in. (71.1 cm), 1993
(Photo: Courtesy of
Linda Kertzman)

artists' dollmaking talents surfaced, they embarked on personal journeys, creating illusions of magical beings that were deeply rooted in their psyches.

Akira Blount of Bybee, Tennessee, believes that the realm of the "faeries" provides answers for what cannot readily be explained. Acclaimed as a master dollmaker, she has always drawn upon what she calls "nature personified" for her dolls. Growing up in Black Earth, Wisconsin, Blount remembers garnering the scraps from her father's woodworking efforts and making things from them. Trips with her grandmother to the farmer's co-op, where she was allowed to choose pieces of fabric for herself from the many colorful bolts on display, instilled a love of fabric that eventually led her into making cloth dolls. The advent of her career came, as with many other dollmakers, with the desire to make a doll or two for her children. "I found cloth dollmaking to be the perfect answer to all of my creative urges, in that it was possible to do the work while tending two small children," she recalls. "I could pick it up and throw it down at a moment's notice. The supplies were accessible, inexpensive, and uncomplicated. It also provided extra income when, several years later, I became a single parent short on funds."

After Blount remarried, she moved to the foothills of the Smoky Mountains in eastern Tennessee. The beauty of her surroundings nourished her creative spirit, and her dollmaking reflected the harmony she found in nature. "I came to sense the spirits of nature who dwelled around me, and I began depicting them in dolls," Blount notes. Her passion for textiles led Blount into making cloth figures that could express the subtleties and contrasts in color, texture, and pattern that Blount found so exciting. "For me, colors have a voice, a vibration that sings," she muses. "When I combine them, they must sing in perfect harmony."

Blount regards herself primarily as a fiber artist whose chosen medium, dollmaking, allows her to pursue her art in an emotionally satisfying way. Her love of natural fibers and her skill in combining them is enhanced by a playful incorporation of found objects that reflect her personality. "Dollmaking is a very personal statement of who I am. It is a compilation of many loves in life, and seems to flow as a natural extension of myself," Blount says. "My work is of an intuitive nature; the figures tend to define themselves, naturally evolving, rather than being planned in detail in advance. I do my best work this way, surrounded by my collections of old, new, and used fabrics, antique trims and laces, buttons and beads, pine cones, acorns, and twigs, leather, feathers, and fur."

The Deerwoman (plates 99) is constructed of cloth and stuffed with polyfill. The hands and face are made of a fine cotton knit, which Blount hand-sculpted with needle and thread. The eyes are embroidered, and facial color and shadow

Plates 99
Akira Blount,
The Deerwoman,
26 in. (66 cm), 1994

were added with pencil. The detachable mask, a trademark of many of Blount's dolls, is one of the most intriguing aspects of *The Deerwoman*. "I guess the masks reflect my desire to make an animal doll without giving up the human form," Blount reveals. "Each mask is made out of cloth, and then gessoed and painted. *The Deerwoman* reflects the thrill I experience when I am privileged to see the deer that live in the woods around me." Blount made the chest plate out of pine cones she collected while walking through the woods. She fashioned a delicate wreath from acorns, sumac berries, and grapevines. The material for the dress, found in a quilting-supply shop, is a print that appears to be a photographic transfer-pattern of grass growing in a field. When the mask is lifted, a hauntingly beautiful face is revealed. Although there is a timeless quality to the face, there is a hint of medieval or Renaissance charm that is in keeping with the Robin Hood spirit of the work.

Blount foresees unlimited opportunities for pursuing what is new and fresh in cloth dollmaking, saying: "Originally, only the most lowly of dolls were made with cloth, and I find that the room for innovation in the medium is wide open.

Through my dolls I can find the child within me and, hopefully, share the emotion, fun, and fantasy with others."

Far from the Smoky Mountains of Tennessee, dollmaker Chris Boston has found her own corner of heaven, the Sunshine Coast of Queensland, Australia. Since childhood Boston has immersed herself in the enchanting world of creatures from the rain forest that wends its way through Boston's "backyard." She remembers spending many hours as a child with her father, scavenging by the sea as he beguiled her with tales of magical creatures living in the caves along the beach and in the rain forest. Years later, using the rain forest as inspiration, Boston created the elaborate fantasy world of "Notsobabillia," inhabited by gnomes, dragons, bunnyips (nocturnal marsupials who centuries ago used to fly), fairies, witches, elves, and fire sprites. Her dolls can be easily identified by their hands, which have three fingers and a thumb, telltale signs of their otherworldliness.

Since making her first creations in the early 1980s, Boston has designed, sculpted, and sewn her one-of-a-kind dolls herself. She eschews molds as she sculpts the heads, hands, and feet of her dolls in Fimo, occasionally incorporating accessories of papier-maché. Boston spends as much time fashioning the clothing of her dolls as she does working on the dolls themselves. She credits her mother with teaching her as a child the meticulous hand-sewing that she now employs in the costumes of her dolls. To obtain just the right look and texture, Boston will treat a fabric by fraying, patching, and layering, until it evokes the dank, mossy rain forest. "I am always finding myself in all manner of stores, searching for bits and pieces of old fabric to recycle through my dolls," Boston confesses. "I prowl about, looking for old doilies, dresses, curtains, or tablecloths."

Chris Boston's dolls reflect her love for the environment and wildlife. *Swamp Ma Hogany* (plate 100), named after swamp mahogany, the Australian eucalyptus tree, is gnarly and stocky like the tree. Boston claims that *Swamp Ma Hogany*'s breath has a eucalyptus smell and that she appears "dirty" from her adventures in the swamp in the back of Boston's house. She says, "At the time I made her there was a fight raging with our government over the use of the land behind my house. They were trying to put a freeway through this precious swamp, endangering many rare species of plant, animal, and bird life. I was inspired to show another species that lives there—Swamp Ma Hogany, a greenie and bunyip baby." She adds, "I've been looking after sick and orphaned wildlife now for over three years, and I guess that's affected my work as these little companions have crept into each piece."

If Chris Boston closed her eyes and somehow found herself in the Morris, New York, studio of Linda Kertzman, she would sense the presence of a kindred spirit. Kertzman's workshop is filled with bins of materials from the nearby woods (flower petals, mosses, bark, and twigs), cabinets brimming over with fabrics, and a paint table holding acrylic paints, boxes of Super Sculpey, and jars of Cernit. Surrounded by materials, Kertzman creates her characters: a winsome group of wizards, fairies, laughing babies, and all manner of children. Like Boston, Kertzman grew up near a forest, often amusing herself by making up stories about "fairies and elves that lived under the roots of trees and in the little groves of sunlight that made magic spots in the woods." Kertzman recalls, "As a child I actually planted a lollypop garden. I took a bag of lollypops out to the woods, and stuck them all in the dirt. Then I rounded up the neighborhood kids and told them the fairies had planted them." Kertzman's childhood preoccupation with fairies is reborn in her work, including a piece entitled *The Lollypop Garden.* Her work often explores themes of childhood innocence, a time when all things seem possible, including fairies. Kertzman also admits that as her own children grew older, her "characters" grew younger, "like the little fairies and sprites I played with as a child and the little babies I loved so much."

Kertzman's dollmaking efforts began in childhood. She remembers, "As a child I used candle wax, soap, and rocks that looked like they had faces. As a teen I saw my first apple doll and was awed that something so real could come from a piece of fruit! My mother and I began experimenting and soon found ourselves teaching together in schools and museums." She continues, "During the time I was raising my four children I experimented with puppetry, clay, and painting. What I really wanted was to create the children and fairies I had seen in the books my mother had brought with her from Germany to America when she was a little girl." In 1985 Kertzman discovered Super Sculpey, and her mastery of the medium led to the exceedingly complex figures that have become her trademark. Later she added Cernit or Cernit mixed with Sculpey to her repertoire.

The Fairy Queen (plate 98) is a three-piece Cernit composition in which the central figure, the fairy queen, is flanked by two young fairy attendants, dressed in silk with wings of preserved magnolia leaves. The blond child offers wild berries to the queen, while the darker-haired child stands on a stump so she can style the queen's luxurious hand-dyed red mohair wig. The fairy queen is swathed in sheer green silk, a magic color to Kertzman, who actually found her inspiration for the piece from the scarf itself. She recalls, "It was a warm and sunny day, and my husband, Pete, and I were on his motorcycle, stopping at antique shops and just enjoying the day. At one shop I found the scarf, and the whole scene flashed from that. We had taken some back roads with woods on either sides, and the light seemed to glitter between the trees. I couldn't wait to start on her! But, I also didn't want to stop riding! So she had to wait for the next day."

Many of the admirers of Linda Kertzman's work are also fans of Stephanie Blythe and Susan Snodgrass, convinced that the two collaborative artists have been touched by fairy dust. Since the late 1980s Blythe and Snodgrass have received accolades for their delicate renditions of fairies in artistic settings that have set new ideals for illusion and beauty. Since the artists envision their fairies dwelling in a land of enchantment, they are as concerned with their backdrops as they are with the dolls themselves. Fairies nestle in the most exquisite antique jewelry boxes, compacts, sewing baskets, miniature Victorian trunks, abalone shells, champagne glasses, ballet slippers, and hats. They also rest on natural objects, such as crystal bases, birds' nests, driftwood, and pieces of coral. A special group of tiny fairies reside in antique china teacups—these pieces have become "signature" works whose fame has made Blythe and Snodgrass famous as the "Teacup Fairy Ladies."

Blythe and Snodgrass learned sculpting, china-painting, and mold-making together from doll artist Sylvia Mobley in the early 1980s; as their work developed, they gradually fell into a division of labor. Now Stephanie Blythe sculpts and paints the graceful porcelain figures, while Susan Snodgrass creates their clothing, drawing upon her background in theater and costume design. While Snodgrass favors antique metallic fabrics and old lace, she also relies on some of the newer, exciting fabrics from India and Europe. Costumes shimmer with sewn-on "jewels" of opals, Austrian crystals, and tiny shells. Attached to the backs of the fairies are the gossamer wings—actual butterfly or African cicada wings for the small figures, and iridescent, hand-painted silk wings for the larger fairies. The artists take turns styling coiffures of raw silk hair or hand-dyed Tibetan lamb's wool. Although both women work in separate studios in Havre de Grace, Maryland, they confer over each piece, sustained by their joint vision of a fairy kingdom.

Plate 101
Stephanie Blythe and
Susan Snodgrass with
Sylvia Mobley,
Dream Voyages,
22½ in. (54.6 cm), 1993

The artists began collaborating in 1977 after a chance meeting. Blythe had visited Snodgrass's Maryland farm in search of some wood for a backgammon board. She stepped into a bee's nest, and while recovering inside the house noticed a bed strewn with antique lace. Blythe and Snodgrass started chatting and discovered they were kindred spirits with a passion for antique lace. "We were both stuck out in the country with all this creative energy, so we decided to make Victorian Christmas stockings together," explains Blythe. After collaborating on a series of miniature rooms peopled by fairies, they decided in 1981 their real love centered on the fairies. The rest, as they say, is history.

Dream Voyages (plate 101) was the answer to a challenge. The 1993 Dollmakers Originals Show of the One of a Kind Salon in New York City invited artists to take part in a "Do Your Dream" contest. Blythe and Snodgrass began by brainstorming—"What is the most fantastic piece we can do?" The artists described some of the elements they wanted to include: an illusion of flying (for which they devised the fairy whispering a secret in the main figure's ear); a fairy on tiptoe; nude porcelain bodies that wouldn't be offensive; fairies integrated into the base; and a feeling of lightness and dreaminess, yet also a natural-looking work.

The idea of incorporating nude porcelain bodies in the piece presented a number of technical challenges. Blythe and Snodgrass called upon their mentor, Sylvia Mobley, who was excited by the project and added her expertise in porcelain dollmaking techniques.

The process began with the selection of a piece of Manzanita burl wood that had been bleached and left in the sun until it achieved a soft-looking, weathered patina. Mobley sculpted the tiny fairies with holes to peg the pieces. The arms were made detachable because of their delicacy, but the problem of covering their joints needed to be solved. The solution came from antique chiffon flower petals that gave the illusion of fluttering wings. The artists chose a monochromatic color scheme (pale colors, opals, an opalescent bottle, and blond hair) to create a soft, ethereal feeling. Snodgrass spent hours gluing on the tiny opals and even tinier Austrian crystals until the whole piece shimmered and glowed.

Dream Voyages not only exemplified the realization of the artists' own dream, but also represented years of collecting "bits and pieces." The exquisite lace covering the pale blue dress was a gift from a friend of the artists. Blythe and Snodgrass found the large opal flowers that constitute the headband at a gem show many years ago, and the smaller ones that adorn the dress several years later. A miniature show yielded the iridescent bottle. All of these elements from the past eventually came together to form one of the most monumental works of their career.

The striking individuality of Paul Robins's fairies piques and captures the imagination at the same time. While never pretty in a conventional manner, they are theatrical without being artificially glamorous. Drawing upon his years as a costume designer, Robins takes in stride laborious tasks of intricate hand-beading and elaborate costuming that demand a month of his time to complete a single outfit. "Working for the theater taught me a number of techniques that have influenced the way my dolls look today," Robins reveals. "I use a lot of beadwork and sequins—they play with light as well as color. In the theater, if you can't find what you need to create an effect, then you just make it, sometimes out of surprising materials. Things are dyed, layered, or painted to make you think you are seeing something that may or may not be there. I use the same techniques when constructing a doll." The wings on Robins's fairies reflect his inventive nature. Although they have the appearance of stained glass, they are really hand-painted tricot material that has been stretched across the wing frames.

As much as Robins loved his earlier work in the theater, he found it stressful, and was looking for something else to do when his sister, an exotic dancer at the time, complained of the astronomical prices she had to pay for shoddy costumes. Robins, sensing an opportunity, started the first design house for professional exotic dancers in Toronto. In three years he had made enough money to close up shop and purchase a piece of property on a small gulf island off the west coast of Canada, where he was determined to devote himself full time to dollmaking. The remoteness and beauty of Gabriola Island, with its many wild creatures roaming the beaches, energized Robins. Working on one piece at a time, he channeled his feelings into a series of dolls that explore every shade of the emotional spectrum. "For me," Robins admits, "dollmaking is more than just creating an interesting object: it means empowering the creation with a soul, and that takes a special kind of magic. Each piece lives in its own little world, frozen in time, an ephemeral snapshot capturing the emotion of the

Plate 102
Paul Robins,
The Promenade,
12 in. (30.5 cm), 1993
(Photo: Courtesy of Pretty
Woman Collectibles)

moment. I strive to capture emotion in my work above all else. I find it difficult to work on more than one piece at a time for precisely that reason. I never make more than twenty-five dolls a year." All of Robins's dolls are either one-of-a-kind or limited to a small series. Robins likes working in a series for it allows him to experiment on the same head. "It is challenging to come up with slightly different solutions in costuming and painting," Robins reveals.

The Promenade (plate 102), one of Robins's most elegant works, reflects his iconoclastic views on the kingdom of fairies. He notes, "It's a misconception that all fairies fly. In many of the fairy courts of Europe, flying is relegated to servants. Although the fairy aristocracy has wings, it is considered common to actually have to use them. For this reason many fairies of aristocratic breeding prefer to travel by other means. What better way is there to spend a leisurely summer's afternoon than to saunter through the woods on a turtle 'Howdah' made of twisted twigs and stretched with a spider's webbing and lace? I love pieces that you have to peer into. This little fairy has even brought her pet turtle along for the ride. It is nestled in among the cushions, but you can only see it when you pull back the curtains and peek inside."

The fantasy dolls of Maggie Finch (see "Figures from Literature") are inspired by gleanings from years spent in scholarly research. Her insatiable curiosity and creative genius sparked the flame that led her to be one of the first contemporary doll artists creating fantasy dolls. Her innovative Phantasmota series, begun in the late 1970s, has been acclaimed by John Darcy Noble, curator emeritus of the toy collection at The Museum of the City of New York. Calling these pieces "streets ahead of anything else," Noble claims Finch helped liberate the doll world from a more narrow view of its artistry.

As the sculptures, "humankind with animal attributes," evolved, Finch came to think of them as "Maggie's Bestiary," based on medieval collections of stories containing physical and allegorical descriptions of animals with interpretations of the moral significance the animals embodied. When asked if she realized at the time the groundbreaking importance of her work, Finch modestly demurred, "I honestly never thought about it. I just felt impelled to express more than the human face alone allowed. I found I could insert a certain humor and subtlety by creating a human face with certain animal attributes." She continued, "Also, the postures of certain animals fascinated me— I could incorporate their poses in my works—make the stances slightly off. In the sculpture Cat Will to Kind, the inspiration for the legs and boots came from watching my own cat."

The second doll in the Phantasmota series, *Cat Will to Kind* (plate 103), got its name from an English proverb. Finch explains, "You can dress a cat in the richest finery, but in the end its true character will out. The bird perched on top of her head better watch out!"

The fantasy dolls of Scott Gray grew out of his career as a theatrical costumer and prop designer for various ballet and opera companies. *Lobster Man* (plate 104) was created as the result of his working on two ballets based on *Alice in Wonderland*, one in his hometown of Seattle and the other in Houston. He designed masks and headdresses for the Seattle production and scenery, props, and dolls for the Houston version that included some giant lobster claws. Gray recalls, "Before I saw the designer's sketches for the lobsters, I imagined what they would look like, and in my imaginings, the idea for *Lobster Man* was born."

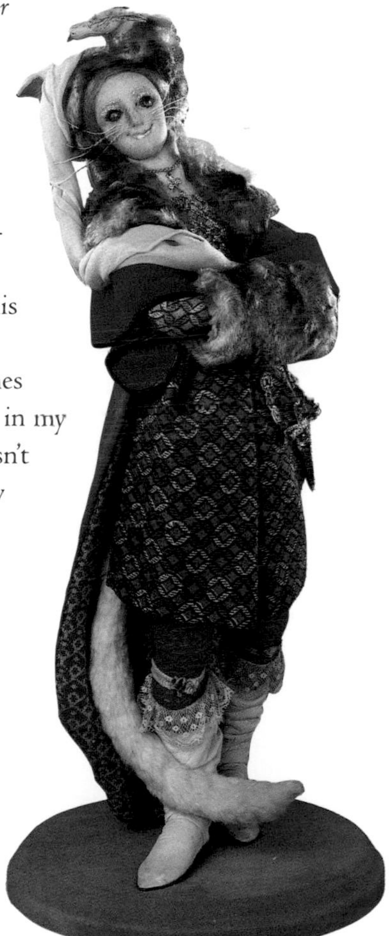

Before sculpting the doll, Gray researched lobster anatomy at his local fish market, where a clerk offered to place a live lobster on top of the tank. Fearing a "crustacean escape," Gray declined and self-consciously leaned over the tank as he sketched. He then went to the children's room at the public library and took out a picture book on lobsters. The subtle colors and shadings of the yellow lobsters particularly impressed Gray, and he incorporated them in his palette. As the doll evolved, Gray changed his original plan for the expression on *Lobster Man*'s face. He says, "As I work, I can sometimes respond better to the piece in progress than I can to the idea I have in my mind's eye. The first head I made didn't suit his personality—it wasn't dancing with the figure, as it was too sullen. Off it came, and is now reincarnated as a surly character sporting a black leather jacket and worn 501s."

Lobster Man, like all of Gray's work, is intended to give the viewer a respite from the mundane, and, perhaps, a bit of a laugh. His mission is accomplished with the skillful placing of familiar elements in unusual combinations. A sense of the dramatic permeates Gray's work: his dolls present themselves as though they are making an entrance, appearing to be on-call for the performance. Gray insists that he aims to convey emotion without being too specific, letting viewers add their own interpretations. "One time I sat in a gallery showing my work," he confides. "I loved it when people would stop in their tracks and make a beeline for a

Plate 103
Maggie Finch,
*Cat Will to Kind:
Phantasmota #2*,
15½ in. (39.4 cm), 1979

Plate 104
Scott Gray,
Lobster Man,
28 in. (71.1 cm), 1993

particular piece. Of course, there were a few who just didn't get it—they would stare at a doll with a totally blank expression. The people who seemed to appreciate my work would finish each piece in their mind's eye."

As a child growing up in Chelmsford, Massachusetts, Gray displayed an interest in art and sewing that foreshadowed his success in costume design and dollmaking. By the time Gray entered college at Boston University, he knew he wanted a career in the theater. In his courses on costume design he learned about pattern making. "When people look at my dolls, they always wonder where the patterns come from," Gray muses. "Well," he continues, "you can't buy them—you have to make your own. My training has made it second nature for me to drape a basic bodice and develop a sense of scale. Scale is what usually trips up a lot of people. You have to be careful that a brocade or a print doesn't overwhelm the figure. There is nothing worse than seeing lace on a doll that looks like it belongs on a woman's blouse." Gray continued work in costume design at Temple University, where he received a master of fine arts degree. "At Temple," he notes, "they really taught me how to see." Gray was on his way to developing a unique vision that has delighted his audiences.

Lisa Lichtenfels's fantasy soft sculptures also deal with contrasting elements by playing upon the tensions inherent in the juxtaposition of human and animal forms. Whatever the form of the piece, a mermaid or a youthful Pan, each subject reflects Lichtenfels's belief that people are composed of warring factions of good and evil. What turned into a recurring theme began by a chance encounter with a green bug perched on the window of Lichtenfels's car at a gas station. "I was sitting in the car," Lichtenfels remembers, "watching my husband pump gas, and this exotic bug caught my eye. I thought it looked like a sensual woman, and it suddenly came to me how much fun it would be to try to combine parts of the bug's body with parts of the human body." Since that moment in 1980, Lichtenfels has created and sold countless human/animal combinations, but she still keeps the original green bug sculpture on the mantel in her home.

Lichtenfels is pleased when her fantasy creations startle and challenge the viewer with contradictory messages. In *Pan* (plate 105), which first appears to be a simple sculpture but is actually an extremely complex work, the tug-of-war between innocence and sensuality is impossible to escape. Pan represents somewhat of a departure for Lichtenfels in that she only occasionally portrays small children. She notes, "I don't do children very often: I'll only do a child if there is an interesting personality to capture. This Pan, I feel, has one of these personalities."

Like Lisa Lichtenfels, Peter Wolf, the Bavarian artist from the fairy-tale town of Würzburg, Germany, has made his share of doll/animal combinations. His pieces have animal bodies and mask heads that when removed reveal dolls' heads underneath. The art of the unexpected characterizes Wolf's fantasy creations, which have delighted his many admirers since the early 1980s. From eighteenth-century automata to nostalgic 1920s dolls in the spirit of Erté and Poiret, the work of Peter Wolf refuses to be typecast. His themes vary and his output reflects a constant race with his imagination, but each piece is stamped with his unique signature. He sums up his quixotic interpretation of the world around him by saying, "I'm happy I can take all of my experiences and make something unusual come out of them."

Growing up in a medieval town, Wolf steeped himself in the romance of its palaces and legends. While still in high school he found an outlet for his creative talents in an internship at the Würzburg theater, where he worked on costumes, props, and scenery. Like many of his fellow doll artists, he began his career making Christmas ornaments for a local gift shop. Wolf's first doll, a harlequin figure, sold immediately, and the many requests by customers for more of his dolls convinced him that he could pursue dollmaking as a livelihood.

Reflecting Wolf's many interests and hobbies, his dolls reveal a passion for collecting jewelry and his love of theater and the opera. Many of Wolf's fantasy dolls glitter with gemstones and crystals incorporated into their costumes and hair. The idea for *The Queen of the Night and General Star and His Starlets* (plate 106) came to him "in a flash," but had its inception in a lifelong fascination with Mozart's opera, *The Magic Flute,* in which the Queen of the Night is a central figure. "Years ago in the early 1980s, I made a Queen of the Night," Wolf recalls, "but it was a much more theatrical piece. This time around, I wanted to explore the magic life of childhood dreams. After making the queen, I decided to portray the starlets as children—a departure from the typical adult male figures." When asked what proved to be the most challenging task in making the group, Wolf answered, "Constructing the hoop! In every piece there are

tedious moments that are countered by unexpected joys." Wolf's eyes brighten
as he recalls unexpectedly finding a box of Christmas ornaments with crystal
stars in a Pennsylvania department store. "After breaking off the stars, I attached
them to the Queen's gown as the final touch."

As an admirer of Peter Wolf's penchant for incorporating unusual elements
in his work, fellow doll artist Nancy Wiley (see "Women of the Imagination")
occasionally consulted with him in the early years of her career. "He encouraged
me to employ the art of surprise," Wiley recalls. "He always suggested adding a
little something here or there to make what was ordinary into something more
interesting." Having spent part of her childhood in Germany because of her
father's foreign-service career, Wiley acquired an eye for medieval and baroque
decoration that would surface in her painting and dollmaking. She continued
to refine her artistic sensibility while studying art in Rome during her college
year abroad. While growing up Wiley was influenced by her mother, whose
hobby was dollmaking, and by Bill Wiley, one of three brothers who Wiley

Plate 106
Peter Wolf,
*The Queen of the
Night and General Star
and His Starlets*,
17 in. (43.2 cm),
15 in. (38.1 cm), and
7½–12 in. (19.1 cm–
30.5 cm), 1994

believed "could make anything." In fact, Nancy Wiley's childhood perception of her brother's talent was prophetic, as Bill Wiley became one of dollmaking's brightest stars in the 1980s before succumbing to AIDS in 1991 (see "Beyond Dolls"). It is not surprising that the *Moon Man* (plate 107), a deeply emotional piece that was made a year after her brother's death, is one of Wiley's favorite dolls. Wiley says the *Moon Man* is the personification of the sadness she felt at the time; she further explains: "The Moon Man's story (which is not from a book, it is my own story) is that he is obliged to hold the moon in the midnight sky forever. He gently guards the moon as a precious thing, but the magnitude of his fate has become a burden. The moon in this case is a symbol of the sadness we all carry around with us. When I look up at the moon at night, a feeling of melancholy sweeps over me—I feel small and lonely. I chose this image along with the colors

Plate 107
Nancy Wiley,
The Moon Man,
24 in. (61 cm), 1992

of the paint and the material to convey my emotions. By making the shoulders and back sloped, I tried to create the effect of a heavy burden weighing down on the figure."

Gail Lackey's business card identifies her as a "Fantasy Sculptor," specializing in "unique one-of-a-kind Fairies, Elves, Santas and other Magical Beings." She entered the dollmaking field in the 1980s with a series of cloth elves, after a long period of experimentation in various art forms, including a stint as a greeting-card illustrator. In college some of her early efforts in art classes displeased her professors, who failed to appreciate her originality. In a pottery class she was criticized for sculpting faces onto her pots, and in a sculpture class she lost points for caricaturing instead of sculpting in a realistic manner. Today, Lackey has found an appreciative audience. Her fascination with the world of gnomes and goblins has been called contagious: people say they can't walk past a Lackey doll without smiling. In 1993, she first showed her dolls at the International Doll Expo (IDEX). "When I signed up for IDEX, I left my job, sculpted thirteen dolls, and brought them to the show, not knowing really what to expect,"

Lackey recalls. She sold every doll she brought to the show and won the prestigious popular vote award.

As an artist who portrays wood sprites and other forest folk, Lackey looks for natural materials to incorporate into her work. On long walks through the Idaho woods, she collects birds' nests, lichen, moss, flowers, twigs, mushrooms, and other objects. She scours antique shops for vintage fabrics and fanciful trims, always on the lookout for an unusual accessory that will "make" a piece. For example, Lackey found a silver pipe from India years ago in a thrift shop, and pulled it out of her stockpile when she began working on *The Elf and His Pipe* (plate 108). "It is obviously the elf's most prized possession," Lackey notes. "He even has a stand for it. I knew I wanted to use a hodgepodge of vintage fabrics for his costume, so I searched through my collection and came up with a Masonic shawl that had seen better days but was perfect for his epaulets." When Lackey uses new fabric, she distresses it, just as she wets down leather to age the quaint-looking shoes she fashions. She selects primitive sheep's wool from Norway for beards, and hand-dyes locks of mohair for wigs.

Plate 108
Gail Lackey,
The Elf and His Pipe,
17 in. (43.2 cm), 1993

Lackey spends as much time on the bodies and costumes of her dolls as she devotes to sculpting the faces. To fashion the expressive hands of her elves, she sculpts them individually, inserting a wire in each finger, thereby allowing the finger to bend. "I want my hands to show character, to show signs of age and wear," she says. "I also want them doing things—holding an accessory rather than just hanging in mid-air." Most of Lackey's elves contain an element slightly askew, such as a mismatched stocking or shoe. "I am not looking to make a person in an elf's costume," Lackey notes. "I want my elves to be a distinct race of their own— to foster this feeling of otherworldliness, I like to incorporate the odd detail." For *The Elf and His Pipe* Lackey couldn't resist sculpting a shamrock for him to wear as a talisman. "After all, even leprechauns need a little luck," Lackey says with a smile.

The lighthearted elves by Gail Lackey could be soulmates to the recent creations of Bill Nelson, who in 1994 added a group of fantasy figures to his portfolio of character dolls (see "Characters"). When Nelson came upon a dwarf-sized gnome named "Hoggle" created by Jim Henson and Brian Froud for the movie *Labyrinth*, he stopped in his tracks. "I found him both ugly and wonderful, and very inspiring to me," Nelson explains. "I couldn't get him out of my mind. I decided to expand my dollmaking into the realm of fantasy." *Phib* (plate 109) represents a transitional piece in which Nelson explores the agelessness and wonder of fantasy figures. He experienced a sense of freedom, especially in the area of costuming, where he did not have to abide by the rules of conventional dress. Nelson adds, "Scale became less rigid. I could experiment with various fabrics and things found in nature. Shortly after *Phib* my scale changed. He towers over the dolls that followed. *Phib* came out of my head and heart, prompted by a desire to grow and change."

Almost every artist has the desire to move on. Yet as in Nelson's case, the core that defines the work of an individual artist shines through multiple refinements and reinventions. Whether Nelson creates character or fantasy dolls, his faces reveal a vulnerability that is both wistful and upbeat. The tension generated by these seemingly opposite emotions is what excites his audience. When Nelson is asked to explain his work, he speaks in poetic terms. "In an age when things are hurried, where everything is becoming high-tech and mass-supplied, where craft has almost been forgotten, I feel it is so very important to be creating something delicate and sweet and endearing with our hands. Handmade dolls become music to the ears of occupants of this fast-paced world. With each of my figures I try to create a unique diminutive personality that exhibits warmth and evokes a good feeling in the viewer. I want them to look as though they have something to say and are about to say it."

In 1993 artist E. J. Taylor (see "Characters"), like Bill Nelson, crossed over from the world of character dolls into the realm of fantasy; the change was made with a Paperclay doll, *Fawn* (plate 110), that he made to bring to the NIADA convention in Chicago. In 1974 Taylor had created a group of half-animal, half-human figures for the windows of Tiffany's on Fifth Avenue in New York City. These anthropomorphic creatures came to mind when Taylor felt the urge to try something whimsical. Years ago the dolls at Tiffany's had caused a sensation and were considered the first of their kind. John Noble, in the August 1993 edition of *Contemporary Doll Magazine*, reviewed the series of windows Taylor

Plate 109
Bill Nelson,
Phib,
14 in. (35.6 cm), 1993
(Photo: Courtesy of
Bill Nelson)

had designed for Tiffany's during the 1970s and 1981, concluding that Taylor had "discovered in his mind a medieval Faerieland, as true and viable as Fifth Avenue itself."

Taylor believes *Fawn* is an example of how new advances in technology influence art. "I wanted to do a full nude figure, but thought it would be very difficult to do in Sculpey. It would be too heavy and wouldn't fit into my small portable oven. The piece really came out of my desire to try Paperclay." Originally Taylor planned a male figure, but as the piece evolved, it became hermaphroditic. "I had finished the genitals and was working on the chest area," Taylor recalls, "and I sculpted what I thought were pecs on a man. When it dried, I looked at the piece again, and the chest resembled the breasts of an adolescent girl . . . so, I thought, okay, I won't start over again; I'll go with it, and make the breasts even more noticeable." *Fawn* reflects Taylor's insistence that a successful work must capture something from within the soul of an artist. "As I sculpt, I know the moment the inert clay becomes alive. From that moment on, the persona dictates the rest of the piece from the figure to the costume."

Plate 110

E. J. Taylor,

Fawn,

18 in. (45.7 cm), 1993

(Photo: Courtesy of

E. J. Taylor)

In Lubbock, Texas, artist Lynn Haney is motivated by a desire to make handcrafted objects that are messengers of good will. Haney's dolls reflect nostalgic childhood memories centering around the Christmas holidays. His characters are collaborations of characters and images from countless childhood hours spent with storybooks of legends, myths, and fantasies. As a child, Haney loved to tinker in his father's workshop, turning piles of discarded wood scraps into toys. He remembers crawling underneath his grandmother's quilting frame, listening to his mother, his grandmother, and their friends gossip as they sewed. As he grew older, he came to appreciate the love of folk art that his parents and grandparents had quietly instilled in him. In college he gravitated toward the arts, enjoying classes in weaving, sculpture, and pottery, and eventually earned a master's degree in art education, which led to a teaching position. If it hadn't been for a chance encounter with an antique Santa Claus figure in 1978, Haney might still be teaching art to junior-high-school students. When Haney thought

Plate 111
Lynn Haney,
Wizard of the Sea,
24 in. (61 cm), 1994

about buying the German Belsnickle, its tattered condition made him think he would be better off trying to make his own version. His first needle-sculptured Santas went to friends and family. Favorable reaction to his work prompted him to join his wife, Sue Haney, in her venture, making and selling a line of stuffed animals and pillows. After working solely in fabric, he became intrigued with resin, appreciating the amount of detail that the medium provides. "With resin," Haney explains, "I can obtain the truest interpretation of my original sculpture in an unlimited number of pieces."

In 1987 the newly formed Lynn Haney Collection introduced three wood-resin Father Christmas characters. The young company's output grew from 250 dolls the first year to the 6,000 dolls he and his staff of twelve craftspeople create currently. After Haney develops the sculpture, a mold is made from the initial piece. Each example is then cast in wood-resin composition, later to be individually painted, detailed, and antiqued with an oil-based stain. The individual sculpted pieces are then incorporated into the complete doll body. Beards and wigs are made by hand from wools and other natural fibers. Haney oversees production, approving every piece before he signs and dates it. Much of his time is spent doing what he likes best, dreaming and designing new dolls in his studio, where he works surrounded by bolts of fabric, trims, and myriad accessories.

In 1994 Haney decided to "stretch his wings" by creating his *Wizard of the Sea* (plate 111), a departure from his Father Christmas figures. Once again he reached back into his childhood for inspiration.

"I remember as a small boy finding seashells at the ocean and the pleasure it brought me," Haney says. "Since I live nine hundred miles away from the ocean, I especially like to go back to the seashore. The *Wizard of the Sea* is my connection to memories of the ocean. I have always been fascinated by shells and sea-related flotsam and jetsam, and combined these elements into a wizard-like character with shells as the primary decorative element. My background in weaving and textiles inspired the use of hand-spun and hand-dyed wools, natural fibers that speak of the sand and the sea."

As Lynn Haney "stretched his wings," so have all the artists whose illusions of whimsy delight while they illuminate a magical world that few are privileged to enter.

Beyond Dolls

 Some artists stretch more than just their own wings; they stretch boundaries, opening their medium to allow the entry of previously alien creations. The definition of the doll is always in dispute. Many of the pieces in this book have nothing in common with the playthings traditionally known as dolls. While some of the artists featured openly acknowledge the influence of the dollmaking tradition, and aim to incorporate an aspect of play in their work, many of them were not aware of dolls until their own pieces happened to cross over into that world.

Why are the pieces in this book referred to as dolls? What is it they have in common that places them under this definition? They all represent human form—except for those with animal heads. They are all posable—except for

Plate 112
Kath Lathers,
Listening Spirit,
7 in. (17.8 cm), 1994

those that have bodies sculpted of one piece. Even if we accept the definition "figural art" for these works, some are beyond that definition as well.

In truth, all of the pieces in this book are "beyond dolls." Bearing this realization in mind, though, it is clear that there are pieces that go even further than the more traditional figures that have been explored in the earlier chapters. The artists whose pieces are featured in this chapter are the ones stretching the boundaries and pushing the limits of this already flexible medium. They are creating pieces that may or may not have human forms, that often are a peculiar mixture of human likeness with odd, surprising aspects. Tracy Stilwell's root-headed piece, *Getting to the Root of the Problem* (plate 113), clearly resembles a human form, except for its almost eerie, unnatural head made, ironically, of natural materials. Kath Lathers's *Listening Spirit* (plate 112), created of shells and fabric, is certainly animal-like in its form, but its presence is strongly human, while Betty Nelson-Daniels's *Mockingbird* (plate 123) appears, at first glance, to have nothing in common with most dolls—except for its pose, its costume, and its strong theatricality.

Some seem to clearly fall into other genres; Elisabeth Flueler-Tomamichel's *Without Words* (plate 114) looks like a three-piece sculpture to most people. In fact, it is. It is missing many of the attributes we look for to define a doll. But Flueler-Tomamichel is a doll artist who has created many traditional dolls, and this piece is part of her body of work. Is this a sculpture by a doll artist? Or should her other works be regarded as dolls by a sculptor? With this piece she goes beyond the traditional boundaries of her other dolls, but does that make it no longer a doll? In considering the works in this chapter, vocabulary becomes much more of an issue than it has been previously.

It will escape nobody's notice that eight of the twelve artists in this chapter work in textiles, thinking of their pieces as collagelike expressions of an abstract spirit. While textiles lend themselves readily to the creation of abstract figural images, even those artists who do not share the commonality of the medium share this spiritual, abstract approach.

Tracy Page Stilwell says she is interested in "expressing spirit, sharing a thought, a word, a reminder. . . . I am not interested in replicating the human body perfectly; I'm looking for new ways to represent the body and express spirit." Stilwell comes to dollmaking from a background of quilts and clothing; the common thread linking all her projects is the great creative joy she finds in embellishment. Mixing yarns, beads, threads, wire, and ribbon in rarely used combinations of material and themes is a rewarding pursuit for the artist. "I think my strength lies in my use of color and sense of whimsy," she reflects.

Plate 113
Tracy Page Stilwell,
*Getting to the Root of
the Problem,*
20 in. (50.8 cm), 1991

Stilwell also looks to more unusual elements for embellishment, what she describes as "found objects from nature and people's lives": twigs, roots, feathers, and bones. *Getting to the Root of the Problem* is typical in being made from such natural found objects, yet it goes a step further in having an enormous, entire root for its crowning glory. The piece has a yarn cone base and is made with cotton, leather, roots, twigs, feathers, and beads, with a face sculpted from Fimo. "The idea of using roots came to me while discussing a harvest ritual in which participants made 'dolls' from whole plants, the roots becoming head and hair," she explains. "The root idea stayed with me. I loved the natural wildness in the shape of the roots and branches. I usually have a loose idea when I begin making something," she continues. "If there is a pattern involved, a certain amount of planning is used in the creation of the body. From that point I make it up as I go along. With the root heads, I have developed a construction style for the base, but the rest is developed in the moment."

Whatever she is making, the Rhode Island artist has a message that is at the same time personal and universal. "I see my dolls as a vehicle for the healing I'm doing in my life," she says. "My work is about the practice of being

Plate 114
Elisabeth Flueler-
Tomamichel,
Without Words,
13 in. (33 cm), 10½ in.
(26.7 cm), 12 in.
(30.5 cm), 1992
(Photo: Courtesy of
W. Donald Smith)

brave—speaking my truth. My work has always been a bit off-center, a reflection of my life, perhaps. Most of my ideas sprout from my political and spiritual work, so I often have a theme in my pieces: the bride, liberty, the healer. I came to this particular medium trying to find a spiritual path that made sense to me, and looking, among other things, for a way to support myself."

Even with such admirable aspirations, Stilwell does not lack for a sense of humor in her work, which shines forth in pieces like *It Seemed Like a Good Idea at the Time*. Another wild root-headed doll, this one wears traditional bridal attire, but has a feather in place of one hand and holds tiny babies dangling on a string from another. This element of sharp humor makes even Stilwell's most overt "message pieces" radiate with compassion and spirit.

Like Tracy Stilwell, Kath Lathers imbues her fabric dolls with a sense of humor, albeit it a lighter one. She, too, has been known to use natural found objects in her work, especially in the fragile *Listening Spirit*, which makes use of a stunning shell for the bottom half of its body. "The listening spirit reminds us that listening is made up of two parts: hearing and understanding," explains Lathers about her piece. "One without the other is the worst kind of deafness. Her magic is what balances the two, so that you can know if what you thought you heard is what was actually said."

The shell was a gift from a friend. "The first thing anybody does with a seashell is put it up to her ear to listen," Lathers says. She has made numerous *Listening Spirits* using different kinds of shells, including one where the doll is actually holding a shell to her ear. "I find it's more effective as a piece, though, when it's coming out of the shell itself," Lathers says. The piece has a wire armature that goes through the shell and head, securing it.

Lathers often looks to her own life for the stories of her dolls. A doll called *Mender of Broken Hearts* came directly from a dream in which the artist encountered a beautiful woman who told her she was the mender of broken hearts and would mend Lathers's. Lathers had been suffering for a long time over the breakup of a very close friendship, and felt, upon waking from the dream, "like I had finally accepted losing my friend." She then made the doll, which, in one hand, held a broken heart with stuffing coming out of it. The other hand held a needle and thread, mending the heart.

Also like Tracy Stilwell, Lathers was first a fabric artist, making quilts and two-dimensional fabric pictures. When she begins to dress the dolls, she plays with the fabrics first, cutting different shapes, twisting and draping, tucking and folding until something interesting happens. "I learned a long time ago not to have preconceived notions when I create something," she explains. She uses a lot of upholstery fabrics in the costuming of her dolls, enjoying their rich and tactile quality, the element of weave and the durability.

She also tries to send messages to others through her work. "Often it's not a good idea to tell somebody something directly, because they need to work through it themselves. So I feel better if I give them a piece that's saying what I want them to hear—and hopefully they'll hear it better."

When Swiss artist Elisabeth Flueler-Tomamichel began making *Without Words,* she conceived of the three characters as sending a message to others. "We sometimes point to someone who is different from what we are," she explains. "We mostly think that how we are used to doing things is best. But sometimes, on a holiday far away, perhaps, we realize that we are the 'foreigner,' the 'different.' It depends from which side we look at the facts." The revelation came upon completion of the piece. "I realized that it also showed myself," Flueler-Tomamichel says. "There is the fat, evil one who points to me, saying, 'Everything has to be correct, proportions, anatomy, statement, technique, etc!' The tall, anxious one: 'Are you sure what you do, don't you want to redo, give up?' And the laughing one says: 'Enjoy yourself making dolls, don't worry too much, just have fun and be a little crazy, life is too short to worry!' It's all these questions, sides also, inside of myself, sometimes working very hard one against the other."

The three-piece sculpture, distinguished by its stark whiteness, is not at all typical of Flueler-Tomamichel's work. She is, in fact, an artist who prides herself on her versatility, known for porcelain babies and children, musicians, dancers, sprites, and more abstract or "statement" dolls, like *Without Words.* "I do not like to be fixed to a certain type of doll nor to a size or a specific material. With my first dolls, I just wanted to create something beautiful, but with the years I tried to bring a statement into some special dolls, too. I wanted them to be acting or to be in the middle of a movement." The broad range of her work is key to her love of dollmaking as a medium, and keeps her from ever feeling any monotony. "When I make a doll through which I would like to show a serious idea, there might be a cheeky spirit dancing behind it," she says, "making a mockery of that seriousness!"

The only boredom she ever found came in making porcelain editions, so she soon found herself altering three heads that should have all been the same. She continues to work in porcelain in appreciation of its lasting quality, but also loves making one-of-a-kind directly sculpted dolls, which she creates of Sculpey, Super Sculpey, papier-maché, modeling powder, or other similar substances.

Without Words is a combination of these sculpting media; the heads and hands are Sculpey, while the bodies are an air-dried, sanded modeling powder over wire armatures. The lack of color is intrinsic to their conception. "With these men I tried to speak with sculpture only, leaving away all color, except for their blue eyes," Flueler-Tomamichel says. "It's these two things all three of them— so different in character—have in common."

Both Flueler-Tomamichel's *Without Words* and the fabric figure *Quietness* (plate 115) by Japanese artist Keiko Yamaguchi bear names that oppose sound. Yet both pieces speak articulately to their observers. *Quietness*, a quilted tapestry stitched into a graceful legless figure, poses with its arms seemingly warding off any approach. The face is smooth and colorless, with delicate Japanese features.

Although Yamaguchi lived for several years in New York City, she was born and raised in Japan by parents who managed kimono shops. This early exposure to beautiful fabrics took firm root in the young artist. While she studied oil painting and printmaking in high school and college, she has also collected old fabrics from kimonos and other clothing for more than a decade and, like many doll artists working in cloth, finds these materials an inspiration for her dollmaking. Her resulting pieces are more sculptural and more tightly structured than those of many other fabric doll artists, however. The delicate form of the face is achieved through her method of first forming it from clay, then covering it with silk and painting it with watercolors. The body is formed from cloth, stuffed with various materials. Yamaguchi's cloths include old kimono fabric as well as cottons and other natural fabrics, which she often quilts and hand-embroiders onto her dolls.

When she works, the artist feels closely involved with her materials. "I interact with my materials as I apply clay, shape the clay, sew and apply cloth, and paint a face," she explains. "While reconciling my own rhythm with the rhythm of my materials, I make changes, and while I create a collage out of the flow of time and memory and cloth, I find that the form which I had originally planned gradually disappears, and a new human form appears before my eyes." If often the form is not quite human, as with *Quietness* or more markedly in pieces that are only heads and arms emerging from half-moon-shaped bases, it is always graceful and evocative.

Yamaguchi uses a broad palette of images and ornaments from Eastern and Western cultures. Her fascination with the sights and sounds of many worlds shines forth in her textural figures. "I enjoy spending my free time at local flea markets," she says. "Whenever I travel, I always search for markets.

I look around at various markets for fruit, daily goods, antiques, and second-hand goods. . . . I watch the local people's faces, listen to the laughing voices, touch those goods that have been handed down for generations, and which the earth has created and brought forward. In this way, I can in a sense feel at one with the stream of time, and touch culture with my own skin. I have seen . . . the traditional Japanese silver hair ornaments and antique cloth in Kyoto, the skin from iguana and the vinyl shopping bag that I bought in Mexico, the fragile frame and beautiful ornamental candlestick in Italy, the spices piled up in the form of mountains that I saw and ate in Thailand—all these things have sometimes influenced my dolls and have sometimes become actual parts of my work. . . . In my work I try to express an image that is constantly evolving. While creating an intersection between the past and the present, and between internal and external experiences, I try to express the human condition and way of life."

The human condition is of primary concern to Olly Copal-Boerboom of the Netherlands. Her gray, bowed piece, which she calls *Amnesty International* (plate 116) in homage to the human-rights organization, is the very picture of misery and hopelessness. She says that with this piece she wanted to bring attention to the group's concerns. The textile work is meant to express "the bad situations all over the world," in terms of political and social issues, explains the artist.

While Copal-Boerboom occasionally creates what she refers to as fantasy pieces, her primary concerns are political and social. She says, "My creations are mostly images of reality; I use issues like the Vietnamese boat refugees, Somalia, Amnesty International, Greenpeace, and environmental pollution." Like *Amnesty International,* these pieces are colorless and bleak; many of them are so relentlessly despairing that the viewer's first reaction is to flinch or back away. While they appear to be clearly sculptural, the artist does not hesitate to call them "textile dolls."

Born in the former Dutch East Indies, Copal-Boerboom came to Holland in 1950, where she married and raised a family. Making her children's clothing led

her to decorating the clothing with appliqué and ornaments, which fostered in her a strong interest in design. She pursued this interest through several media—pottery, clay modeling, watercolor painting—but finally found making dolls out of textiles the most satisfying. Over the years she developed her own technique of shaping the dolls' heads out of textile, with needle and thread, much like modeling clay. The dolls' bodies are then loosely draped around a frame of iron wire. The shaping of the heads is the most time-consuming, and most rewarding, task; it can take several days of intensive work. "It's most interesting to model the right expression, in textile with needle and thread," says the artist. "My favorite part of the work is making the head and face—but it's also the most difficult, giving the dolls the right expression."

Because her messages are so overt, Copal-Boerboom begins with a clear idea of what she wants to create. "Before I start I know exactly what to make," she says. "Then I take my fingers into the work with heart and soul."

Grace Forrest, a New Mexico artist with a background in Jungian psychology, uses a different vocabulary to explain what she puts into her work, but she too brings her heart and soul through her fingers into her work. "My dolls are a visual and tactile language for experience I can communicate in no other way," she says.

In 1988, the artist left behind her family and life in Ann Arbor, Michigan, where she was a teacher and part-owner of a bookstore, to travel through the United States for four years. She journeyed "across the land to Oregon, down the West Coast, and finally into the Southwest, coming to rest in New Mexico," Forrest relates. "I have had the opportunity to live in isolated and solitary places, mountaintops, rain forests, and deserts, and out of this experience the figures came to be. They began out of fear and loneliness, and have become my family, my tribe." Forrest's daily companions are her three dogs and an elderly burro, although her daughter and two grandchildren have now followed her to the state.

John Darcy Noble, Curator Emeritus of the Toy Collection of the Museum of the City of New York, in a 1994 article in *Contemporary Doll Magazine*, likened Forrest's art to that of another woman who came to New Mexico. "Her art is of a very feminine kind," Noble wrote, "and I am reminded of another artist, Georgia O'Keeffe. She too forsook her 'other life' for the wilderness, and for a pure, even austere communication with nature. And like Grace's fabric sculpture, Georgia's paintings took on a spiritual intensity entirely of their own." Forrest's figures are fabric-bodied with clay masks and hands, and many of them, like *The Lovers* (plate 117), are wall hangings.

"They begin with the 'mask' of plaster gauze upon which are random layers of modeling paste," Forrest explains. "This is left to dry in the sun or on the wood stove. When it has achieved a certain point of dryness a certain crack will call attention and I begin to carve with a jackknife, following line to line as you would with a drawing. As I work, the story begins and I come to know 'who' is appearing. The story and the face indicate the form of the body, the fabric and enhancement that will express this particular energy. The face and hands are painted with oils and the bodies hand-sewn. Each is one-of-a-kind, though certain archetypal energies repeat."

All of Forrest's figures have a flowing, organic existence. With names like *Dancing Coyote, Wandering Spirit,* and *In Celebration of the First Toad Moon,* they embody both the physical and the inner journey the artist has embarked on—the kind of journey that does not have a final destination. "It remains difficult to put into words," Forrest says, "even after all this time, but a way to say it is that I have followed a need to come into an experiential relationship with 'the God thing,' with Spirit, with the Mystery. I study Native American teachings and Buddhism and in these find wisdom and assistance, but it is the Earth itself that is my greatest teacher, and from the Earth, the elements, and all archetypal form come the dolls."

Lenore Davis's lively fabric sculptures come from her fascination with the universal gesture. Animated and colorful performers, they bring smiles to the viewer. "There is a performance nature in many of the figures," agrees Davis. "They play to the viewer like performers on a stage; others perform ordinary human activities and are caught in their genre postures. I have moved frequently between these two themes, dividing the world into on- and off-stage characters. I am interested in recognizing the comedic element, and strive to make it classic. The dancer and choreographer Alvin Ailey said, 'Dance is a natural outpouring of what you are as a person, your culture, your background, your family, your heritage,' and this speaks to me in the making of figurative sculpture."

Her medium is fabric and paint. "They temper my ideas with their own demands," says Davis. The energetic pieces have aluminum armatures that capture the essence of the movement; the bodies are linen, stuffed with polyester fiberfill. The vibrancy of her figures is achieved by her textile painting technique. "The richly colored surface is a mingling of textile paint and the fabric," explains the Kentucky artist. "The linen is an elegant neutral background, like a miniature canvas, with its natural color and texture breaking through the thin layers of transparent paint. The figures are painted as if for the stage, to be seen at a distance, or as if they were in a painting. Flat color areas are dry-brushed with layers of transparent colors, shadows are painted on, definitions between color areas are soft edge. Patterns are used to express the character of the piece and to contribute to the feeling of movement."

Her inspiration ranges from her own regular exercising to photographs, television, and her basic "interest in gestures, large and small." *One Arm Jump* (plate 118), a playful flax-haired acrobat, is in a position inspired by a dance photo taken by Lois Greenfield and shown in *The New York Times*. Davis likes the performance skill, humor, and physical ability of the clown image, and has several pieces entitled simply *Clown Exercise*, in which the figures execute knee-bends or splits.

Where many artists are trying to express something at once personally and universally spiritual through their dolls, Davis finds that "story within" in a person's physical expression, and endeavors to capture it through depicting a moment of movement. "Every human body tells a story," she reflects. "One only has to see to learn from the gestures and motion how a person is meeting life. Every part of the body is expressive; there are enough bones, muscles, and body variations to provide a lifetime of fascination. I work for making the essence of the movement, to find the gesture that expresses the 'moment' and more. The ordinary motions of daily life are graceful and expressive when isolated as sculpture. The desire to move, to dance, to physically express a feeling

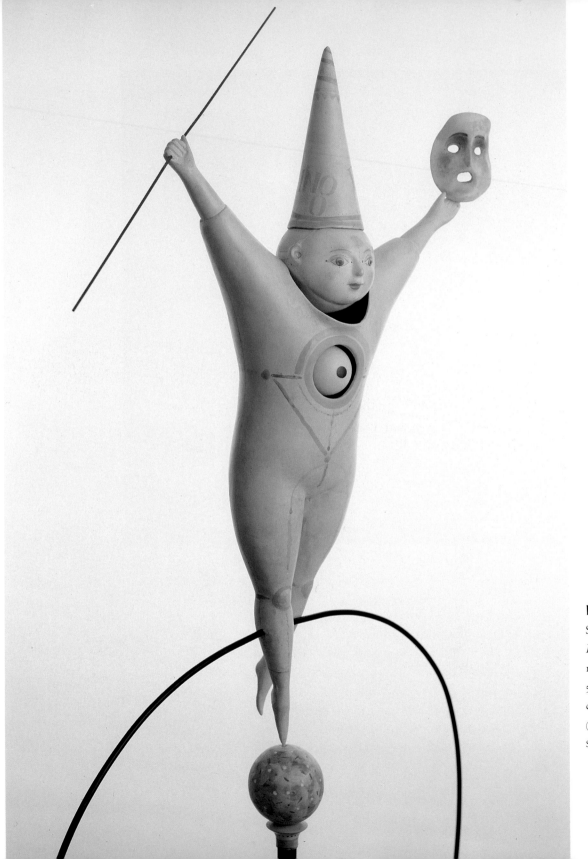

Plate 119
Sylvia Wanke,
Ballerino,
19½ in. (49.5 cm) on
50½-in. (128.3 cm)
column, 1989
(Photo: Courtesy of
Sylvia Wanke)

is the story within, that is what I try to embody in the figures. This search has taken me through many evolutions in form, fabric, and coloration in the fabric sculpture medium in the past twenty-four years. I live vicariously through the small figures," Davis concludes. "I do as much as I can and stretch for more, the figures go further."

Akin to Davis's fabric sculptures in their playful theatrical sensibility are the papier-mâché figures of the German artist Sylvia Wanke. Like Davis, Wanke is fascinated with theater and circus themes and with the acrobats, artists, clowns, and dancers whose being is taken up with the performance of movements. Where Davis's work is also characterized by its use of color, though, Wanke's is distinguished by its lack thereof. The German artist prefers to focus on the sculptural form, keeping her figures free of fabric clothing or any accessories. Their only decoration is occasional lightly painted embellishments, usually in pale pastel colors.

Plate 120
William Wiley,
Jack-in-the-Box,
32 in. (81.3 cm), 1990

Wanke studied sculpture, and considers herself a sculptor. She creates a variety of works, ranging from life-sized sculptures to what she calls small kinetic objects, moving figures she names *Kunst-Spiel Zeug* (artistic toys for adults, by her translation), which include puppets on sticks, climbers, cyclists, balancers, and theater puppets. *Ballerino* (plate 119), says Wanke, "is the smallest of my tall balancers who stand on a thin column on the ground. He shows the crucial moment, when also the second foot is about to rise and the contact with the earth has become as small as possible. But, being an artificial person, he has found his balance forever in this position of extreme effort. By the way," she adds, "it is a real balance. He is standing free on his tiptoe, can turn around and rock to all sides, and you can lift him."

Wanke traces her interest in theater and circus to her year of study at the academy of theater and puppetry in Prague, Czechoslovakia, where she focused on pantomime and set design. She loves to dance and specializes in the Spanish flamenco. She feels a strong link between her work and earlier traditions of theatrical figures. "My figures are kindred both to the types of the commedia dell'arte and to the old German or Czech puppet theater. And as a sculptor,"

she says, "I have been influenced by the work of Oskar Schlemmer, who himself was a sculptor, painter, dancer, and choreographer."

Ballerino is at once light and airy, plump and substantial. The figure could be either male or female. It is caught in an uplifted moment; having achieved its precise pose, it has flung off its neutral face mask to reveal a gentle, rounded face. The only vivid spot on the figure is the ball inset in the middle of its chest, decorated by a bright red central dot. It is like a naked heartthrob exposed to the audience at this moment of delicate balance.

The late William Wiley (1957–1991) was a wildly imaginative, versatile artist with a special love for playthings. His body of work, like that of Elisabeth Flueler-Tomamichel, includes beautiful women, endearing children, well-known characters (always seen through his own slightly quirky vision), and more serious, sometimes frightening figures. The grinning *Jack-in-the-Box* (plate 120) was made late in his career, in 1990, after Wiley had already created his own fresh versions of nursery characters like Humpty-Dumpty, looking in open-mouthed horror and anger at a broken egg, dolls and toys for Maurice Sendak's film of *The Nutcracker,* and a set of three bakers and the "pudding boy" from Sendak's book *In the Night Kitchen.*

Some of Wiley's work has been described by Louise Fecher in an article in *Dolls* magazine ("Wiley in Wonderland," September/October 1988) as "a collision of expert doll artistry and imagination gone amok." Whatever the soft-spoken young artist made, he thought of it as light-hearted. "Even the scary ones are absurd and silly," he told Fecher in 1988. Many of his dolls—one could actually say all his work—grew from his love of old toys, fairy tales, and children's books.

His sister, Nancy Wiley (see "Women of the Imagination" and "Fantasies") explains that in making the *Jack-in-the-Box,* her brother was trying to make dolls that looked like old toys, "but to add a little something different to them. He looked at Punch-and-Judy puppets for inspiration for the face of this *Jack-in-the-Box,*" she recalls. The inspiration is clear in Jack's big chin and big nose. To achieve the look of age, Wiley distressed the figure's porcelain eyes with cracks, and used distressed velvet for the clothes. He painted and then weathered the box, and sanded the porcelain face until it no longer bore the look of the medium. The hat is made of ribbons sewn together; the hands are simply wire covered with velvet. The letters on all sides of the box spell out Jack. "Bill wanted to make a piece that was somewhere between a doll and a toy," explains his sister.

After this *Jack-in-the-Box*, which is almost menacing, with its oversized chin and overbearing grin, Wiley went on to make several other jack-in-the-boxes with more openly frightening themes. Marie Antoinette springs out of her box with a piece of cake on her head; a red devil carries away a young pale maiden. In his brief, rich career, William Wiley coaxed pieces from his imaginative dreamland. His disarming creations came forth from dreams of childlike delight, but also from nightmares of menacing absurdity.

California artist Tammy Lavanty says she is "charmed by the world of the illogical and the absurd," and sees her work as "a playground for my imagination." A fiber artist who also makes quilts, Lavanty's first medium was ceramics, but she explains that she always worked it as though it were fabric—"draping, rolling, tucking, and working textures into it." A friend who was making cloth dolls gave Lavanty the idea to try the same. She immediately realized that fabric was her natural medium.

"I'm intrigued by the tactile appeal, the softness and pliability," she says. "Fabric is a sensuous hands-on medium filled with magical qualities and infinite possibilities. My work combines every different fabric, fiber, and color imaginable. Colors and textures begin to take on a life of their own as they mix and mingle. Each new piece of cloth or trim brings with it dazzling suggestions."

Lavanty's pieces are bright, gay, and fun-filled. She covers them with a colorful variety of images, shapes, trims, textures, and baubles. *The Baby Angel* (plate 121) is a typically rich collage, with added significance for the artist, who created it while she was pregnant. "*The Baby Angel* is a strong maternal figure who cares for and watches over the children," explains Lavanty. "She is made from a variety of fabrics, some of which are hand-painted, and is embellished with beads and trims. She cradles a baby figure on one arm. I was pregnant while creating this piece, so I myself was filled with thoughts of providing a secure nest where children could thrive. I carried all these feelings into the process of creating this piece."

Usually, though, the California artist doesn't think much about symbolism as she works. "It is always there," she admits, "but usually I get caught up in the excitement of the piece. As I work, colors and textures interrelate and direct themselves, taking on a life of their own. I start with a fairly clear image, which I then begin to refine by sketching and visualizing each new stage of development." She sees one of the trademarks of her dolls as their asymmetry; often a doll will have just one wing, or one eye open and one closed. The asymmetry appeals to Lavanty's personal sense of design and expresses a figure's dual nature.

While *The Baby Angel* has two fairly similar sides, the asymmetry is expressed in her side-closing robe.

"Fabric is an important means for my emotional expression," Lavanty reflects. Her dolls exude spontaneity and fun, which the artist finds in full measure in her work. "It's a playful, uncomplicated place which allows me to create fanciful creatures and to instill life into a piece of cloth," she says.

For the German artist Irmgard Wilhelm, her fabric dolls emerge from the mood she is in as she creates. "I usually do not have a specific picture in mind," she notes, "It just develops and grows while I am working on it." She first makes the bodies: the head, torso, and limbs, as well as the hands, fingers, and nose, are usually made from cotton, which she bunches and wraps together. She covers all the individual parts with a material of a base color, then sews them together to build a body. "The face gets its expression through additional applications and embroidery," Wilhelm explains. "Mouths and eyes are also created with embroidery, and the nose is sewn on. I compose the hairstyle with a sense of fun and fantasy, using knotted strips of material or wool threads, or I sew material in pleats very closely together. I usually adapt the dress out of something I've bought in the flea market." To make the face, Wilhelm waits until the body is finished. "Then I spread a multitude of materials around me," says the artist, "and from this pile I select pieces that 'smile' at me to make a face of them."

Wilhelm traces her interest in making dolls back to an early childhood orthopedic problem, which forced her to spend a year in the hospital when she was three years old. "Since I could not explore the world by walking like other children," she recalls, "I developed manual dexterity with the help of my mother. While forced to stay in bed, I busied myself making figures out of pieces of material and colorful handkerchiefs by tying knots in them. These figures kept me company and I talked to them. I refused to play with the toys provided by the hospital." Once she was allowed to return home, the child learned a great deal more about sewing from her mother, who was a seamstress.

The interest in art stayed with her; she pursued drawing and painting as she grew older, but once pregnant with her son, she found herself designing and making dolls with heads and limbs of Plasticine. Eventually she started exploring other materials, and came back to her love of fabric both for dollmaking and for designing embroidered wall hangings, which she now pursues as well. "Embroidery is a meditative and calming activity," muses Wilhelm.

Her wall-hangings are often inspired by her favorite artists, Picasso,

Chagall, and Nolde. But, as with dollmaking, she begins by playing with the materials to see what will emerge. "In that way the most inconspicuous scrap may conjure up a picture in my mind." When she began to create the doll she calls *Without* (plate 122), she knew only that she wanted to make an "all-white doll, with friendly and light features." The figure mixes handkerchief linen, cotton laces, and a fabric embroidered in a peasant style. The sock fingers are unnaturally long; the prominent nose is three-dimensional. Long hair is suggested by a single long lock of curly black wool. The piece is clearly a female figure, yet a most loosely constructed one, which seems to have formed itself of its own accord. "The creative process is similar to dreaming," says Wilhelm, "I cannot influence my unconscious nor the course of the story told in my dream."

The exotic Mockingbirds of Betty Nelson-Daniels make no pretense of being human figures. They are clearly birds, carefully constructed, extravagantly costumed in leathers, suedes, and velvets, and posed in dramatic, often swashbuckling attitudes. Some are dancers; some are simply theatrical figures. One series is dressed to represent Native Americans, bedecked in thickly feathered costumes. Each mockingbird is a rich harmony of colors and textures. "Mockingbirds originated from a conglomeration of fanciful trimmings collected over a span of ten years," notes the Canadian artist. "Each figure is designed from a variety of colored and textured materials spontaneously placed, creating a completely unique piece each time."

Nelson-Daniels describes the *Mockingbird* shown here (plate 123) as being "in a dramatic pose, wings spread, ready to lift off." A mere seven inches high, the compact, vividly colored *Mockingbird* is made of wire, leather, snakeskin, and feathers. "To those who view them, they possess dramatic qualities, mimicking vestiges of human attitudes," their creator notes. She credits her travels to the Caribbean as playing a strong part in her aesthetic inspiration: "Traveling to the Caribbean and staying for a period of time had a direct influence on my work. I enjoyed the freedom of dance and costume throughout the island. A warm carnival spirit prevailed." There is certainly a carnival spirit to Nelson-Daniels's creations, but there is a tight elegance of form, as well, that lends them a sophistication and cosmopolitan air and distances them from the primitiveness of much island art.

The Mockingbirds have found favor in art galleries throughout the United States and Canada and have been commissioned by performing arts groups such as the Pittsburgh Opera, the National Ballet of Canada,

Plate 122
Irmgard Wilhelm,
Without,
39 in. (99.1 cm), 1993

and the Canadian Stratford Shakespeare Festival to serve as thematic elements. Nelson-Daniels says that "My aspiration for the future is to continue developing Mockingbird designs, always striving to create amusing and wondrous sculptures more outrageous than yet achieved."

The Mockingbirds are certainly "beyond dolls." What is it that gives them a place in this book? They are, as John Darcy Noble wrote of them in *Contemporary Doll Magazine* (February 1993) "the outer limits" of dollmaking. More than any creation featured here, they raise the question of what makes a doll.

Usually books about dolls begin with the *Webster's Dictionary* definition of the word. It seems right, somehow, to end this book by looking at the definition, having now looked closely at a very broad range of dolls. *Webster's* says a doll is "A small-scale figure of a human being, used especially as a child's plaything." Most of us are accustomed to this idea of dolls as playthings. Usually, they are meant for a child's amusement, but clearly none of the dolls in this book were made to be children's toys. They are, however, meant to be playthings—for adults, who play very differently than children, but who do need to play, whether through the creation or the appreciation of their toys.

The dollmaker and teacher Elinor Peace Bailey argues vehemently for calling a doll a doll; her assertion is that the aspect of play in a doll is intrinsic to the object, and to the emotional and aesthetic experience the artist and viewer has of the piece. "Play," she wrote in her 1990 book *Mother Plays with Dolls*, "is the very center of the creative act." John Darcy Noble has long stood by his early definition of what constitutes a doll (*Contemporary Doll Magazine*, May 1993), and it is perhaps his long-tested understanding that best sums up the explorations this book has taken.

"A doll," Noble wrote, "is a plaything, and its physical attributes are irrelevant. Its qualification depends on your definition of play, but, to my mind, play is a natural human function. The very making of a doll can be play, and so can the collecting of dolls, the preserving and displaying of dolls, the cherishing, and, above all, the sheer thrill and delight in the possession of dolls. All this, to my mind, is an exalted form of play."

Exalted, yes. Through the creation of dolls, artists are discovering a new way to celebrate the human form, imagination and experience, and the endless possibilities of artistic expression.

Plate 123
Betty Nelson-Daniels,
Mockingbird,
7 in. (17.8 cm), 1994

Glossary

Armature A framework serving as a supporting core in a doll's body, usually metal, wire, or wood.

Bisque Unglazed porcelain with a matte finish.

Cernit A polymer clay from Germany characterized by its waxlike look that gives the feeling of a warm, fleshlike translucence. It can be sculpted like clay and cured in boiling water as well as in a home oven.

Fimo A polymer material available in small colored blocks that make it easy to mix colors and achieve various shades of flesh tones. May be cured in a home oven.

Fired (or Cured) A term applied to a ceramic product heated in a kiln or oven for the purpose of hardening, binding pigment, or glazing its surface.

Glaze A glasslike finish applied to pottery and porcelain.

Hydrostone A plasterlike material resembling dental plaster that is used for making molds of teeth. It is also used for interior architectural moldings. Doll artists like its hardness and durability.

Limited-edition Doll A doll that is one of a numbered, finite edition.

Mold A hollow form, usually metal or plaster, into which porcelain slip, melted wax, or another liquid is poured; also used for malleable materials, such as porcelain clay or composition, which are pressed to shape doll heads or other body parts.

Paperclay A modeling material made from paper pulp, water, talc, starch, volcanic ash, and preservatives. It has the advantage of drying in open air while being extremely durable. It is considered the most versatile material as it can be sculpted wet or dry.

Papier-maché A material made from shredded paper and ground paper pulp combined with water and, sometimes, glue.

Plasticine An oil-based clay that cannot be hardened, but is used for fine sculpture because it can be shaped and buried in wet plaster to make molds.

Polyform Another term for Sculpey.

Polymer Clays By-products of industrial engineering that were originally conceived for design prototypes and models. Types include Sculpey, Super Sculpey, Fimo, and Cernit.

Poured-wax Doll A doll with a head and sometimes limbs made from wax that is poured into a mold in successive layers.

Sculpey A white, nontoxic, resin-based plastic material that has most of the attributes of Plasticine modeling clay and can also be fired in a home oven.

Super Sculpey Resembles Sculpey but is harder than Sculpey after firing. It also comes in several flesh tones and has a waxier surface appearance than the granular Sculpey.

Terra-cotta A water-based ceramic clay that is a mixture of ground earth and clay.

The Artists

Malou Ancelin
96 bis rue Porte Poitevine
37600 Loches, France

Martha Armstrong-Hand
575 Worcester Drive
Cambria, CA 93428

Janie Ashcraft
Highway North, Box 1429
Qulin, MO 63961

Roxanne Becker
3385 Sam Rayburn Run
Carrollton, TX 75007

Gina Bellous
3629 Helms Avenue
Culver City, CA 90232

Akira Blount
P.O. Box 87
Bybee, TN 37713

Stephanie Blythe and
Susan Snodgrass
217 North Washington Street
Havre de Grace, MD 21078

Martha Boers and
Marianne Reitsma
1890 Parkside Drive, Pickering,
Ontario L1V 3S4, Canada

Chris Boston
29 Cormorant Crescent
Peregian Beach, Queensland
Australia 4573

Anna Avigail Brahms
116 Thorndike Street
Cambridge, MA 02141

Elizabeth Brandon
5916 West Fifty-third Street
Mission, KS 66202

Uta Brauser
873 Broadway, No. 4B
New York, NY 10003

Patricia Ryan Brooks
P.O. Box 1290
Summerton, SC 29148-1290

Barbara Buysse
9630 Almena Road
Kalamazoo, MI 49009

Mary Alice Byerly
1497 Roslyn Road
Grosse Point, MI 48236

Beth Cameron
1000 Washington Avenue
Oakmont, PA 15139

Christa Canzio
Ravenspurgerstra. 41
86150 Augsburg, Germany

Jane Cather
P.O. Box 1073
Carmel Valley, CA 93924

Antonette Cely
P.O. Box 52043
Atlanta, GA 30355

Lois Clarkson
P.O. Box 28
Buckingham, PA 18912

Holly Conrad
84 East River Bend Road
Fredericksburg, VA 22407

Olly Copal-Boerboom
53 Rozengaard, 5283 GE Boxtel
The Netherlands

Van Craig
417 West Forty-sixth Street
New York, NY 10036

Jodi and Richard Creager
105 Berryman Street
Grass Valley, CA 95945

Paul Crees and Peter Coe
124 Alma Road
Bournemouth BH9 1AL
Dorset, England

Edna Dali
17A Hatayasim Street
Ra'anana 43264, Israel

Jane Davies
Amber, The Street
Walberton Nr. Arundel
West Sussex BN18 0PH, England

Lenore Davis
655 Nelson Place
Newport, KY 41071

Brigitte Deval
Podere Casanova
53020 Trequanda
Siena, Italy

Jacques Dorier
93 Shirley Street
Winthrop, MA 02152

Susan Dunham
36429 Row River Road
Cottage Grove, OR 97424

Pat Eagan
1119 Corvallis Drive
San Jose, CA 95120

Terry Lynn Eaton
18 Elwyn Road
Portsmouth, NH 03801

Helen Facto
630 Oakton
Evanston, IL 60202

Margaret Finch
106 Liberty Avenue
New Rochelle, NY 10805

Marta Finch-Kozlosky
9 Catamount Lane
Old Bennington, VT 05201

Dan Fletcher
4761 Broadway
New York, NY 10034

Marla Florio
24373 Fairway Hills Drive
Novi, MI 48374

Elisabeth Flueler-Tomamichel
Bodenacherstrasse 87
CH-8121 Benglen, Switzerland

Grace Forrest
7 Gordon Road
Los Lunas, NM 87031

Mary Ellen Frank
P.O. Box 021137
Juneau, AK 99802

June Goodnow
2324 Ashley Drive
The Village, OK 73120

Scott Gray
1101 Seventeenth Avenue
Seattle, WA 98122

Lynn Haney
2211 University Street
Lubbock, TX 79410

Clark Hanford
151 Hills Point Road
Westport, CT 06880

Janis Harris
23 Pohutukawa Avenue
Cockle Bay, Howick
Auckland, New Zealand

Héloise
18 rue Guillard
44100 Nantes, France

Paula Hemsley
301 Shenks Lane
Millersville, PA 17551

Linda Horn
HC-64, Box 222
Trout Run, PA 17771

Dorothy Hoskins
1411 Mary Ann Street
Fairbanks, AK 99701

Maggie Iacono
2 Raymond Circle
Downingtown, PA19335

Linda Kertzman
37 West Main Street
Morris, NY 13808

Virginia Killmore
4168 Bussey Road
Syracuse, NY 13215

Helen Kish
10253 West Geddes Circle
Littleton, CO 80127

Jutta Kissling
Oettingenstrasse 4
80538 Munich, Germany

Gail Lackey
11716 Emerald Road
Nampa, ID 83686

Michael Langton
P.O. Box 1122
North Hampton, NH 03862

Kath Lathers
37220 Eight Mile
Farmington, MI 48335

Tammy Lavanty
1495 West Ninth Street, No. 603
Upland, CA 91786

Lisa Lichtenfels
P.O. Box 90537
Springfield, MA 01139

Gretchen Lima
1419 South Twentieth Street
Sheboygan, WI 53081

Gabriele Lipp
Lange Strasse 2
87541 Bad Oberdorf, Germany

Ann McNichols
824 Fifth Avenue South, Suite 6
Naples, FL 33940

Michele Malpica
Isinglass Studio
Height of Land Road
Canaan, NH 03741

Lorna Miller
5130 La Honda Road
El Sobrante, CA 94820-1471

Anne Mitrani
51 rue du Théâtre
75015 Paris, France

Jocelyn Mostrom
16311 Black Rock Road
Darnestown, MD 20874

Bill Nelson
107 East Cary Street
Richmond, VA 23219

Betty Nelson-Daniels
233½ McIntosh Street
Scarborough, Ontario M1N 3Z2
Canada

Susanna Oroyan
3270 Whitbeck Boulevard
Eugene, OR 97405

Kazuyo Oshima
c/o Solange Strawczynski,
A.P.P.C.
12 rue de la Marne
86000 Poitiers, France

Hal Payne
1017 North Twelfth Street
Coeur d'Alene, ID 83814

Harry Perzyk
2860 Chiplay Street
Sacramento, CA 95826

Marilyn Phillippi
R.D. 2, Box 351
Homer City, PA 15748

Carole Piper
73 Fairlawn Drive
East Grinstead
Sussex RH19 1NS, England

Jeff Redford
3912 Willowcrest Avenue
North Hollywood, CA 91604

Kathy Redmond
319 Wright Avenue
Kingston, PA 18704

Paul Robins
Box 28, Site 14, R.R. #1
Gabriola Island
British Columbia V0R 1X0
Canada

Beverly Roessel
1099 Peter Anderson Road
Burlington, WA 98233

Alexander and Marina Royzman
570 Fort Washington Avenue,
No. 2B
New York, NY 10033

Karin Schmidt
Lindenseestrabe 9
65428 Russelsheim-
Konigstadten, Germany

Rotraut Schrott
Spitzingrasse 1
8001 Baldham, Germany

Nerissa Shaub
5295 Centennial Trail
Boulder, CO 80303

Tracy Page Stilwell
39 Hall Street
Newport, RI 02840

E. J. Taylor
6 Layer Gardens
Acton W3 9PR
London, England

Robert Tonner
Kripplebush Road
Stone Ridge, NY 12484

Carol Trobe
116 Mainsail Drive
Grayslake, IL 60030

Ken Von Essen
305 Emerald Street
Redondo Beach, CA 90277

Kathryn Walmsley
8041 Shady Road
Oldenburg, IN 47036

Nancy Walters
690 Trinity Court
Longwood, FL 32750

Sylvia Wanke
Gebelbergstrasse 22
D70 199 Stuttgart, Germany

Charlene Westling
3228 NW Alice Drive
Topeka, KS 56618

Faith Wick
4800 Amelia Island Parkway,
Suite B108
Amelia Island, FL 32034

Nancy Wiley
300 Observer Highway,
Fifth Floor
Hoboken, NJ 07030

Irmgard Wilhelm
Tegernseer Landstrasse 19a
D81539 Munich, Germany

Peter Wolf
Leistenstrasse 1
97082 Würzburg, Germany

R. John Wright
15 West Main Street
Cambridge, NY 12816

Keiko Yamaguchi
1316-11 Kojikadai Haibara-cho
Uda-gun, Nara 633-02, Japan

Fawn Zeller
8825 East Ren Place
Inverness, FL 34450

Bibliography

Books

Many books have been published on the history of dolls. There are also many how-to books for people who would like to try their hand at dollmaking. This bibliography is limited to books that feature, or at least include, the work of contemporary doll artists, as well as how-to books written by artists featured in this book.

Anderton, Johanna Gast. *The Collector's Encyclopedia of Cloth Dolls.* Des Moines: Wallace-Homestead Book Company, 1984.

Bahar, Ann. *Santa Dolls.* Cumberland, Md.: Hobby House Press, 1992.

Bailey, Elinor Peace. *Mother Plays with Dolls.* McLean, Va.: EPM, 1990.

Baten, Lea. *Japanese Dolls: The Image and the Motif.* Rutland, Vt.: Charles E. Tuttle Company, 1986.

Brooks, Patricia Ryan. *Babes in Wood: An Introduction to Doll Carving.* (Patricia Ryan Brooks, P.O. Box 1290, Summerton, S.C. 29148-1290.)

Bullard, Helen. *The American Doll Artist.* Vol. 1. Boston: Charles T. Branford, 1965. Vol. 2. Kansas City, Mo.: Athena, 1975.

——. *Dorothy Heizer.* New York: National Institute of American Doll Artists, 1972.

——. *Faith Wick: Doll Maker Extraordinaire.* Cumberland, Md.: Hobby House Press, 1986.

——. *My People in Wood.* Cumberland, Md.: Hobby House Press, 1984.

Cely, Antonette. *Cloth Dollmaking.* (Antonette Cely, P.O. Box 52043, Atlanta, Ga. 30355.)

Cochran, Dewees. *As If They Might Speak.* Santa Cruz, Calif.: Paperweight Press, 1979. (Dewees Cochran Museum, R.F.D. No. 1, Royce Hill Rd., Orwell, Vt. 05760.)

Coleman, Dorothy S., Elizabeth A. Coleman, and Evelyn J. Coleman. *The Collector's Encyclopedia of Dolls.* Vol. II. New York: Crown Publishers, 1986.

Directory to Limited Edition Collectible Stores. (Collectors' Information Bureau, 2420 Burton SE, Grand Rapids, Mich. 49546.)

Erikson, Rolf, and Faith Wick. *Sculpting Little People.* 2 vols. Oneonta, N.Y.: Seeley Ceramic Services, 1988.

Fainges, Marjory. *The Encyclopedia of Australian Dolls.* Cincinnati: Seven Hills Book Distributors, 1994.

Forek-Schmahl, Marion. *Kunstobjekt Puppe.* Weingarten, Germany: Kunsterverlag Weingarten GmbH, 1990. (German-language edition only.)

Goodfellow, Caroline. *The Ultimate Doll Book.* New York: Dorling Kindersley, 1993.

Hand, David. *Martha Armstrong-Hand's Living Dolls.* Cumberland, Md.: Hobby House Press, 1983.

Lasky, Kathryn. *The Eyelight and the Shadow.* New York: Scribner's, 1982.

Laury, Jean Ray. *Dollmaking: A Creative Approach.* New York: Von Nostrand Reinhold, 1970.

Lavitt, Wendy. *American Folk Dolls.* New York: Alfred A. Knopf, 1982.

——. *The Knopf Collector's Guide to Dolls.* New York: Alfred A. Knopf, 1983.

Lentz, Mary Jane. *The Stuff of Dreams.* New York: Museum of the American Indian, Heye Foundation, 1986.

McFadden, Sybil. *Fawn Zeller's Porcelain Dollmaking Techniques.* Cumberland, Md.: Hobby House Press, 1984.

McKinley, Robert. *Dollmaking: One Artist's Approach.* (Nelson/McKinley Books, 107 East Cary St., Richmond, VA 23219), 1991.

——. *Sculpting Dolls in Paperclay.* Livonia, Mich.: Scott Publications, 1994.

National Institute of American Doll Artists. *The Art of the Doll.* (M. Barrie, Route 1, Box 9640, Loomis Hill Rd., Waterbury Center, Vt. 05677), 1992.

Oroyan, Susanna. *Dollmaker's Notebook: Working with Sculpey.* Eugene, Oreg.: Fabricat Designs, 1983.

——. *Dollmaker's Notebook: Working with Paperclay.* Eugene, Oreg.: Fabricat Designs, 1992.

——. *Dollmaker's Notebook: Working with Polymer Clays.* Eugene, Oreg.: Fabricat Designs, 1993.

——. *Fantastic Figures.* Lafayette, Calif.: C & T Publishing, 1994.

Oroyan, Susanna, and Carol-Lynn Rössel Waugh. *Contemporary Artist*

216

Dolls: A Guide for the Collector. Cumberland, Md.: Hobby House Press, 1986.

Perkins, Myla, ed. *Black Dolls: An Identification and Value Guide, 1820–1991.* Paducah, Ky.: Collector Books, 1992.

Purlsey, Joan Muyskens, and Karen Bischoff. *The World's Most Beautiful Dolls.* New York: Konecky and Konecky, 1994.

Revi, A. Christian, ed. *Spinning Wheel's Complete Book of Dolls.* 2 vols. Hanover, Pa.: Everybody's Press, 1975.

Richter, Joachim. *Kunstlerpuppen.* 3 vols. Munich: Magica Lanterna Press, 1986, 1989. (German-language edition only.)

Rustam, Phillis A. *Cloth Dolls.* South Brunswick and New York: A. S. Barnes and Company; London: Thomas Yoseloff Ltd., 1980.

Schrott, Rotraut. *Making Original and Portrait Dolls in Cernit.* Cumberland, Md.: Hobby House Press, 1993.

Sorensen, Lewis. *Doll Scrapbook.* Alhambra, Calif.: Thor Publications, 1976.

The Best of Doll Reader. 3 vols. Cumberland, Md.: Hobby House Press.

Waugh, Carol-Lynn Rössel. *Petite Portraits: Miniature Dolls by Contemporary American Artists.* Cumberland, Md.: Hobby House Press, 1982.

Publications

Cieslik's Puppen Magazine
Theodor-Heuss-Strasse 3D-5170
Julich, Germany
(GERMAN-LANGUAGE EDITION ONLY.)

Collectible Dolls and Miniatures International
P.O. Box 1023 Tweed Heads
New South Wales 2485
Australia

Contemporary Doll Collector
Scott Publications
30595 Eight Mile Road
Livonia, MI 48152

Doll Crafter
Scott Publications
30595 Eight Mile Road
Livonia, MI 48152

Doll Designs
House of White Birches
306 East Parr Road
Berne, IN 46711

Doll Forum Japan
3-27-57 Kumegawa
Higasimurayama, Tokyo 189
Japan
(JAPANESE-LANGUAGE EDITION ONLY.)

Doll Reader
Cumberland Publishing
6405 Flank Drive
Harrisburg, PA 17112

Dollmaker's Journal
2900 West Anderson Lane,
No. 20-150
Austin, TX 78757

Dollmaking: Projects and Plans
Jones Publishing
121 North Main Street
P.O. Box 337
Iola, WI 54945

Dolls, The Collector's Magazine
Collector Communications
Corporation
170 Fifth Avenue
New York, NY 10010

International Doll World
House of White Birches
306 East Parr Road
Berne, IN 46711

Newsletter of the Association for People Who Like to Play with Dolls
1779 East Avenue
Hayward, CA 94145

Puppen & Spielzeug
Verlag Puppen & Spielzeug
Stresemannstrasse 20-22
47051 Duisburg, Germany
(GERMAN-LANGUAGE EDITION ONLY.)

Sources

❧ Organizations for Artists and Collectors

British Doll Artists Association
June Rose Gale, President
49 Cromwell Road
Beckenham, Kent BR3 4LL
England
(*Juried membership, exhibits*)

Doll Artisan Guild
Seeley Ceramics Services
9 River Street
Oneonta, NY 13820
(*Courses, exhibits, magazine, annual meeting*)

International Dollmakers Association (IDMA)
Lucille Gerrard
16770 Wilderness Court
Jackson, CA 95642
(*Newsletter, annual conference*)

National Institute of American Doll Artists (NIADA)
Robert Tonner,
Standards Chairman
Kripplebush Road
Stone Ridge, NY 12484
(*Juried artist membership, patron membership, newsletter, annual conference*)

National Original Doll Artists of Australia
Susie Pitt, President
30 Killarney Avenue
Robina, Queensland 4226
Australia

Original Doll Artist Council of America (ODACA)
Sandra Justiss, President
720 Maplewood Avenue
Ambridge, PA 15003
(*Juried artist membership, patron membership, newsletter, annual conference*)

United Federation of Doll Clubs (UFDC)
10920 North Ambassador Drive
Kansas City, MO 64153
(*Local collector clubs, magazine, national and regional conferences*)

❧ Museums Displaying Dolls by Contemporary Artists

Doll collections exist in numerous museums throughout the world; this list focuses only on those collections that include dolls by contemporary artists. This list is by no means inclusive, however, as museums are constantly in the process of acquiring new pieces.

United States

Alfred P. Sloan Museum
1221 E. Kearsley Street
Flint, MI 48503

Denver Museum of Miniatures, Dolls and Toys
1880 Gaylord Street
Denver, CO 80206

The Dewees Cochran Foundation Museum
R.F.D. #1, Royce Hill Road
Orwell, VT 05760

The Enchanted World Doll Museum
615 North Main
Mitchell, SD 57301

The Hobby City Doll and Toy Museum
1238 South Beach Boulevard
Anaheim, CA 92804

The Carole and Barry Kaye Museum of Miniatures
5900 Wilshire Boulevard
Los Angeles, CA 90036

The McCurdy Historical Doll Museum
246 North One Hundred East Street
Provo, UT 84601

The Museum of the City of New York
1220 Fifth Avenue at 103d Street
New York, NY 10029

The Margaret Woodbury Strong Museum
One Manhattan Square
Rochester, NY 14607

The Toy and Miniature Museum of Kansas City
5253 Oak Street
Kansas City, MO 64112

Wenham Historical Association and Museum
132 Main Street
Wenham, MA 01984

The Rosalie Whyel Museum of Doll Art
1116-108th Avenue NE
Bellevue, WA 98004

**Yesteryears Doll and
Toy Museum**
Main and River Streets
Sandwich, MA 02563

Europe

**Bethnal Green Museum
of Childhood**
Cambridge Heath Road E21
London, England

Musée des Arts Décoratifs
107 rue du Rivoli
75001 Paris, France

Musée de Poupées
3 rue de Trente
56120 Josselin, France

Coburg Puppen Museum
Ruckerstrasse 2-3
8630 Coburg, Germany

Deutsche Spielzeug Museum
Beethovenstrasse 10
96515 Sonneberg, Germany

Hessiches Puppenmuseum
Park Promenade
Hanau Wilhelmsbad, Germany

Sasha Morgenthaler Museum
20-22 Barengsse
Zurich, Switzerland

Puppenmuseum
Schwarzhorngasse 136
8260 Stein am Rhein
Switzerland

 Dealers

Alabama

Enchanted Attic
3716 Lorna Road
River Oaks Village,
Riverchase
Birmingham, AL 35216
(205) 988-3716

Alaska

We Two
1411 Mary Ann Street
Fairbanks, AL 99701
(907) 452-2688

Arizona

Children of the Artist
16719 East Palisades Boulevard,
Suite 201
Fountain Hills, AZ 85268
(602) 939-4578

Arkansas

Melodys Choices
NW Arkansas Mall
Fayetteville, AR 72703
(501) 521-5480

California

The Artist's Doll
510 Waverly Street
Palo Alto, CA 94301
(415) 324-1300

Best Friends Collectables
17141 Marilla Street
Northridge, CA 91325
(818) 993-8873

**Dollsville Dolls and
Bearsville Bears**
461 North Palm Canyon Drive
Palm Springs, CA 92262
(619) 325-2241

Lee's Collectibles
P.O. Box 19133
Sacramento, CA 95819
(916) 457-4308

Pretty Woman Collectibles
12190½ Ventura Boulevard,
Suite 381
Studio City, CA 91604
(818) 763-5058

Colorado

Rainbow Connection I
7657 West Eighty-eighth
Avenue
Arvada, CO 80005
(303) 424-3988

Rainbow Connection II
201 University Boulevard,
Suite 101
Denver, CO 80206
(303) 393-1443

Connecticut

The Country Doll House
7 Sodom Road
Canaan, CT 06018
(203) 824-7739

Olde Towne Doll Shoppe
227 Main Street
P.O. Box 78
Wethersfield, CT 06109
(203) 563-3049

Florida

**Celia's and Susan's Dolls
and Collectibles**
800 East Hallandale Beach
Boulevard
Hallandale, FL 33009
(305) 458-0661

**The Little People
Company**
P.O. Box 311
Bristol, FL 32321
(904) 643-2424

Patt & Billy's
3045 North Federal
Highway
Fort Lauderdale, FL 33306
(305) 568-9066

Georgia

Cabbages and Kings
6330 Lawrenceville Highway
Tucker, GA 30084
(404) 934-0055

Magic in Medium
3299 Ashburton Chase
Roswell, GA 30075
(404) 552-8669

Illinois

Dolls . . . Etcetera
3605 Pebble Beach Road
Northbrook, IL 60062
(708) 564-3543

**Gigi's Dolls & Sherry's
Teddy Bears**
6029 North Northwest
Highway
Chicago, IL 60631
(312) 594-1540

Heirloom Dolls and Treasures
226 South Washington Street
Naperville, IL 60540
(708) 717-5995

Jan Dolls
1326 State Street
Springfield, IL 62704
(217) 523-4880

Indiana

Antique & Modern Doll Shop
136 North Second Street
Decatur, IN 46733
(219) 728-2377

Turner Doll Shop
4743 East State Road 46
Bloomington, IN 47401
(812) 336-5210

Louisiana

Oh Susannah
528 Saint Peter Street
New Orleans, LA 70116
(504) 586-8701

Maine

Petit Mon Ami
R.R. #3, Box 319
Wiscassett, ME 04578
(207) 882-6656

Porter Emporium
P.O. Box 5, Route 25
Porter, ME 04068
(207) 625-8989

Maryland

Galerie Les Enfants
(street address not available)
Glenwood, MD
(410) 795-0772

Massachusetts

Baby Me
730 Boston Road (Route 3A)
Billerica, MA 01821
(508) 667-1187

Eden Gallery Ltd.
P.O. Box 6
North Quincy, MA 02171
(617) 472-3911

Forever Dolls
13 Providence Road
Sutton, MA 01590
(508) 865-0779

McKay's Secret Garden
P.O. Box 52
Weymouth, MA 02190
(617) 337-2248

Mann Gallery
39 Newbury Street, Suite 211
Boston, MA 02116
(617) 696-6666

Pick & Poke
10 Still Drive
Hudson, MA 01749
(508) 562-6671

Michigan

Forever Friends
422 East Michigan Avenue,
Suite 2
Saline, MI 48176
(313) 944-DOLL

Marj's Doll Sanctuary
5238 Plainfield Avenue NE
Grand Rapids, MI 49505
(616) 361-0054

Reme Collectibles
42839 Ford Road
Canton, MI 48187
(313) 981-7500

Rikki Schaffer Gallery
6897 Orchard Lake Road
West Bloomfield, MI 48322
(313) 855-9494

Victorian Doll Shoppe
117 North Center Street
Northville, MI 48167
(313) 347-4810

Minnesota

**Mary D's Dolls and
Bears and Such**
8407 West Broadway
Minneapolis, MN 55445
(612) 424-4375

Missouri

Dolly Dears
1972 Highway 165 S.
Suite K
Branson, MO 65615
(417) 339-3655

New Jersey

Best of Everything
199 Main Street
Hackettstown, NJ 07840
(908) 850-4858

Bright's Dolls
706 Foxcraft Drive
Cinnaminson, NJ 08077
(800) 3-OUR-DOLLS

**Corbett's Collectable
Dolls . . . and Such**
120 King's Highway
Maple Shade, NJ 08052
(609) 866-9787

Doll Parlor
7 Church Street
Allentown, NJ 08051
(609) 259-8118

Meyer's
595 Route 18
East Brunswick, NJ 08816
(908) 257-1720

Simply Lovely Gift Shoppe
572 New Brunswick Avenue
Fords, NJ 08863
(908) 738-4181

New York

Alisa's Dolls
Ramapo Cirque
3 Arapho Court
Suffern, NY 10901
(914) 368-2509

The Angel Keeper
56 Midchester Avenue
White Plains, NY 10606
(914) 428-1236

Anneliese's Dolls
36 Ruben Road
Poughkeepsie, NY 12601
(914) 463-2144

Dear Little Dollies
2880 Merrick Road
Bellmore, NY 11710
(516) 679-0164

The Enchanted Room
65-67 Sheather Street
Hammondsport, NY 14840
(800) 544-0198

Harbour Doll Gallery
61 North Country Road
Setauket, NY 11733
(516) 689-2565

Julie's Artisans' Gallery
687 Madison Avenue
New York, NY 10021
(212) 688-2345

Ann Michaels Collectibles
P.O. Box 721
Setauket, NY 11733
(516) 751-0109

Little Switzerland Dolls
267 Main Street
Huntington, NY 11743
(516) 549-8743

Puppen Stube
P.O. Box 44
East Amherst, NY 14051
(716) 639-0822

Barbara Steiker
1463 Granada Place
Far Rockaway, NY 11691
(718) 471-7075

Today's Treasures
655 Seventy-third Street
Niagara Falls, NY 14304
(716) 283-1726

Tomorrow's Heirlooms
42 Apple Hill Drive
Peekskill, NY 10566
(914) 736-6188

Yesterday's Yields
65 East Main Street
Avon, NY 14414
(716) 226-8360

Ohio

Hickory Dickory Dolls
124 East Aurora Road
Northfield, OH 44067
(216) 468-2085

The Toy Store
Franklin Park Mall
Toledo, OH 43623
(419) 473-9801

Treasures in the Attic
263 South Main Street
Amherst, OH 44001
(216) 988-2626

Oklahoma

The Doll House
5022 North May Avenue
Oklahoma City, OK
(405) 943-1498

Pennsylvania

Bear N Wares
312 Bridge Street
New Cumberland, PA 17070
(717) 774-1261

The Doll Room
228 Main Street
Berlin, PA 15530
(814) 267-4484

Fantastic Fantasies
44 Locust Street
Macungie, PA 18062
(215) 966-4314

Lynne-Art's Doll House
Route 202, Box 242
Lahaska, PA 18931
(215) 794-0605

Sweetness and Light
7 West Afton Avenue
Yardley, PA 19067
(215) 321-9095

Zip's Toys to Go
16 West Lancaster Avenue
Ardmore, PA 19003
(610) 649-2555

Rhode Island

Dolls and Daffodils
761 Bald Hill Road
Warwick, RI 02886
(401) 822-3655

Texas

Blue Willow Collections
1801 Royal Oak
Tyler, TX 75703
(903) 581-5133

The Doll Collection
6959 West Arapaho, No. 509
Dallas, TX 75248
(214) 458-7823

Virginia

Biggs Limited Editions
5517 Lakeside Avenue
Richmond, VA 23228
(804) 266-81489

The Toy Shoppe
1003 Sycamore Square
P.O. Box 28
Midlothian, VA 23113
(800) 447-7995

Acknowledgments

 The authors would like to thank all the artists who so enthusiastically cooperated with us in the preparation of this book, sharing with us not only their own work but that of their colleagues as well. Special thanks are due to Ursula Driskell, who translated texts from German-speaking artists for their inclusion in this book. In addition, the authors are deeply grateful to all those who participated in this project by sharing information, ideas, and photographs, and by lending dolls for photography; in particular: Alisa of Alisa's Dolls, Louise Fecher, Maggie Finch, Anna Galli of *Contemporary Doll Collector,* Helen Ginns, Deborah Hellman of Dolls . . . Etcetera, Carol-Lynn Hutton of the Dewees Cochran Foundation Museum, Julie of Julie's Artisans' Gallery, Malcolm Magri, Shirley and Monroe Paxman of The McCurdy Historical Doll Museum, Riki Shaffer, Danny and Barrie Shapiro of European Artist Dolls and The Toy Shoppe, W. Donald Smith, Barbara Spadaccini-Day of the Musée des Arts Décoratifs in Paris, Barbara Steiker, Robert Tonner, Suesanna Voorhees, Anne Votaw, Cynthia Webb, Nancy Wiley, Susan Hedrick and Rosalie Whyel of The Rosalie Whyel Museum of Doll Art, and Robert Campbell Rowe and the staff of *Dolls.* We would also like to acknowledge the inspired writings of John Darcy Noble, which have changed the way we all think about dolls.

Index

Page numbers in *italics* refer to illustrations.

A

Adam, Ludwig, 130
Afghanistan Child (Deval), 102–3, *103*
Alice Fantasy (Bullard), 25
American Couple Circa 1708 (Bullard), *24, 25*
American Doll Artist, The (book; Bullard), 22, 25, 155
American Folk Dolls (book; Lavitt), 76
America's Children dolls (Cochran), 16
Aminabad (Davies), 57–58, *58*
Amnesty International (Copal-Boerboom), 199, *200*
Ancelin, Malou, 112–13; work by, *112*
Angelique, Lawan, 99–101; work by, *90*
Armstrong-Hand, Martha, 138–40; work by, *139*
Art Dolls (exhibition), 10
Art of the Doll, The (Brandon), *151*
Ashcraft, Janie, 84–85; work by, *86*
As If They Might Speak (book; Cochran), 15

B

Babushkas (Florio), 133, *141*, 142
Baby Angel, The (Lavanty), 206, 207–8
Bahar, Ann, 137
Bailey, Elinor Peace, 211
Ballerino (Wanke), *204, 205*, 206
Becker, Roxanne, 60–62; work by, *61*
Bellous, Gina, 47–49; work by, *48*
Bellous, Jaymie, *48*, 49
Ben (Westling), 122, *123*
Benny (Nelson), 156–57, *157*
Berta (Frank), 93, *93*
Betsey Sheffield (Thompson), 21, *22*
Blount, Akira, 92, 172–74; work by, *173*
Blue Ball Bouquet (Buysse), 148, *149*
Blue Ribbon, A (Hoskins), 137, *137*
Blythe, Stephanie, 176, 178–79; work by, *177*
Boets, Martha, 34–36; work by, *35*
Bolivian Girl with Brother (Lipp), 122–23, *124*
Boston, Chris, 174–75; work by, *174*
Brahms, Anna Avigail, 115, 131, 144–46; work by, *145*

Brandon, Elizabeth, 149, 151; work by, *151*
Brauser, Uta, 116–17; work by, *110*
Brooks, Patricia Ryan, 46–47, 161; work by, *47*
Bullard, Helen, 21, 22–23, 25–26, 155; work by, *24*
Buysse, Barbara, 147–48; work by, *149*
Byerly, Mary Alice, 73, 75; work by, *75*

C

Cameron, Beth, 71–73, 157–58; work by, *74, 158*
Canzio, Christa, 103–4; work by, *104*
Carnivale (Wiley), *132*, 146
Caroline of 1880 (Bullard), 25
Cather, Jane, 87, 89; work by, *89*
Cat Will to Kind: Phantasmota #2 (Finch), 180–81, *181*
Cely, Antonette, 133, 142–43; work by, *142*
Children and Dolls dolls (Royzman), 37
Christmas Angel (Mostrom), 78–80, *79*
Christmas Carol, A (novel; Dickens), 67

Cindy (Cochran), 17
Clarkson, Lois, 70–71; work by, *71*
Clown Exercise (Davis), 202
Cochran, Dewees, 15–17; work by, *17*
Coe, Peter, 20, 38–40; work by, *40*
Concours Lepine, 10–11
Conrad, Holly, 159–60; work by, *160*
Contemporary Doll Magazine, 62, 188, 201, 211
Copal-Boerboom, Olly, 199–201; work by, *200*
Coper, Hans, 58
Cora Mae Sanborn (Brooks), *47*, 47
Countess of Central Park, The (McKinley), 155, *156*
Courtesan, The (Fletcher), 106, *107*, 108
Cowslips (Finch and Finch-Kozlosky), *55*, 56
Crab Man (Wiley), 147
Craig, Van, 165–67; work by, *152*
Creager, Jodi, 86–87, 98–99; work by, *88, 99*
Creager, Richard, 86–87, 98–99; work by, *88, 99*
Crees, Paul, 20, 38–40; work by, *40*

D

Dali, Edna, 113–15; work by, *113*

Dancing Coyote (Forrest), 201

Daphne (Dali), *113,* 113–14

Davies, Jane, 57–58; work by, *58*

Davis, Lenore, 202–3, 205; work by, *203*

Deaconess, The (McNichols), 36, *37*

Deerwoman, The (Blount), 172–73, *173*

Delilah: Folies 1924 (Craig), 152, 166–67

Delineators (magazine), 21

Deval, Brigitte, 102–3, 133–34; work by, *103, 134*

Diana McManus (Cochran), 17, *17*

Dickens, Charles, 67

Doll I (Kruse), 9, *12*

Dollcrafter Magazine, 73

Dollmaker's Magic (exhibition), 60

Dollmaking: A Creative Approach (Laury; book), 82

Dolls (magazine), 147, 206

Dolls—The Collector's Magazine, 6

Dolls of Yesterday (book; St. George), 20

Dorier, Jacques, 104–6; work by, *106*

Dream Voyages (Blythe, Snodgrass, and Mobley), *177,* 178–79

Dunham, Susan, 62–63; work by, *62*

E

Eagan, Pat, 162–63; work by, *163*

East Wind on Cherry Tree Lane (Walters), 58, *59,* 60

Eaton, Terry Lynn, 161–62; work by, *162*

Ebony (magazine), 78

Elf and His Pipe, The (Lackey), *187, 187*

F

Facto, Helen, 136–37; work by, *136*

Fairy Queen, The (Kertzman), 175–76, *170*

Fatal Interview (book; Millay), 55

Father and Son (Malpica), *94,* 94–95

Fawn (Taylor), 188–89, *189*

Fawn Zeller's Porcelain Doll-making Techniques (book; McFadden), 27

Fecher, Louise, 147, 206

Finch, Maggie, 27, 54–56, 180–81; work by, *55, 181*

Finch-Kozlosky, Marta, 54–56; work by, *55*

Fine Woodworking (magazine), 96

Fletcher, Dan, 106, 108; work by, *107*

Florian, Gertrude, 22–23; work by, *23*

Florio, Marla, 133, 140, 142; work by, *141*

Flueler-Tomamichel, Elisabeth, 194, 197–98; work by, *195*

Forrest, Grace, 201–2; work by, *200*

Fourth of July (Ashcraft), 85, 86

Fourth of July (Creager and Creager), 87, 88

Fowles, John, 53

Frances's Children—1953 (Shaub), 41, *43, 43*

Frank, Mary Ellen, 91–93; work by, *93*

Frank Sinatra (Hanford), 40–41, *41*

French Lieutenant's Woman, The (book; Fowles), 53

Froud, Brian, 188

G

Gertrude (Conrad), 159–60, *160*

Getting to the Root of the Problem (Stilwell), *194, 195, 195*

Gift Giver, The (Roessel), *77, 77*

Girl (Morgenthaler), *13, 15*

Girl with Braids (Mitrani), 131, *131*

Girl with Her Doll (Ancelin), *112, 113*

Gloria (Crees and Coe), *40, 40*

Goff, Susie, 145

Goldsmith, Oliver, 57

Goodnow, June, 158–59; work by, *159*

Gray, Scott, 181, 183; work by, *182*

Great American Button Box Wars, The (Payne), *114, 115*

Greenfield, Lois, 202

Grow-Up dolls (Cochran), 17

H

Haney, Lynn, 189, 191; work by, *190*

Haney, Sue, 191

Hanford, Clark, 40–41; work by, *41*

Hansel and Gretel (Mostrom), 65–66, *66*

Happy Birthday Grandma (Goodnow), 158–59, *159*

Harper's Weekly Magazine, 71

Harris, Janis, 97–98; work by, *98*

Heart Fairy (Horn), *81, 81*

Heizer, Dorothy, 17, 19; work by, *18*

Helbeck, Paul, 16

Héloïse, 120; work by, *121*

Hemsley, Paula, 160–61; work by, *161*

Henson, Jim, 188

Henry VIII (Heizer), *18,* 19

Himalayan Fluteman (Phillippi), 96–97, *97*

Home Boys (Brauser), *110,* 117

Horn, Linda, 80–81; work by, *81*

Hoskins, Dorothy, 137–38; work by, *137*

I

Iacono, Maggie, 11, 123–24; work by, *125*

In Celebration of the First Toad Moon (Forrest), 201

In the Night Kitchen (book; Sendak), 206

Isabella (Schmidt), *44, 45, 46*

It's a Mighty Fine Day, Miss Ruby (Hemsley), 160, *161*
It Seemed Like a Good Idea at the Time (Stilwell), 196

J

Jack-in-the-Box (Wiley), 205, 206–7
Jaymie (Bellous), *48*, 48–49
Jessie (Taylor), 168, *169*
Johl, Janet, 23
Johnson, Jack, 161, *162*
Jouets Artistiques (exhibition), 11

K

Kate's Santa (Cameron), 73, *74*
Kaulitz, Marion, 10
Kertzman, Linda, 63, 65, 175–76; work by, *64*, *170*
Killmore, Virginia, 75–77; work by, *68*
Kish, Helen, 53–54; work by, *50*
Kissling, Jutta, 124–25; work by, *126*
Klee, Paul, 14
Koh, Anna, *136*
Kruse, Käthe, 10, 11–13; work by, *8*
Kruse, Max, 12
Kunst-Spiel Zeug (Wanke), 205

L

Labyrinth (movie), 188
Lackey, Gail, 186–87; work by, *187*
Lady in Green Velvet (Deval), 134, *134*
Langton, Michael, 34, 95–96; work by, *33*, *94*
Lathers, Kath, 194, 196–97; work by, *192*
Laury, Jean Ray, 82
Lavanty, Tammy, 207–8; work by, *206*
Lavitt, Wendy, 76
Leonardo da Vinci (Boers and Reitsma), *35*, 35–36
Leonie (Kissling), 125, *126*
Letter, A (Facto), 136, *136*
Lichtenfels, Lisa, 101–2, 183–84; work by, *101*, *184*
Lima, Gretchen, 133, 143–44; work by, *143*
Linni (Kissling), 125, *126*
Lipp, Gabriele, 122–23; work by, *124*
Listening Spirit (Lathers), *192*, 194, 196
Little Bo Peep (Walters), 60
Little Brother (Thompson), 21
Little Lady Ready for a Walk (Schrott), 127, 129, *129*
Little Prince, The (Wright), 52–53, *52*
Little Women dolls (Thompson), 22
Lobster Lady (Wiley), 147
Lobster Man (Gray), 181, *182*
Lollypop Garden, The (Kertzman), 175
Look-Alikes dolls (Cochran), 16
Lovers, The (Forrest), 200, *201*
Lucille (Cely), 133, *142*, 142–43

M

McFadden, Sibyl, 27
McKinley, Robert, 154–55; work by, *156*
McNichols, Ann, 36–37; work by, *37*
Madge Overbee (Brandon), 149, 151, *151*
Magic Flute, The (opera; Mozart), 184
Malpica, Michele, 93–95; work by, *94*
Marie Antoinette (Cely), 142
Martha, An American Flag Doll (Cather), 89, *89*
Mender of Broken Hearts (Lathers), 196
Mercer Girl (Florian), 23, *23*
Midsummer Night's Dream, A (play; Shakespeare), 63
Millay, Edna St. Vincent, 54–55
Miller, Lorna, 117–19; work by, *117*
Mine! (Trobe), 119
Minerva Mulliner in Halloween Costume (Oroyan), 82, *83*
Miniature Collector (magazine), 137
Mitrani, Anne, 130–31; work by, *131*
Mi-Zhou (Canzio), 104, *104*
Mobley, Sylvia, 176, 178; work by, *177*
Mockingbird (Nelson-Daniels), 194, 209, *210*
Model 1991 (Tonner), 133, 149, *150*
Moon Man, The (Wiley), 186, *186*
Moore, Clement, 71
Moore, Gene, 167
Morgenthaler, Ernst, 14

Morgenthaler, Sasha, 10, 13–15; work by, *13*
Mormon Pioneers dolls (Sorensen), 20
Mostrom, Jocelyn, 65–66, 78–80; work by, *66*, *79*
Mother and Baby in the Rocking Chair (Florian), 22, *23*
Motherhood 1784 (Armstrong-Hand), 138, *139*
Mother Plays with Dolls (book; Bailey), 211
Music, Maestro, Please! (Eagan), 162–63, *163*
My People in Wood (book; Bullard), 23, *25*

N

Nast, Thomas, 71
National Institute of American Doll Artists (NIADA), 15, 25, 151
Nefertiti (Cely), 142
Nelson, Bill, 155–57, 187–88; work by, *157*, *188*
Nelson-Daniels, Betty, 194, 209, 211; work by, *210*
New York Times, 202
Nigerian Earth Mother (Angelique), 90, 99–100
Nijinsky, Vaslav, 28, 38
Nino the Clown (Eaton), 161–62, *162*
Noah's Ark (Iacono), 123–24, *125*
Noble, John Darcy, 62, 102, 167, 180, 188, 201, 211
Noufflard, Berthe, 10, 11
Nutcracker, The (film; Sendak), 206

O

Old Tom Morris (Langton), 33, 34
One Arm Jump (Davis), 202, 203
Oroyan, Susanna, 81–82, 154; work by, 83
Oshima, Kazuyo, 125, 127; work by, 128
Othello (Dunham), 62, 62–63

P

Paris Babe (Von Essen), 135, 135
Pan (Lichtenfels), 183–84, 184
Payne, Hal, 115–16; work by, 114
Père Nöel (Clarkson), 70–71, 71
Perkins, Ellen, 145
Perzyk, Harry, 109; work by, 108
Petite Fille Debout, La (Héloise), 120, 121
Petit Prince, Le (book; Saint-Exupéry), 52–53
Phantasmota series (Finch), 180–81, 181
Phib (Nelson), 188, 188
Phillippi, Marilyn, 96–97; work by, 97
Piper, Carole, 31–32, 34; work by, 32
Polly Piedmont (Zeller), 26
Poppins, Mary, 58, 59, 60
Portrait Dolls (Cochran), 16
Portrait of a Young Japanese Girl (Oshima), 127, 128
Princess, The (Walmsley), 56, 56–57

Princess and the Pea, The (fairytale), 56–57
Promenade, The (Robins), 179, 180
Puppen Reform, 10

Q

Queen Anne (Sorensen), 20, 21
Queen Elizabeth (Piper), 32, 32
Queen of the Night and General Star and His Starlets (Wolf), 184–85, 185
Quietness (Yamaguchi), 198, 199
Quilted Father Christmas (Killmore), 68, 76–77

R

Rapunzel (Becker), 60–62, 61
Rasha, the Crystal Gazer (Lima), 133, 143, 144
Redford, Jeff, 67, 162; work by, 66
Redmond, Kathy, 30; work by, 31
Reitsma, Marianne, 34–36; work by, 35
Robins, Paul, 179–80; work by, 179
Roche, Lynne, 123
Roche, Michael, 123
Roessel, Beverly, 77–78; work by, 77
Royzman, Alexander, 37–38; work by, 28
Royzman, Marina, 37–38; work by, 28

S

Saint-Exupéry, Antoine de, 52–53
Saketo (Perzyk), 108, 109
Scarecrow, The (Wick), 84, 84
Schmidt, Karin, 44–46; work by, 45
Schreiber, Max, 10
Schrott, Rotraut, 127, 129–30; work by, 129
Scrooge (Redford), 66, 67
Selephi (Creager and Creager), 98, 99
Sendak, Maurice, 206
Shakespeare, William, 63
Shaub, Nerissa, 41–44; work by, 43
She Stoops to Conquer (play; Goldsmith), 57
Snodgrass, Susan, 176, 178–79; work by, 177
Snowshoe Santa (Byerly), 75, 75
Somali Man (Lichtenfels), 101, 101
Sorensen, Lewis, 20–21; work by, 20
Spencer, Dolly, 92
Standing Tot in Pink Undershirt and Saggy Diaper (Trobe), 118, 119–20
Stilwell, Tracy Page, 194–96; work by, 195
Studyvin, Virginia, 149
Suitor, The (Walmsley), 164–65, 165
Swamp Ms Hogany (Boston), 174, 174–75

T

Taylor, E. J., 167, 169, 188–89; work by, 168, 189
Thompson, Martha, 21–22; work by, 22
Titania and Bottom (Kertzman), 63, 64, 65
Tonner, Robert, 16, 133, 148–49; work by, 150
Toy Trader (magazine), 21, 25
Travers, P. L., 58
Trobe, Carol, 119–20; work by, 118
Trouble (Trobe), 119
Turtle Shaman (Langton), 94, 95–96

U

United Federation of Doll Clubs (UFDC), 22

V

Vargas, Rudolf, 135
Vaslav Nijinsky (Royzman and Royzman), 28, 38
Velveteen Rabbit, The (Cameron), 157–58, 158
Victoriana (Kish), 50, 53, 54
Viking Woman (Becker), 60
"Visit from Saint Nicholas, A" (poem; Moore), 71
Von Essen, Ken, 134–36; work by, 135
Von Essen, Norma, 135

W

Waiting for Santa (Brooks), 46

Walmsley, Kathryn, 56–57, 163–65; work by, *56, 165*

Walters, Nancy, 58, 60; work by, *59*

Wandering Spirit (Forrest), 201

Wanke, Sylvia, 205–6; work by, *204*

Washi paper dolls, 104–6, 108

Westling, Charlene, 121–22; work by, *123*

Wick, Faith, 82, 84; work by, *84*

Wiley, Nancy, 146–47, 185–86, 206; work by, *132, 186*

Wiley, William, 146, 185–86, 206–7; work by, *205*

Wilhelm, Irmgard, 208–9; work by, *209*

Wiremu and Marama (Harris), 98, *98*

Without (Wilhelm), 209, *209*

Without Words (Flueler-Tomamichel), 194, 197–98, *195*

Wizard of the Sea (Haney), 190, *191*

Wolf, Peter, 102, 184–85; work by, *185*

Wright, R. John, 11, 52–53, 123; work by, *52*

Wright, Susan, 52

Y

Yamaguchi, Keiko, 198–99; work by, *199*

Yoshitsune (Dorier), 105, *106*

Young Queen Victoria (Redmond), 30, *31*

Young Woman Seated (Brahms), 145, *145*

Your Dolls and Mine (book; Johl), 23

Ysah (Miller), 117, *117–19*

Z

Zeller, Fawn, 26–27; work by, *26*